MH00778403

FREEDOM AND RESISTANCE

Contested Boundaries

UNIVERSITY PRESS OF FLORIDA

Florida A&M University, Tallahassee
Florida Atlantic University, Boca Raton
Florida Gulf Coast University, Ft. Myers
Florida International University, Miami
Florida State University, Tallahassee
New College of Florida, Sarasota
University of Central Florida, Orlando
University of Florida, Gainesville
University of North Florida, Jacksonville
University of South Florida, Tampa
University of West Florida, Pensacola

FREEDOM

AND

RESISTANCE

A Social History of Black Loyalists in the Bahamas

CHRISTOPHER CURRY

University Press of Florida
Gainesville · Tallahassee · Tampa · Boca Raton
Pensacola · Orlando · Miami · Jacksonville · Ft. Myers · Sarasota

Copyright 2017 by Christopher Curry
All rights reserved
Printed in the United States of America on acid-free paper

This book may be available in an electronic edition.

First cloth printing, 2017
First paperback printing, 2018

23 22 21 20 19 18   6 5 4 3 2 1

Library of Congress Cataloging-in-Publication Data
Names: Curry, Christopher, 1971– author.
Title: Freedom and resistance : a social history of black loyalists in the Bahamas / Christopher Curry.
Description: Gainesville : University Press of Florida, 2017. | Includes bibliographical references and index.
Identifiers: LCCN 2016055641 | ISBN 9780813054476 (cloth)
ISBN 9780813064871 (pbk.)
Subjects: LCSH: African American loyalists—Bahamas. | Slavery—Bahamas—History. | Blacks—Bahamas—History. | Bahamas—History.
Classification: LCC F1660.B55 C87 2017 | DDC 972.96—dc23
LC record available at https://lccn.loc.gov/2016055641

The University Press of Florida is the scholarly publishing agency for the State University System of Florida, comprising Florida A&M University, Florida Atlantic University, Florida Gulf Coast University, Florida International University, Florida State University, New College of Florida, University of Central Florida, University of Florida, University of North Florida, University of South Florida, and University of West Florida.

University Press of Florida
15 Northwest 15th Street
Gainesville, FL 32611-2079
http://upress.ufl.edu

CONTENTS

FIGURES

ACKNOWLEDGMENTS

The completion of a project of this size required the assistance and encouragement of many people. First, I wish to acknowledge the preliminary suggestions and substantive critique of my manuscript provided by Melina Pappademos, Blanca Silvestrini, and Richard D. Brown.

I am also grateful for the encouragement I received from the University of The Bahamas, particularly from colleagues in the School of Social Sciences and Dean Sumner, whose support contributed to the completion of this project. Donell Johnson and Samantha Pratt, administrative assistants in the School of Social Sciences, provided institutional backing that made completing this project easier. I also owe a great deal of gratitude to Marjorie Downie in the School of English Studies, who ably assisted in copyediting an earlier draft of this project. Many students at the college are to be thanked for graciously accepting their role as the testing laboratory for this material. The History B.A. majors in particular deserve credit for providing insightful and timely comments on selected portions of this project and for attending the various public presentations where these ideas were discussed. Additionally, I must highlight the work of Clethra Dean, an education major and student researcher who ably assisted me in collecting illustrations and maps for the manuscript.

I am also thankful for the support provided from the community of scholars and intellectuals outside the college, most notably Marion Bethel, Gail Saunders, Tracey Thompson, Rosanne Adderley, Jim Lawlor, Keith Tinker, Philip P. Smith, Ean Maura, Grace Turner, and Patricia

Glinton-Micheolas. Many archivists and librarians from across the United States and the Bahamas also provided valuable assistance, although lack of time and space prevents me from listing them all. Of particular importance, however, were Mrs. Elaine Toote, Patrice Williams, and Sherriley Strachan and the staff at the Bahamas National Archives; the staff and archivists at the Saint Augustine Historical Society; the Georgia Historical Society, the State Archives in Columbia, South Carolina; the Charleston Historical Society; and the New York Public Library. I also wish to thank Timothy Stewart and Bethel Baptist Church for allowing me to share some of my research findings with them.

I would also like to thank Sian Hunter, Michele Fiyak-Burkley, Ali Sundook, Lucinda Treadwell, and the other professionals at the University Press of Florida. Without their support, this project might have been consigned to the dustbin of history. Finally, I want to express my sincere gratitude to my family, my mom, dad, and sister, and especially my wife, Raquel, and daughter, Chrisselle, for their patience and support in seeing this project completed.

INTRODUCTION

In 1786, Caesar Brown, a free black residing in Nassau, delivered a "bill for the sum of 360£" to his employer, John Wood, a white Loyalist who had migrated to the Bahamas in 1783. Apparently, Brown had worked for Wood on a variety of tasks for three years without pay. The invoice that surfaced in the Registrar's Office does not indicate whether Wood ever paid Brown, but it does meticulously record both the type of work performed and the payment due. Some of Brown's work included "building an overseers house" valued at 20£; "clearing 18 acres, my part, 9 £"; "making a fence around the plantation," valued at 8£; and "making a kitchen table 7 ft by 4ft," assessed at 7£ for labor. Brown's demand for payment is particularly interesting in light of his relationship with John Wood. While they were still in East Florida, Caesar Brown had "bought his freedom for 20 pounds and went to work for John Wood." When Loyalists evacuated Saint Augustine in 1783, both of them moved to the Bahamas, where Brown continued to work for Wood.[1] The migration and subsequent settlement experiences of both men in the Bahamas exemplify the larger global movement of people that occurred as a consequence of the evacuation of Loyalists from garrisoned seaports in colonial America. Indeed, the migration of Loyalist refugees across the Atlantic world "reminds readers that the history of the British Empire involved an even wider world in motion."[2]

Equally important, however, was the racial politics that shaped the fortunes of both men when they crossed colonial borders. As a white man,

Wood could claim his right to land grants of forty acres and an additional twenty acres for each dependent. He was also entitled to vote and partici-pate as an active citizen in the political affairs of Bahamian society. Brown, on the other hand, was probably poor and in debt. His destitute condition not only disqualified him from owning land but also most likely forced him into some kind of contracted indenture to Wood. Moreover, in spite of his legal status as a free black, Brown was excluded from an active po-litical role in Bahamian society. Evidently both men experienced freedom in the Bahamas, but to very different degrees. Caesar, as a black Loyalist, had to fight for his liberty and the right to earn wages while Wood, as a white Loyalist and property owner, attempted to expand his fortune by exploiting the labor of blacks such as Brown.

The tension between Bahamian newcomers such as Caesar Brown and John Wood underscores a number of significant issues that faced black Loyalists seeking freedom and better opportunities in the Bahamas at the end of the American Revolution. First, as this study will show, racial iden-tities inscribed in law, customs, and practice became the source of friction between black and white Loyalists in the Bahamas. Such friction in fact was initiated during the course of the Revolutionary War, when thousands of enslaved men and women flocked to the British lines in order to claim freedom based on promises made by British officials. The sheer number of free and enslaved African Americans who escaped to British strongholds in Savannah, Saint Augustine, Charleston, and New York reveal that the American Revolution was not simply a war between Patriot and Loyalist, but a fulcrum of slave resistance.[3] By the end of the war, those African Americans in service to the British cause may have numbered between 80,000 and 100,000, including women and children, enslaved and free. Yet serving the British during the Revolution did not mean that black Loyalists were necessarily aligned with metropole politics or politicians. Instead, black Loyalists were motivated by their own desire for freedom rather than a commitment to any place, people, or abstract cause.[4] In es-sence, blacks and other persons of color often aligned themselves with the Loyalists rather than with Patriots simply because the British promised them the best opportunity to live in a world without bondage. In aban-doning their former residences, traveling great distances, and staking out a position behind British lines, they made their own declarations of inde-pendence from slavery.[5]

Recent debate between Barry Cahill and James St. George Walker has clarified our understanding of the term *Black Loyalist*.[6] Cahill's contention is that most of the approximately 3,000 black persons who arrived in Nova Scotia from New York were enslaved fugitives belonging to Patriot owners, not Black Loyalists. He argues that their primary goal was achieving freedom from slavery, not loyalty to Great Britain.[7] In responding to Cahill's assertion that the term Black Loyalist is essentially a myth created by intellectuals and academics in the 1960s and 1970s, Walker suggests that there is substantial evidence that the term—or variations of it—was appropriated by various groups (white Loyalists, Patriots, and black refugees) in exiled communities across the Atlantic world at the time of the Revolutionary War.[8] Walker affirms that when individuals such as Thomas Peters and Murphy Stiel referred to themselves as "loyal black refugees" in their petitions, the term did not mean refugees from slavery but rather was common parlance in the 1780s for "Loyalists."[9] Beyond self-identification as loyal refugees, Black Loyalists were defined by wartime policies as enslaved persons (or fugitive slaves) who had escaped to British lines and came under the protection of various British proclamations. The term "Black Loyalists" would also include manumitted or freeborn blacks who allied with the British during the Revolutionary War; however, others would not be considered Black Loyalists. One example was "sequestered property," those unfortunate enslaved persons belonging to Patriots captured during the course of the war. Likewise, enslaved persons owned by white Loyalists would still be considered chattel and therefore removed and evacuated with their enslavers to various British territories around the Atlantic basin. Walker succinctly notes that during the course of the Revolutionary War, British officers made a distinction between enslaved fugitives who came voluntarily to the British, and those who simply fell into British hands during the course of their campaigns. The former were, in theory, to be treated as free British subjects; the latter, captured from the rebels, would be kept as enslaved persons or sold for the benefit of the captors.[10]

Moving beyond the Cahill and Walker debate, it is important to conceptualize Black Loyalists in ways that avoid reifying a dichotomous relationship between Yankee rebel and loyal subjects to the British Crown. In truth, there was always a degree of elasticity to the concept of Black Loyalist as individuals working in a British imperial world. Some were more self-conscious than others, writing and articulating their political views in pamphlets and broadsides. On the other hand, many blacks were far less politically engaged, pragmatically choosing the British side simply because they wanted the easiest path to freedom and economic autonomy. Additionally, time and space shifted the boundaries of who self-identified as Loyalist to the point where the term became less self-evident and useful by the 1820s. Notwithstanding the fluidity of the nomenclature, the revolutionary world birthed a movement that allowed persons of color to make self-conscious decisions about their future aspirations. For the purpose of this study, I define Black Loyalists as those enslaved and free persons of color who actively sought freedom and protection by responding to British proclamations during the American Revolutionary War, beginning with Lord Dunmore's November 7, 1775, proclamation and culminating with Sir Guy Carleton's evacuation orders of April 1783.

Yet upon exile the concept of who constituted a Black Loyalist was marked by fluidity, often changing as black royal refugees traversed various colonial borders and legal systems throughout the Atlantic world. In the case of the cohort of Black Loyalists entering the Bahamas, they were often redefined by whites as enslaved fugitives, or, as the barrister William Wylly caustically noted, as "black persons arriving from America who are either free or pretending to be so."[11] In time, the equivocal status of Black Loyalists would be tested and sometimes clarified by various proclamations, laws, and legal court rulings in the Bahamas. Despite these legal changes, their presence remained in many ways ambiguous in relation to the existing white power structure as well as to the free black and enslaved populations that intermingled and crossed paths within the porous city boundary of Nassau. Put another way, the settlement of Black Loyalists in the Bahamas was complicated by the presence of a small free black population in Nassau that had emerged during the pre-Loyalist period of enslavement by way of manumission and miscegenation, but who faced, in common with the new refugees, exclusionary restrictions by the first decade of the nineteenth century.[12] In the end, a central concern of this project is both to demonstrate the distinctiveness of Black Loyalist communities, as well as to highlight the interactions between black refugees, enslaved persons, and other free populations in the Bahamas.

Caesar Brown's case also reminds us of the global dimensions of the struggle for freedom that emanated from the American Revolution. The struggle for liberty was embraced by Black Loyalists in various receiving societies throughout the Atlantic world, including London, England, Nova Scotia, Sierra Leone, Jamaica, and the Bahamas.[13] In the case of the Bahamas, the global dimensions of the American Revolution are evidenced by the fact that the war itself was waged within the Bahamian archipelago. The capital of Nassau was in fact attacked twice: first by American Patriot forces in 1776 under the command of Ezekiel Hopkins and a fleet of eight ships, and later, in 1781, when the Bahamas was seized and held by Spanish forces until the Treaty of Paris in 1783 restored the colony to Great Britain. Additionally, before the signing of the Treaty of Versailles was generally known in the thirteen colonies, Colonel Andrew Deveaux and a number of East Florida Loyalists launched a successful campaign to retake the Bahamas for the British.[14] Sailing from Saint Augustine in April 1783, Deveaux stopped on Harbour Island and Eleuthera in order to recruit local inhabitants to fight the Spanish. Nassau was also attacked during the course of the war by a number of privateers. One particular instance is noteworthy for the involvement of free blacks in defending the city against American Patriot invaders. According to a survey report intended to persuade Loyalists to immigrate to the Bahamas, Lieutenant John Wilson noted that "the black people have always proved themselves willing and friends to Government, particularly those who are not subject to the control of a master." Wilson further observed that during an attack on Fort Nassau by an American sloop in January 1778, the "free mulattoes and negroes" were so outraged that they "voluntarily embodied themselves with an intention to storm the fort."[15]

While such loyalty to the British cause was evident during the conflict, the immigration of Black Loyalists at the end of the war demonstrates the ways in which the revolutionary ideals of liberty and freedom were carried beyond the continental borders of the thirteen colonies. In practice, Black Loyalists in the Bahamas continued their discursive battle for "freedom"—the war of words—in the face of challenges to their status as free persons in the Bahamas.[16] Yet, crossing the Atlantic from seaports in colonial America to the Bahamas most certainly altered the concept of freedom as understood by Black Loyalists. While "freedom" is normally associated with civil liberties, enfranchisement, and the ability to live independently, it can also be altered based on local circumstances. Indeed, freedom can best be understood as a dynamic and elastic concept, shaped as much by local conditions—labor, law, and access to land and resources—as by larger political and socioeconomic forces within the

Atlantic world. In the end, freedom and liberty were not fixed concepts, but "evolve[d] over time into dramatically different end states."[17]

Even as the meaning of freedom was transformed by local circumstances it is equally telling that Black Loyalists functioned as cultural carriers of a revolutionary experience that had spread across the entire Atlantic basin. Black Loyalists were uniquely positioned as purveyors of revolutionary ideas precisely because they functioned as Atlantic Creoles, a term developed by historians to describe culturally conversant Africans who effectively navigated and traversed multiple destinations and languages within an evolving Atlantic world.[18] Such a framing underscores the complex ways in which Black Loyalists were imbued with traditions inherited from colonial America, which were then transplanted and reinscribed in new host societies such as Jamaica, Nova Scotia, and the Bahamas. In essence, as Black Loyalists moved across multiple colonial borders, they became resourceful, culturally flexible, adaptable and able effectively to refashion their identities and institutions within the larger geopolitical matrix of the Atlantic littoral.

Additionally, the complex nature of Black Loyalist migration calls attention to "the circulation of ideas and activists as well as the movement of key cultural and political artifacts." Such movements reflect an "outer-national, trans-cultural re-conceptualization" of the African Diaspora.[19] Clearly, Black Loyalists embarking for the Bahamas from the British-controlled seaports of Saint Augustine, Charleston, Savannah, and New York fit squarely within this outer-national movement. Beyond complicating notions of diaspora, these trans-Atlantic movements of ideas challenge those scholars who see black resistance as nation-bound or who conceptualize the American Revolution as a singular continental struggle between rogue colony and crown, effectively ending with the surrender of Cornwallis and the signing of the Treaty of Paris. Arguably, the American Revolution did not end either with the cessation of armed conflict in 1781, or with the Treaty of Paris in 1783; rather it continued and mutated in unusual places, a revolution often carried on by those who had the most to lose by being denied the freedom promised at the outset of the war.

Though Nova Scotia appeared to be the preferred destination for black refugees trekking across the Atlantic, a sizable number settled in Jamaica and the Bahamas. Contemporary estimates suggest that 8,000 to 10,000 Black Loyalists left colonial America, with about 3,000 settling in the maritime provinces of Canada, a much smaller contingent (amounting to fewer than 200) arriving in the slave society of Jamaica, and the remaining portion disembarking in Great Britain and the non-plantation colony of the Bahamas.[20] Those Black Loyalists settling in the tropics encountered very different environments. Both Jamaica and the Bahamas had long been British possessions, though each evolved in very different ways. Jamaica, acquired by Great Britain in 1655, had developed into a slave society in which the production of sugar had by the mid-eighteenth century made it the most prosperous British colony in the Caribbean.[21] Coinciding with the rise of sugar was a dramatic increase in the number of enslaved blacks, soaring 100-fold in fifty years, from 514 in 1661 to 55,000 by 1713.[22] This demographic pattern continued to accelerate throughout the eighteenth century, with the total number of enslaved reaching 127,881 by 1750.[23] In contrast, the Bahamas, settled by British immigrants from Bermuda in 1648, remained a marginal territory economically, with little or no export economy, though firmly established as a slaveholding society. In the pre-Loyalist period in the Bahamas, not only was the ratio of enslaved to master fairly equal, but enslaved persons tended to work in a range of environments, often laboring alongside their owners in maritime activities.[24] Despite their substantial socioeconomic differences, both colonies had adopted slave codes and customs that mirrored legislation passed in the older slave colonies of Barbados and Virginia. Thus, the Bahamian slave codes of 1729 and 1767 owed much of their content to the earlier Barbadian law of 1665. They also reflected the general trend whereby the enslavement of Africans was justified on the grounds of racial and cultural inferiority.[25] Such sociopolitical factors inevitably shaped the experiences of Black Loyalists arriving in the Bahamas and Jamaica after 1783.

A close examination of the Bahamian Black Loyalist experience is warranted given the peculiar slaveholding society that had emerged in the colony by the 1780s. Indeed, the central focus of this study is to investigate the struggles for freedom that Black Loyalists experienced in the non-plantation colony of the Bahamas, located on the periphery of the Caribbean region.[26] By focusing on Black Loyalists such as Caesar Brown, this study not only aims to recover the social history of Black Loyalists, but also seeks to examine the nature of their contributions to Bahamian society. Additionally, this project explores the racial discord that erupted in the Bahamas between black and white Loyalists. Ironically, though black and white Loyalists shared the common experience of being on the losing side of the Revolutionary War, their racial identities reflected manifold differences that would be expressed in their subsequent settlement of the Bahamas after 1783. At the center of their differences were conflicting future aspirations: one group seeking greater freedom under the protection of British promises and proclamations, and the other, already possessing liberty, seeking economic advantages as potential slave-owning planters.

Upon settlement in the Bahamas, such divisions became fully expanded and codified throughout the archipelago, forming the basis for the exploitation, coercion, and even outright re-enslavement of Black Loyalists at the hands of white Loyalists. Two episodes are worth highlighting for the incendiary violence between black and white Loyalists during the formative stages of their settlement in the Bahamas. In Abaco in October 1787 a small-scale revolt was reported in which "a number of blacks went about with muskets and fixed bayonets, robbing and plundering" the property of whites.[27] Despite efforts to quell the spirit of insurrection, by May of the following year, it was once again reported that blacks were absenting from their work, hiding in the woods and swamps, and encouraged to declare themselves freemen.[28] Evidently defending or seeking freedom often led to uneasy tension if not outright violence, particularly in a society increasingly stratified along racial lines. This was clearly evident in the case involving a Black Loyalist woman in Nassau who was attacked in her home by white vigilantes after she had successfully defended her right to freedom in a magistrate's court. Though the attackers beat and abused the woman and her children, their position as powerful white men (with at least one actually holding office as Surveyor-General) precluded punitive judgments for these acts of violence. Indeed, after spending a night in the public jail, not only were the offenders released without an official charge, but the ring leader, John Tattnall, also vowed he would "burn every house belonging to the free Negroes in that quarter of the town."[29] This incident indicates that the question of freedom in general for blacks—both men and women—became a contentious and violent issue in Bahamian society.

Such tensions were neither isolated nor contained to the colonial capital of Nassau. Consequently, this project explores the racial discord that erupted in the Bahamas between black and white Loyalists in two distinct locales: the previously uninhabited islands of Abaco, and the older, urban center of Nassau, located on the island of New Providence. Situated in the northeast quadrant of the archipelago, Abaco has a land area of 649 square miles (about half the size of Rhode Island), comprising mostly limestone rock with only small pockets of soil able to sustain vegetation such as pine, Madeira (mahogany), and lignum vitae. Though Great Abaco Island is the second largest of the Bahama Islands, much of its western shore is not well defined and is almost wholly taken over by mangrove swamps, which serve as breeding grounds for fish and crawfish.[30] Despite these harsh geographical conditions, early reports emanating from New York City described glowingly the potential of Abaco as a place of settlement for Loyalist refugees. Sir Guy Carleton, in a letter to Lieutenant Wilson, observed that Abaco "is reported to be more fertile and valuable than Providence and is likely to become settled." Apart from its large tracts of uncultivated land, Abaco possessed a desirable climate and a harbor reported to be even "better than the one at Providence."[31]

Whereas Abaco was unsettled prior to the Loyalist arrival, Nassau, New Providence, had emerged by the early eighteenth century as the colonial capital and principal town of the colony. Named after William of Orange in 1695, Nassau was the logical choice for the capital, boasting a protected harbor and a central location within the archipelago. Its strategic importance was borne out by the fact that it emerged by the beginning of the eighteenth century as a key port city in the Caribbean, located within the major trade routes of the Atlantic and a popular destination for pirates and other seafaring adventurers.[32] By the early 1780s and just before the arrival of the Loyalists, Nassau was described as small, consisting mostly of wooden huts clustered around a single muddy road (Bay Street) overlooking the harbor. Its townspeople consisted of sailors and fishermen, "a few royal officials, divers merchants and what laborers are needed." Despite its diminutive size, Nassau held a single parish church, various courts, administrative buildings, and Government House, built on a small ridge overlooking the town.[33] The town and harbor were protected by two forts: to the east by Fort Montagu, built in 1742 by German engineer Peter Henry Bruce, and to the west by Fort Nassau, completed in 1695 and home to the British regular troops stationed in the colony. Because New Providence lacked a staple export crop, most of the wealthier estate owners lived on the returns of their lands located within or just outside the limits of the town.

Beyond the borders of the town and hugging the coast to the east were scattered houses occupied by sailors and fishermen. Further east and along the northern seaside end of the island lay a small village of free blacks aptly named New Guinea. Directly south of the city of Nassau, in

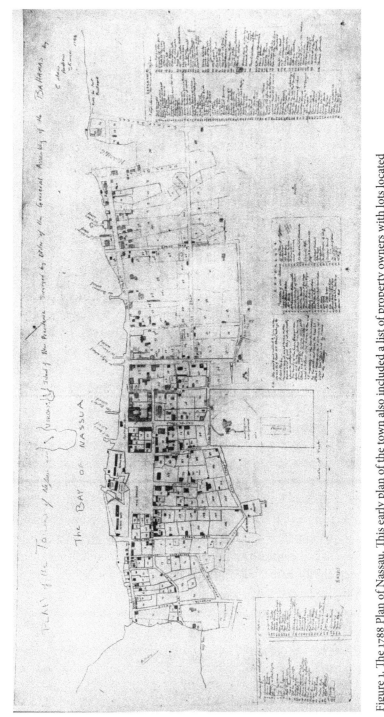

Figure 1. The 1788 Plan of Nassau. This early plan of the town also included a list of property owners with lots located westward and eastward of the town. By permission of Special Collections, Department of Archives, Nassau, Bahamas.

an area later called Over-the-Hill were large uncultivated woodlands. Further south and encompassing the rest of New Providence was flat bushy terrain, interspersed with a few small ponds and lakes and an additional ridge running east to west of the 21- by 7-mile island. By the time of the arrival of the Loyalists, these wooded areas would serve as convenient sites for the development of semipermanent communities of escapees, seeking momentary refuge and relief from the bonds of slavery.

Contemporary writers noted that the inhabitants of Nassau and its adjoining communities appeared healthy and easygoing, earning a living by way of privateering during wartime but in peacetime subsisting by means of wrecking and fishing. Though racial distinctions were codified in Nassau by laws dating back to 1723, the relative poverty of both free blacks and whites and the lack of a plantation commodity allowed for common subsistence labor to emerge—particularly in fishing and woodcutting—in ways that leveled social and class distinctions.[34]

In general, before the arrival of the Loyalists, the Bahamas remained severely underdeveloped, with only three major islands settled: New Providence, Harbour Island, and Eleuthera. Thus, the migration of black and white Loyalists at the end of the Revolutionary War had a transformative effect on the colony, with 5,700 enslaved and free blacks, along with 1,600 whites arriving. This demographic revolution not only led to the settlement of new islands such as Abaco, Long Island, and Cat Island, but it also doubled the white population (3,500) and tripled the black population (6,500) by 1790.[35]

Beyond numbers, the story of the Black Loyalist experience in Abaco and Nassau highlights the efforts of black refugees to extend their newfound liberties to a marginalized British colony in the Age of Revolutions. Arriving at the end of the American Revolution and before the eruption of the Haitian Revolution in 1791, Black Loyalists occupy a peculiar space in the history of the region—defending in courts their right to freedom in ways that foreshadowed a more advanced black abolitionism expressed in wide-scale revolts that erupted within the British Caribbean in the last decades of formal slavery. The conflicts that emerged between black and white Loyalists were also complicated by the people and circumstances they encountered upon settling in the Bahamas. I argue that their lives were shaped by complex crosscutting identities expressed in relation to other African-descended people as well as to white inhabitants in the Bahamas. Black Loyalists entering the Bahamas from either Saint Augustine or New York encountered African-born as well as other free and enslaved black populations. Black Loyalists also negotiated and navigated relationships of power with various segments of the white Bahamian population.

In doing so, Bahamian Black Loyalists became politically engaged individuals, often acutely aware of the constraints on their rights as loyal black subjects functioning within a society of slaves on the periphery of the British Empire. Like Thomas Peters, Boston King, and other loyal blacks dispersed throughout the Atlantic, Black Loyalists entering the Bahamas took advantage of the fissures of the Revolutionary War to assert their right to be free. They also understood the value of their work as freemen and women, and appreciated the rights and privileges afforded to them as subjects of the British Crown. Like those who settled in Nova Scotia, Black Loyalists in Abaco and Nassau struggled to live independently outside the influence and control of white enslavers. Their effort to remain free from relations of dependency was both personal and political. By claiming their right to protection under various British proclamations and defending their freedom in courts, Black Loyalists established a foundation of political activism in the Bahamas rooted in the revolutionary and antislavery discourses emerging across the larger Atlantic world.

Beyond contributing to the political development of the Bahamas, Black Loyalists also established important social and religious institutions, including churches and schools that were inspired by the Black Loyalist experience in colonial America. Evidently, Black Loyalists throughout the Atlantic basin built on revolutionary traditions: demanding the right to land and equal opportunities, establishing churches based on evangelical religion, and generating a strong sense of self-reliance within their communities.[36] It will be demonstrated that these developments applied to the Bahamas but with peculiar variants based on the social, economic, and political landscape of the archipelago at the time. Thus, Black Loyalists played a critical role in the evolution of Bahamian society.

Additionally, this project seeks to fill an important historiographical void by reframing the view of Black Loyalists from a Bahamian and Caribbean perspective without losing sight of their roots in colonial America. In essence, the Black Loyalist experience in the Bahamas is discussed within a broader Atlantic world and Caribbean framework. Scholars of Caribbean history have long argued that the region was particularly important as the first site where a fully regimented and modernized plantation system was so organized that it fueled the growth of the Industrial

Revolution in England. The central characteristics of the region's history were a consequence of the forced importation of slave labor and the industrial organization of plantations. Though this focus on the development of the plantation system is necessary for understanding the general conditions that existed in much of the Caribbean region, it also obfuscates the presence of slavery in important locales where plantation labor was not the dominant labor system. Evidently, the plantation model has so dominated the historiography "that it often masks the fact that diversification was a significant feature of Caribbean society and economy even in the age of sugar." This study engages recent scholarship that has alluded to other sites where racial antagonism and oppressive conditions existed outside the plantation system.[37] Arguably, the hostility that emerged between black and white Loyalists in the Bahamas suggests the remarkable durability and flexibility of racial ideologies that emerged in various slave-holding societies in the Atlantic world.

This study also intersects with broader debates among scholars of comparative slave systems in the Americas. Recent scholarship on Latin America has revisited Frank Tannenbaum's early study, *Slave and Citizen,* in which he argues that access to courts of law and Catholicism in Iberian colonies provided a more benign and less severe form of slavery, particularly evident in high manumission rates and an enlarged free colored population.[38] Though rejecting Tannenbaum's flawed epistemological and dichotomous construction of Latin America versus the U.S. South, these scholars have, nevertheless, seen much value in exploring the resourceful and creative ways that enslaved persons and free blacks used various civic and ecclesiastical courts to advance individual liberties and secure freedom from the brutality of slavery. Studies of Louisiana, Spanish Florida, Colonial Mexico, the British Caribbean, and even the Andean Highlands have demonstrated that while enslaved persons may have utilized various courts and Roman law to assert their rights as subjects of the crown, not as chattel, the institutional system of slavery often remained brutal.[39] Local circumstances, demographic patterns, and material conditions often proved more significant than laws and ecclesiastical authority in shaping the contours of enslavement experienced by enslaved persons across the Americas. Recent scholarship in North America has called attention to the historical contingencies of slavery as an institution, noting that regional shifts in the transition from slaveholding to slave society were varied and did not always follow a linear model.[40]

It is within this framework that the Black Loyalist generation exiled to the Bahamas needs to be considered. Like enslaved persons who made good on the institutional promises of freedom in Spanish Florida, Black Loyalists in the Bahamas creatively fashioned freedom through aligning themselves with British imperial policies and local proclamations.[41] Black Loyalists in the Bahamas inhabited a unique geopolitical space: a non-plantation slaveholding society that bordered the Anglo-American world to the north and the sugar islands of the Caribbean to the south. Thus, Black Loyalists operated within a complex interlinked colonial world, pragmatically drawing on various received traditions in order to advance their rights as subjects of the British crown. In transporting these notions of subject-citizen to the Bahamas, Black Loyalists entered court spaces (much like their Latin American counterparts) to agitate for freedom and civil liberties. Yet even as Dunmore's proclamations provided Black Loyalists with direct and immediate access to "Negro Courts" to have their cases heard, the rulings did not always lead to freedom and greater liberty. In many ways, Negro Courts in the Bahamas upheld planter interests rather than softening the slave system or creating more benign conditions as suggested by Tannenbaum. Yet despite the negative rulings and other punitive measures, Black Loyalists forged new adaptive strategies to achieve that which was denied them by the law.

In more general terms, it is important to recognize that black responses to racial slavery in the Bahamas reflected a range of pragmatic political strategies. Several Black Loyalists in the Bahamas confronted the racial inequalities they faced by opportunistically seeking out white patronage and mimicking white values as a way to achieve personal advancement. Thus, these Black Loyalists developed an accommodationist strategy, applying their trades and skills in such a way as to gain entry into the world of white Bahamians, acquiring land, and even becoming slaveholders.[42] The case of Betty Watkins and Timothy Cox, both Bahamian Black Loyalists and slaveholders, is instructive for demonstrating the difficulty in assuming that all Black Loyalists adopted an antislavery posture in their politics. Indeed, moving beyond simple accommodation, Cox and Watkins represent individuals who upheld rather than opposed the slave system from which they themselves had only recently been disentangled. Others such as Joseph Paul may have adopted a moderate posture, attempting to remove the stain of slavery by focusing on the educational needs of the black masses. This position was much like that of Elizabeth and Anne Hart, free black missionaries to Antigua who in writing about faith, slavery, and freedom espoused a restrained view that was more ameliorationist than abolitionist.[43] Still others chose a more radical approach, defending the autonomy of their sacred institutions against the influences of white missionaries or government regulations. Such was the case with men like Prince Williams (1763–1840) and Frank Spence (?–1846), who not only established independent black Baptist churches in Nassau, but also defiantly worked to keep them under the control of black leadership.

Such varied strategies suggest that Black Loyalists entering the Bahamas creatively adapted their politics to the social and political realities of a territory that remained strongly allied with the imperial system and slave labor. For those individuals whose liberty was extended in the course of the Revolutionary War but later had it denied upon entry into the Bahamas, their struggle for freedom in the Negro Courts can best be understood as a conscious political act rooted squarely in an antislavery discourse. In this respect they advanced their cause for freedom in a language that reflected a mixture of British conservatism regarding their place as worthy subjects of the Crown and their desire for freedom from bondage. Yet, in many ways the strategies of the Black Loyalists in the Bahamas, whether slaveholder, accommodationist, or radical, were fragmented and constrained precisely because of the persistence of slavery in the Bahamas.

Arguably, it was the enduring specter of enslavement that made the Black Loyalist struggle for freedom in the Bahamas so complex and unpredictable. The fluidity of this slaveholding society allowed Prince Williams, cofounder of Bethel Baptist Church, to be redefined as an enslaved person and escapee in 1785, despite his service to the British cause during the war; but it also afforded Anthony Wallace, a founding Methodist, to be elevated to the status of slaveholder.[44] For Williams and countless others who had to fight for freedom a second time, their ideology was not inscribed in words or documents as much as they were articulated in their praxis. Where archival records exist it is evident that these liberty-seeking black refugees espoused a strong sense of individual freedom particularly manifested in the demands they articulated in legal documents and before the courts. Nevertheless, the few petitions that can be ascribed to Black Loyalists are worth considering as important political documents.[45] Written at a time of increasing abolitionist activity throughout the British Empire, both the 1816 petition on behalf of Methodists in the Bahamas and

Prince Williams' 1826 petition to the Governor represent ideas grounded in the sense that these individuals saw themselves as English subjects accorded the same rights and privileges of other Englishmen across the British Empire. Thus the political ideas inscribed in these documents coupled with their assertive actions suggest a people who were keenly aware and awakened to the ideas of liberty circulating the Atlantic.

This study locates the Black Loyalists and their lived experiences within a British imperial system in which their day-to-day struggles epitomized their quest for liberty.[46] Similar to the experience of Black Loyalists who settled in Australia, the process of achieving liberty was not only a slippery and tenuous process, but also deeply personal.[47] Particularly germane is the story of Randall, whose sense of satisfaction was drawn from the fact that despite being born in slavery, his three surviving children would grow up in New South Wales as freeborn English subjects, with rights guaranteed by custom and law.[48] Randall's case and countless others highlight the fact that Black Loyalists deployed multiple strategies to achieve individual liberty. This project focuses on the personal, political, and paradoxical: the fact that in fleeing republicanism and the rhetoric of liberty that denied them their aspirations in colonial America, Black Loyalists in the Bahamas animated the idea of liberation from bondage and coincidentally found freedom in a slave colony controlled by the British Crown. But navigating freedom required adaptability, pragmatism, and, above all, moving away from a doctrinaire ideological position.

Although individual efforts to secure freedom were more common and widespread in the Bahamas, there were moments when collective resistance surfaced among persons who shared the experience of having their quest for freedom denied. In discussing Black Loyalist political mobilization, I utilize the concept of collective resistance, which often takes shape within the groundswell of the hidden transcript. Hidden transcripts are those expressive cultural practices and individual performances that not only reinforce a sense of solidarity, but often surface in overt acts of rebellion.[49] Black Loyalists in the Bahamas undoubtedly fit within this definition of resistance. Their collective expressions of resistance included holding clandestine nocturnal meetings; escaping to the woods to form maroon communities; and close to the town of Nassau, collecting and keeping "together in the neighborhood of Government House, and Fort Charlotte, in open and flagrant violation of the laws of the colony."[50] Likewise the landholding practices of Black Loyalists—squatting on uncultivated land, holding untitled land in common, and selling produce grown on garden plots at the marketplace—can also be conceived as a kind of black resistance, an adaptive strategy operating in counterpoint to the dictates of colonial officials and local mercantile elites.

While such subversive acts are small in scale compared with the magnitude of the Haitian Revolution that erupted by 1791, the Black Loyalist experience, nevertheless, drew upon a radical tradition of resistance that went beyond individual effort. Emblematic of the ways in which these refugees acted within a black radical tradition was the 1788 Abaco insurrection, in which, after hiding in the woods for a considerable time, Black Loyalists took up arms against whites in order to defend their liberty. In this respect the 1787–1788 Abaco insurrection, represents a turning point, the apex of Black Loyalist agitation. It is telling that after May 1788 the next major collective upheaval in the Bahamas occurred during the late 1820s and '30s, when enslaved persons across the Bahamas sent a resounding antislavery message by taking up arms and fighting for freedom.

For various reasons, historians have tended to focus on the larger and more wide-scale revolts of the latter period without giving much attention to the place of the Abaco insurrection and its antecedents in Bahamian history. Perhaps the lack of a recognized ringleader or the shortness of the affair has led to this obfuscation. Such considerations ignore the fact that Black Loyalists, much like those who later fought against slavery, made discernible choices—both collective and individual—that spoke to a maturing political consciousness, one that was forged in the crucible of slavery and directed against the system that bound them to oppressive conditions and denied them rights as subject-citizens.[51] This process of political awakening did not occur in a vacuum but was shaped by the politics of the black Atlantic in an Age of Revolutions.[52] Significantly, both Black Loyalists and enslaved rebels of the formative period of rebellion were acutely aware of the activities taking place in the Atlantic world, to the point that they could direct their self-assertiveness toward those who could most readily remedy their situation. In the case of the Exuma uprising (1829–1830) the leader, Pompey, along with his coconspirators, stole their master's dinghy and headed for Nassau where they hoped to have their case heard before an allegedly sympathetic governor, Carmichael Smyth.[53] Similarly, in 1833, on Johnson's estate in Eleuthera, news of impending freedom led enslaved persons to "assert that they were free," refuse to work, and thereby force a magistrate and soldiers of the Second

West Indian Regiment to intervene with promises of improved working conditions.[54] Yet beyond the political acumen and self-determination evident in these two episodes, no other pattern can be discerned between the events that feature Black Loyalists in the late eighteenth century and the substantial slave revolts that erupted on Family Islands in the Bahamas from 1828 to 1832. Nonetheless, the lack of patterns or causal connections should not be reason to feature prominently one set of antislavery struggles over another. The Black Loyalist case ought to stand on its own as a study of nascent abolitionist activities in an Age of Revolutions. Given the global dimension of the Black Loyalist diaspora, this study provides insight into a previously ignored group of refugees forced to navigate a unique local terrain—both socioeconomic and geopolitical—within an evolving black Atlantic.

Precisely because of their unique politics and the geopolitical space they inhabited, the Black Loyalist quest for liberty in the Bahamas raises a number of important questions related to individual and collective identity formation and the particular ways in which people negotiate and navigate inequalities across international borders.[55] To what extent did the experience of war shape Black Loyalists' sense of being British subjects in the Bahamas? Further, what kind of black communities evolved in British-garrisoned cities, and how, if at all, were they reconstituted in the Bahamas? How did the revivalism of the Great Awakening inform Black Loyalists' religious and political thinking in the Bahamas? Moreover, given the fact that the Bahamas emerged as a nonplantation slaveholding society, how did Black Loyalists navigate relations of power with whites of various classes? Finally, did their responses to oppressive conditions mirror forms of collective and individual resistance found throughout the Caribbean region and broader Atlantic world?

Bearing these questions in mind, chapter 1 focuses on the roots of black political and religious thought as expressed by those Black Loyalists who settled in the Bahamas. It highlights the ways in which their wartime experiences in the garrisoned seaport cities along the Atlantic were routed to the social, political, and religious landscape of the Bahamas after 1783. Experiences in these cities provided a blueprint for the kind of politics and institutions that Black Loyalists would develop in the Bahamas. Chapter 1 also examines the distinctive social and political terrain of the Bahamas in the pre-Loyalist period as a way to bring into relief the transformative effect that their arrival had on the islands in 1783.

Chapter 2 explores the political activism of Black Loyalists as they fought for their freedom in various courts established in Nassau and Abaco by 1787. This chapter also explores the contentious issues that arose in Abaco, leading to outright rebellion in 1788. Beyond this, chapter 2 examines alternative strategies taken up by Black Loyalists who by the late 1780s had developed a deep antipathy toward the notion of legal redress.

Chapter 3 focuses on the emerging Black Loyalist social institutions, including churches and schools that supported the development of self-reliant communities in Nassau and Abaco. Chapter 4 turns to the importance of work conditions for Black Loyalists as well as their struggles to gain access to land. It argues that freedom for Black Loyalists was shaped in large part by the socioeconomic conditions in which they lived and labored. Chapter 5 examines the political contests emerging in the early nineteenth century over whether full citizenship and inclusion in the body politic would be extended to Black Loyalists. In the end, I argue that Black Loyalists in the Bahamas played a critical role in the development of nineteenth-century Bahamian society: advancing political ideas related to personal freedom; building important institutional structures, including churches and schools; and asserting an important role in the emerging local market economy.

1

ROOTS AND ROUTES

The journey embarked upon by Black Loyalists destined for the Bahamas was not marked by a rupture from their past experiences in colonial America, but rather reflected a continuity shaped by conditions of enslavement and their entry into a British colony as persons of color. Like West African victims of the transatlantic slave trade, Black Loyalists arriving in the Bahamas did not come as a tabula rasa, but rather brought with them various ideas about religion, land, politics, and even freedom. Thus, upon arrival in the Bahamas the lessons of the Revolutionary War were appropriated and reinterpreted by Black Loyalist men and women in a variety of ways, often with varying consequences. Such complex transmutations within the Bahamas invite an analytical approach that examines the roots of such thought as it emerged out of the social and political world of colonial British North America.

A brief examination of leading Black Loyalists in the Bahamas demonstrates that the world they lived in was indelibly shaped by the world they left behind. Prince Williams' remarkable story began in colonial Georgia where he was born free, but was later "cheated out of his freedom and sold to an American."[1] Although his slave owner is never mentioned by name, Williams' account reveals that he was forced to serve "this man" when "the British troops came to Georgia." Taking advantage of the chaos of the American Revolution, Williams, in an act of self-assertion, escaped to the British side in order to claim freedom as a Black Loyalist. As Williams tellingly admitted in his claim, "by this circumstance he gained his liberty and is in a better situation than he would have been if the war had not happened."[2] As proof of his loyalty to the British cause, it was noted by the Loyalist Claims Commission that Williams had served six years in the 60th regiment under the command of General Prevost at Savannah. It was also in the environs of Savannah that Williams came into contact with black Separate Baptist preachers George Liele (1752–1825), and Amos Williams (?–1799). With the war ending, Prince Williams was most likely part of the massive evacuation of Loyalists from Savannah to Saint Augustine. Williams eventually embarked on a sea voyage in the 1780s to New Providence in an open boat with another Black Loyalist and Baptist preacher by the name of Sharper Morris.[3] Even as he escaped to freedom in the Bahamas, Williams was still identified as a runaway based on the 1785 advertisement published in the *Bahama Gazette*. In the advertisement, Williams was described as a "Negro Man named Prince," to be found along with another escapee identified as Sambo Scriven, "well known as a Baptist preacher." Williams' tenuous and torturous status eventually was resolved but only after he had petitioned the government and defended his claims in the Negro Court. Accordingly, Williams was finally declared free by way of Lord Dunmore's Certificate, issued in 1793 and recorded for posterity in the Negro Freedoms Register, an addendum to the Executive Council Minutes. Confirmation of Williams' hard-won free status was further evident in the fact that in 1801 his signature appeared on the property purchased for Bethel Baptist church.[4]

Amos Williams had a similar journey to freedom. Likely an enslaved person living on the Galphin plantation, Williams was first exposed to the doctrine of Separate Baptists from the preaching of George Liele. At the outbreak of the Revolutionary War, Amos Williams fled to Savannah and worshipped at Yamacrow or Brumpton, congregations established by Liele outside of Savannah. Eventually, Amos was evacuated from Savannah for East Florida where he apparently was identified in the Registry Office Records as a Black Loyalist, having received a free pass from Saint Augustine, dated 1784 and authorized under the proclamation order of General McArthur.[5] Subsequent to his departure from East Florida in 1784, Amos arrived in New Providence where he along with Prince Williams and Sambo Scriven established Bethel Baptist Church.[6]

A third example of a journey to freedom in the Bahamas also relates to the Galphin plantation. In a decision made before Dunmore's Negro Court on January 2, 1788, "the claims to freedom set up by Hannah a

negro woman formerly the property of George Galphin of South Carolina," were upheld.[7] Though the historical record on Hannah is relatively
slim, her life story indicates much about the Black Loyalist experience.
First, it reveals the fact that despite aligning herself with the British and
claiming freedom as a full British subject during the war, Hannah was
forced to defend her right to freedom in a court in the Bahamas. Moreover, her connection to George Galphin—most likely her slave owner—
also suggests a possible link to the Separate Baptist congregation in Silver
Bluff and by extension Bethel Baptist Church in the Bahamas.

Taken collectively, these three cases highlight the complex geopolitical
space of the Black Loyalist diaspora. As sojourners, all three had lived in
multiple locations throughout the Atlantic world, often moving between
and through national boundaries such as Spanish Florida or British-
controlled Savannah. As these individuals moved beyond the emerging
boundaries of Anglo-America, they carried the ideas that shaped their
particular worldviews. In this regard, Black Loyalists were culturally informed individuals operating in a larger Atlantic world in which they not
only carried peculiar ideas about faith and politics but also were forced to
navigate various colonial boundaries and borders. These beliefs were not
static and immutable notions timelessly fixed in the past. Instead, they
were shaped and reshaped as much by the people and communities they
encountered as by the peculiar sociopolitical environments they experienced in their travels. Utilizing the image of the ship as a fluid space con-
necting Atlantic ports, this chapter traces the roots and routes of the experiences of Black Loyalists in colonial America and how particular political
and religious traditions were eventually transmitted and refashioned to
the Bahamian sociopolitical landscape.[8] Notably, this process of adapta-
tion and transmission to the Bahamian environment was both unique and
common to the larger Black Loyalist diaspora. Thus, in order to sharpen
the distinctiveness of the Black Loyalist experience in the Bahamas it is
necessary to expand our optics to the larger world of the Black Loyalist
diaspora. This approach captures the multifarious and multilayered experiences of the Black Loyalist diaspora, underscoring the sinews of ideas
and institutions that were carried collectively by royal refugees, without
losing sight of local peculiarities. By extension, the narrative will naturally
involve placing Bahamian Black Loyalists such as Joseph Paul and Prince
Williams alongside others with a similar experience. In this regard, the
rooted colonial experience of George Liele, David George, John Marrant,

Boston King, and other Black Loyalists will be examined alongside the featured black refugees that eventually were *routed* to the Bahamas. Beyond contextualizing Black Loyalist thought in colonial America, it is equally important to explore the peculiar local terrain of the Bahamas. In this respect an effort will be made to link both the world left behind and the new world that Black Loyalists entered when they were evacuated from various colonial seaports to the Bahamas at the end of the Revolutionary War. In this respect, examining the local conditions that existed in the pre-Loyalist Bahamas will allow for a more measured assessment of the acute and dramatic changes that occurred upon the arrival of Black Loyalists in 1783. In the end, this chapter focuses on the development of religious and secular institutional structures in colonial America and how they were eventually routed by Black Loyalists to the Bahamas, a peculiar slaveholding society on the margins of the emerging Atlantic world.

The roots of Black Loyalist thinking in the Bahamas and throughout the Atlantic were shaped by a number of significant intellectual and religious currents, most notably the Revolutionary War and the religious upheavals of the Great Awakening. Where the revolutionary fervor of the American Revolution broke the bonds of monarchical rule, the revivalism of the Great Awakening worked on leveling the ecclesiastical order in colonial society.[9] The Great Awakening can best be defined as an evangelical Christian movement that began in the 1740s, initially disseminated by enthusiastic white itinerant preachers in the North, including Jonathan Edwards, George Whitefield, and John Wesley. Driven by a deep sense that God's divine power could be immediately experienced by persons from all stations in society, these men preached a redemptive message that not only broke the traditional denominational boundaries and creeds, but also embraced a religious experience open to all believers. By the 1780s the religious fervor had spread to the South. Spurred by the black missionary David Margate (who had arrived in Charleston in January 1775), evangelical Christianity would eventually be embraced by free blacks and enslaved persons living along the swampy waterways and rivers of South Carolina and Georgia. Among the new converts and purveyors of Great Awakening revivalism were black men such as John Marrant (1755–1791), David George (1742–1810), George Liele (1750–1828), Joseph Paul (1753–1802), and Amos Williams (?–1799). These men not only founded chapels in the South, but also led Black Loyalists in the establishment of sectarian churches in Jamaica, Nova Scotia, Sierra Leone, and the Bahamas.[10]

Much of the black evangelical work that would eventually be transmitted across the black Atlantic originated on the Galphin plantation, on the
border between South Carolina and Georgia. Of particular importance
for the Black Loyalist diaspora was the emergence of George Liele as a
leader among free black and enslaved congregants in the Silver Bluff and
Burke County frontier area along the Savannah River. Liele had initially
been exposed to Separate Baptist teachings through the efforts of his
enslaver Harry Sharpe, a devout man who shared the Great Awakening
enthusiasm of George Whitefield, Daniel Marshall, and Shubal Stearns.
Upon settlement in the Kiokee area in Georgia, Harry Sharpe employed
Matthew Moore as a plantation pastor, and encouraged Liele and other
enslaved persons to attend gospel meetings. Under Moore's tutelage, Liele
was converted to the Separate Baptist faith by age twenty-three. Apparently, Liele also was taught how to read and write. Moore also played a
critical role in credentialing Liele as an itinerant preacher. By 1775 Liele
was ordained by a ministers' council presided over by Matthew Moore,
Harry Sharpe, and Daniel Marshall.[11]

From the outset it appears that Liele's missionary work targeted the
free black and enslaved populations in the immediate area. Liele, in fact,
worked with a white missionary, Wait Palmer, in establishing a meetinghouse on the Galphin plantation, owned by an Irishman, George Galphin. The plantation was located almost directly across the Savannah
River from Augusta, Georgia, in the area known as Galphinton and Silver
Bluff. Though the exact date of the establishment of the church is hard to
determine, it is evident that the congregation had been formed a year or
two before the Revolutionary War broke out.[12] It was here that George
Liele came into contact with David George and Jesse Palmer. Together,
these men would not only constitute the Silver Bluff Church—the first in
North America directly controlled by blacks—but in the case of George
and Liele they would be linked together as itinerant black preachers and
Loyalists during the American Revolution.[13]

The outbreak of war in the South dramatically altered the work of black
evangelicals and their supporters in the rural areas of Georgia and South
Carolina. Silver Bluff, as the incubator for much of the Separate Baptist
teachings, was in fact disbanded as a result of the war. Though the fissures of war ruptured the Silver Bluff congregation, the end result was not
entirely negative, as it allowed George Liele and others to expand their
evangelical work to British-controlled spaces in and around Savannah. In

this way, "the vicissitudes of war drove the church into exile—but only to multiply itself elsewhere."[14] Indeed, it was in the British-occupied area of Savannah and the outlying regions that Black Loyalists David George and George Liele converged to establish close informal networks of black congregants and lay preachers that would later extend across the Atlantic to Jamaica, Nova Scotia, and the Bahamas.[15] Of significance for the establishment of Separate Baptists in the Bahamas was the influence of these men on Amos Williams. The latter had initially been exposed to the evangelical message of Liele while a member of the Dead River Church, located on the Galphin plantation.[16] During the war, Amos Williams fled to the British lines at Savannah, where he reconnected with Liele and other black itinerants. It was possibly in the immediate vicinity of Savannah and behind British lines that Prince Williams also came into contact with Amos Williams, George Liele, and David George. Such informal ties would take on greater significance once these Black Loyalist men were forced to evacuate Savannah with the British in 1782. Despite being dispersed to various locales throughout the Atlantic world, George Liele, David George, and Amos Williams maintained communication with one another. In a letter written by George Liele to John Rippon, the editor of the Baptist Annual Registry, he mentions correspondence received from friends in Savannah with news that "Brother Amos" had organized a Baptist congregation and constructed a church building for worship services.[17] Clearly, within the Separate Baptist faith, close ties were established between black Baptist preachers dispersed throughout the Atlantic world.[18] Perhaps more telling of the linkages between the Separate Baptist faith emanating out of the Galphin plantation and loyal black Baptists who settled in the Bahamas was the list of names in the Negro Freedoms Register, an addendum to the larger Executive Council Minutes of the Bahama Islands. Listed in the Register in 1783 were Cyrus Galphin, Charlotte Galphin, Clarinda Galphin, Chloe Galphin, and Jamo Galphin, all recorded as free according to a "Justices Certificate." This document is important for two reasons: first, it bears witness to the freedom earned by these Black Loyalists who allied with the British during the Revolutionary War; second, it also gives a clear indication that much of the Separate Baptist church at Silver Bluff was reconstituted not just in Jamaica under Liele, but also more impressively and directly in the Bahamas.[19]

However, the rapid growth and spread of revivalism among enslaved and free blacks throughout the Atlantic world was not limited to the influence of George Liele and the Separate Baptist denomination. Indeed, black evangelicals of the Methodist persuasion became carriers of a colonial American religious experience that was later grafted onto Atlantic world sites inclusive of Nova Scotia, Jamaica, Antigua, England, and the Bahamas. Most significantly for the study of Black Loyalists in the Bahamas was the journey of Joseph Paul. Paul's roots began in South Carolina, where as a young boy he had heard George Whitefield preach. Sometime shortly before, or perhaps even during the American Revolution, Paul was moved to New York with his owner Richard Cartwright.[20] During the war, Paul was able to purchase not only his own freedom but also the freedom of his wife and three children.[21] It is also quite possible that during his time in British-occupied New York, Paul would have come into contact with other black evangelicals of the Methodist persuasion such as Boston King (1760–1802), Murphy Stiel, and Moses Wilkinson (1747–?). Though no written correspondence exists between these men, all four were evacuated from New York and recorded in the *Book of Negroes*.[22]

Notwithstanding these possible connections, Paul, his wife Susannah, and their three children left New York onboard *The Nautilus* on August 21, 1783 for the island of Abaco. In time, Paul and his family migrated to Nassau, New Providence, where he preached in the open to a congregation of three hundred every Sunday afternoon.[23] By 1791 Paul and his congregants had built a permanent edifice in the heart of Delancey Town (on the corner of Augusta and Hetherfield streets) that was used as both a Methodist meeting-house and a school.[24] It is worth noting that even as Paul established evangelical roots in New Providence, much of his congregation was drawn from the Black Loyalist population in New York City and the New England area. William Gordon, an Anglican priest stationed in New Providence, observed the presence of black Methodists, noting that many were originally from New England and included several "Negro Preachers."[25]

Whereas Paul had acquired roots within a larger swath of the Eastern seaboard of colonial America, it appears that Anthony Wallace had more direct connections with the religious revivalism spreading across Georgia and South Carolina. Likely a follower of Primitive Methodism, as a free black, Wallace was eventually elevated to lay preacher and worked among the Methodists in Charleston before being evacuated with the British to Saint Augustine sometime between 1782 and 1783. Though little detail is available in colonial America regarding Anthony Wallace, his marriage to a co-congregant Igbo woman living in Charleston and his later connections with black missionary efforts to the Bahamas in the 1790s suggest Wallace likely had fairly deep roots in the black Methodist world of Charleston. It is also worth noting that the Register of Negro Freedoms confirms Wallace's free status in the Bahamas. In 1799 it described him as an exhorter of James Wallace.[26] Arguably both Wallace and Paul used their experience in the Atlantic world as trans-Caribbean evangelicals to effectively navigate relations with black and white church leaders within the fold of Primitive Methodism.[27]

The broad trans-Atlantic connections expressed in the lives of Joseph Paul and Anthony Wallace mirrored those of other Black Loyalist evangelicals of the Methodist persuasion. Evidently, "Afro-Protestants in the eighteenth century forged evangelical networks which spanned the Atlantic to places as scattered as Sierra Leone, the West Indies, North America and Europe."[28] Similar to Joseph Paul and Anthony Wallace in the Bahamas, men like Moses Wilkinson, Boston King, and John Marrant were carriers of an evangelical revivalism that reflects this trans-Atlantic trajectory. Born enslaved in 1760 to Richard Waring, King grew up in the rural areas surrounding Charleston, South Carolina. With the outbreak of war and the capture of Charleston by the British in 1780, Waring became apprehensive and moved King to a more remote plantation at some distance from the estate where his parents resided. This unfortunate circumstance turned fortuitous for King as he used the opportunity to escape as an enslaved fugitive to the British side. Despite a number of harrowing experiences including bouts with smallpox and near recapture, he eventually found his way to New York, where he worked precariously as a British privateer, even while facing the specter of being re-enslaved by Patriot raiders. It was this series of fortunate experiences that led King to believe that God had providentially intervened in his life.[29] This spiritual narrative would later legitimize his calling as a lay preacher.[30] Evacuated in 1783, King would embrace the Wesleyan brand of evangelicalism in Nova Scotia through the work of Moses Wilkinson, an aged, near-blind, and lame lay preacher who converted him.

Wilkinson's journey as a Black Loyalist evangelical had begun in Virginia, where he had absconded from Mills Wilkinson, a merchant in Suffolk County, and joined Dunmore's Ethiopian Regiment. Despite falling victim to smallpox, Wilkinson perfected his evangelical preaching skills, relying on his oral communication and spontaneous emotive expressions even while working within the fold of Wesleyan Methodism. Once he found his way to the security of British-occupied New York City, Wilkinson continued to preach, utilizing spellbinding renditions of Old Testament stories to attract followers drawn from the refugee population that proliferated in the city.[31] Upon exile, Wilkinson would remain a fervent evangelical, arriving in Nova Scotia in the summer of 1783 and eventually establishing one of the largest Wesleyan congregations in the black Atlantic.

Although King and Wilkinson remained connected with the Wesleyan Methodist work in Nova Scotia, the experience of the black evangelical John Marrant was much different. Marrant's initial foray into evangelical religiosity began in Charleston, South Carolina, where as a young violinist he was converted after stumbling upon a meetinghouse where George Whitefield was preaching.[32] Following his conversion, Marrant was eventually evacuated to London, England, where he became ordained as a preacher attached to the Huntingdon Connection of Calvinist Methodists. Marrant epitomized the global treks of Black Loyalists, returning to British North America briefly to serve a Black Loyalist community in Nova Scotia before moving on to Boston in 1788 and then back to England where he died at age thirty-five.[33] Echoing the work of other black evangelicals caught up in the fervor of revivalism in colonial America, Marrant preached a message tailored to the specific social and political needs of blacks throughout the Atlantic world. Yet Marrant's Zionist vision was also unique given his short life span and his extremely prolific writing. In sermons, pamphlets, and broadsides, Marrant articulated a discourse of black redemption and the principles of social justice instilled in him during his experience as a Black Loyalist and revolutionary living in colonial America.[34]

Even as Marrant developed a peculiar Zionist message in his printed works and sermons, his call was not uncommon among black evangelicals across the black Atlantic who preached a message of hope and spiritual regeneration with direct links to the revivalism of the Great Awakening. What attracted this chorus of black evangelicals to the religious experience of the Great Awakening? Black itinerants throughout the Atlantic world spurned orthodoxy and ignited a democratic revolution in American religion founded on egalitarian principles.[35] Within the Methodist and Baptist denominations in particular, black and white congregants participated as spiritual equals in unprecedented fashion. The preachers, men such as George Whitefield, Francis Asbury, and John Wesley, not only encouraged blacks, whites, and native Americans to participate together, but in their sermons also emphasized a common evangelical experience based on the authority of scripture and the importance of preaching instead of liturgy. Great Awakening preachers also expressed a spiritual form of egalitarianism by emphasizing salvation by faith rather than the efficacy of the sacraments.[36] In this respect the Great Awakening revivalism highlighted the fact that the church was to comprise the regenerate, "those whom God had saved and who had experienced God's precious dealing with their souls in ways they could recount to others." This experience of being born again represented the clearest example of the leveling effect of revivalism. As such, "a slave could certainly experience saving grace, even when his owner had not."[37]

Likewise, among both Separate Baptists and Methodists, blacks could more easily rise to positions of leadership in the church because of the lack of institutionalized obstacles. In other words, "the self-validating quality of Methodism provided for those furthest on the peripheries of organized American religion, most notably women and blacks, the means with which to exercise greater influence than they had ever been allowed to command in more established churches."[38] Regarding the Baptists, "the lack of strict educational requirements for the ministry, with the emphasis upon being called to preach rather than upon educational preparation" was one of the factors that explained why the Baptists attracted the largest following among blacks.[39] In addition to the egalitarian ethos of the revival meetings, Baptist and Methodists attracted large followings among the enslaved and free populations in colonial America because of the congregational structure of church organization that facilitated the development of an independent church body.[40]

Apart from the egalitarian church structure, Methodists and Baptists shifted away from the rituals and catechism instructions of Anglicanism which had by the late eighteenth century come to represent a far more staid and formulaic form of religiosity that was associated with the white slave-owning class. Baptists replaced the learning of catechisms with the yearning for ecstatic spiritual experience, and the celebration of the Lord's Supper at Christmas, Easter, and Whitsunday, with frequent love feasts where the bread and wine were brought to the people. Methodist revival meetings also tended to reproduce similar ecstatic and emotional experiences. As such, a number of early Methodists believed in the efficacy of prophetic dreams, visions, and supernatural impressions and were not afraid to base their daily decisions on such phenomena.[41]

Such ecstatic experiences underscore the ways in which the Great Awakening drew upon cultural practices that resembled religious rituals originating in West African societies.[42] In this regard, despite variations within African societies, evangelicals did have a "closely shared set of perceptions" that made possible the shaping of an African-derived culture under the impact of British North American slavery.[43] While West African cultures were certainly not monolithic, it is nevertheless quite possible that within the colonial American world, Africans and descendants of Africans born in America began to share similar cultural practices based on West African principles often working synchronously within Christian evangelical religion.[44]

A number of examples serve to highlight the ways in which Black Loyalists synthesized West African and Judeo-Christian religious practices. Of particular importance are the various accounts of conversion experiences by Black Loyalists that occurred within the context of the revivalism of the Great Awakening. David George's narrative reflects the ways in which Christian revivalism reflected an ecstatic experience whereby the initial depraved condition of the seeker is transformed by a personalized encounter with a transcendent God. Born in Essex County, Virginia, to parents "who were brought from Africa," George was initially exposed to the revivalism of the Great Awakening as an enslaved person on the Galphin plantation at Silver Bluff, South Carolina. Accordingly, after living a "bad life" George came to the realization that "if I lived so, I should never see the face of God in glory." The depraved condition of his soul had in fact led him to become physically sick to the point where George could no longer wait "upon my master."[45] Realizing the total depravity of his life of sin, George noted that he prayed earnestly that the Lord would take away his distress. As a testament to his conversion experience, George recounted how not only did the Lord intervene and "take away my distress," but "I had such pleasure and joy in my soul, that no man could give me."[46]

John Marrant's conversion echoed a similar ecstatic expression. Marrant recounted how his initial interest in attending a meetinghouse in Charleston where George Whitefield was preaching was purely vain and foolish, given that he wanted only to disrupt the meeting by blowing his horn. However, upon hearing the sermon preached by Whitefield—on the text, "Prepare to meet thy God, O Israel"—Marrant was instantly "struck to the ground, and lay both speechless and senseless near half an hour."[47] When he eventually recovered, Marrant observed that "every word I heard from the minister was like a parcel of swords thrust in to me, and what added to my distress, I thought I saw the devil on every side of me." Unable to walk or stand, Marrant was eventually carried to the vestry office where Whitefield would later confront him with the words, "Jesus Christ has got thee at last." Though Whitefield would eventually depart Charleston, Marrant remained bedridden for three or four days until some ministers called on him to relieve him of his distress. After several hours of arduous praying and exhorting, Marrant was finally relieved of his condition through the divine intercessions of God Almighty. As Marrant aptly noted, "the Lord was pleased to set my soul at perfect liberty, and being filled with joy, I began to praise the Lord immediately: my sorrow were turned to peace and joy and love."[48]

Apart from conversion testimonials, Black Loyalists expressed a religious experience that reflected a sense of direct and personal contact with God through night visions and trances. Such religious expressions harkened back to beliefs about the ancestral spirit world that were predominant in West Africa. While at the barracks of his company on Water Street in New York City, Murphy Stiel, a sergeant in the Black Pioneers, heard a voice "like a man's (but saw no body)." Apparently, however, the voice had instructed Stiel to inform the British General, Sir Henry Clinton, that "he should send a special message to George Washington. Stiel heard the voice say several times that Washington must surrender his troops immediately or the 'wrath of God would fall upon him.'" God's condemnation, Stiel understood, meant that he "would raise all of the blacks in America to fight against him." In a letter to Clinton that followed, Stiel made it clear to Clinton and Lord Cornwallis that they need not worry because "the Lord would be on their side."[49] Stiel's prophetic vision speaks to the ways in which an African Sacred Cosmos was reinscribed and reinterpreted by people of African descent during the Great Awakening. Indeed, Stiel most likely believed in "soul talk," the African-derived concept that ancestral spirits often roamed freely in the world and could be accessed through dreams and trances.[50] While Stiel's vision was unique in its political undertones, it also represents the ways in which Great Awakening revivalism had so deeply penetrated the religious lives of people of African descent. In the end, the revivalism of the Great Awakening appealed to African-descended people for multiple reasons: the egalitarian nature of revival meetings; the emphasis on experience rather than pedigree as the basis of faith; the early embrace of blacks as itinerant preachers; and the ecstatic practices that provided a mnemonic image of West African traditions. Undoubtedly, such religious permutations had far-reaching repercussions, imbuing black evangelicals and their followers with a deep desire to transmit these traditions and practices to various host societies they entered at the end of the Revolutionary War.

If the evangelical movement associated with the Great Awakening had a far-reaching impact on the religious ideas of Black Loyalists dispersed to the Bahamas, equally important was the political thought shaped during the Revolutionary War and the subsequent evacuation process from British-occupied cities. In ways never before presented, the chaotic circumstances of the Revolutionary War opened and exposed ruptures in American colonial society. Such discursive spaces, no matter how small, provided African Americans with opportunities to claim freedom as a legitimate right. In responding to pronouncements made by British officers beginning with Lord Dunmore's November 7, 1775, proclamation, and culminating with Sir Guy Carleton's evacuation orders in April of 1783, Black Loyalists demonstrated their desire to establish an autonomous life outside the control of white colonial hegemony.

From the British perspective, the decision to use enslaved persons in a military capacity was never meant to destroy the edifice of slavery itself but rather was purposely directed toward undermining and weakening the Patriot cause.[51] This point is evident in the ambiguous and contradictory actions of British officers in battle and their hesitancy to embrace the claims to freedom articulated by enslaved Africans. The decision to arm enslaved persons was not based on any preexisting policy but was formulated for the most part by individual commanders and leaders acting independently and according to local circumstances. As such, plans to arm enslaved blacks were regularly proposed, opposed, and discarded in a rather ad hoc manner. Ultimately, the development of a formal policy on arming and later freeing blacks and persons of color serving in various capacities under the British flag grew out of the circumstances of war, not as a unified and cohesive pattern.[52]

Considered in this context, the earliest proclamation promising freedom to enslaved Africans willing to fight for the British cause by Lord Dunmore, then governor of Virginia, reflected neither an attempt to overthrow slavery nor an effort to make war on it.[53] This is evident from the proclamation issued on November 7, 1775, in which only "indentured servants, negroes or others (appertaining to rebels) free, that are able and willing to bear arms," would be encouraged to join the British forces in "restoring the colony to a proper sense of duty."[54] When examined closely, Dunmore's proclamation was designed primarily to encourage the defection of useful or able blacks willing and able to bear arms.[55] From a tactical standpoint, Dunmore's strategy was to encourage the defection of useful blacks without provoking a general insurrection, and to disrupt the psychological security of Patriot whites without unleashing the full military potential of blacks. In the end, his policy was pragmatic rather than moral, rooted in political expediency rather than humanitarian zeal.[56] Put another way, in an empire determined to maintain the institution of slavery and the continuation of the slave trade, "the Dunmore proclamation and Britain's subsequent extension of it can only be viewed in isolation as a desperate attempt to bring the rebellious colonies to their knees by any available means."[57]

If Dunmore's proclamation was squarely rooted in the politics of a military campaign, then later proclamations were extensions of this peculiar wartime condition. This is borne out by Henry Clinton's policy of July 1776 in which he pledged to free any rebel-owned black aligned with the Loyalist cause while simultaneously insisting that Loyalist-owned enslaved persons be returned to their owners, adding that masters should refrain from punishing these escapees. In 1779, Clinton issued his famous Philipsburg proclamation promising "to every negro who shall desert the Rebel Standard, full security to follow within these lines, any Occupation which he shall think proper."[58] Here, Clinton departs from Dunmore's earlier proclamation in one substantial area: previously, only those blacks capable of military service had been accepted as refugees, and consequently numbers had been kept relatively small. After 1779, however, the inclusion of *every negro* meant that even those unfit to bear arms, including women and children, could now technically qualify for British protection, not to mention men who had previously hesitated to join the ranks of the British, knowing they were leaving their families behind.[59] However, like Dunmore's earlier proclamation, Clinton's policy was never meant to destroy slavery as an institution. Rather, it was simply a ploy to destroy the southern slave-owners' livelihood, and, by extension, to weaken the military strength of the Patriot cause.

In contrast, for enslaved blacks and free persons of color who joined the British forces, their decision was grounded in the hope of freedom and a better life. Simply put, African Americans were by no means passive recipients of British proclamations. Through their actions and determination to seek freedom behind British lines, Black Loyalists voted with their feet.[60] However, the decision to ally with British forces was complicated and risky for a number of reasons. Many faced the very real possibility of being captured in the midst of their flight by one or the other contending forces and in many cases re-enslaved under different auspices.[61] In addition, both enslaved and free person alike, in taking this action, were tacitly acknowledging their allegiance to the British, the very colonial power that had made possible their enslavement. Yet despite the risks, and the provisional and tentative nature of the reward, many enslaved blacks were motivated and inspired by the promise of freedom.

If escaping to British lines inspired a desire for freedom on the part of enslaved blacks, then their experience in British-controlled cities such as Charleston, New York, Savannah, and Saint Augustine afforded them the opportunity to defend their newfound liberty, establish social and religious institutions, and develop strong, self-reliant communities. In particular, in all four cities the war allowed Black Loyalists the chance to effectively reconstitute important social networks, or even create new ones. For New York City, *The Book of Negroes* indicates a substantial number of blacks who seized the moment to either reunite families divided by slavery or establish new ties while in New York City. Take for instance, a man named simply Prince, born enslaved in New Jersey, who was able to purchase his freedom from Joseph Stokes of New Jersey. Prince eventually found his way to New York with his freeborn wife, Margaret, and their son Mintard. In New York City, they connected with their daughter, Elizabeth, her small child, and her husband, Samuel Van Nostrandt, who had escaped from his former master in Essex County, New Jersey.[62] These cases suggest that despite the continuation of slavery in New York, it appears that many blacks were able to take advantage of the war to reestablish familial links or even forge new ones.

In Savannah and its environs, Black Loyalists established important networks based on work and religious affiliation. George Liele in particular made use of the fissures of the Revolutionary War to extend his itinerant preaching to black communities along the Savannah River located within British lines. Liele also worked as a cart man, traveling to remote areas within the South Carolina backcountry in order to transport important supplies to the British troops in Savannah. Of particular importance were the links between Liele and David George. Not only did David George assist Liele for two months in his Savannah ministry, but they also worked together on a plantation as cart men during the war.[63] Liele's connection with David George is but one of many accounts of Black Loyalists forging important links during the war.[64] Likewise, in Charleston, Black Loyalists established significant social, religious, and familial contacts even while the city was garrisoned by British troops. An advertisement in the March 9, 1782, edition of the *Royal Gazette* reveals the extent of social networks forged during the war. According to the advertisement, "a mustee wench, named Kate, about forty years of age," had run away on February 25. Escaping with her was "a negro boy named Marcus." The two, it was alleged, were harbored along with "another negro named George," who had arrived in Charleston from Pensacola, in West Florida. The three were intending to travel to New York and therefore the subscriber warned all masters of vessels against "harbouring, or carry[ing] off the said negro and her child."[65] Although Marcus is never identified as Kate's son, it would appear from the advertisement that they did have a familial connection. Most telling are the connections between Kate, Marcus, and George. Not only do these domestic ties suggest a wide social network that extended beyond the immediate parameters of Charleston, but they also demonstrate that blacks were acutely aware of where freedom resided in the North.

Not only did British-occupied cities provide for families and social networks to be either formed or reconstituted, but they also afforded substantial economic opportunities during the war that would otherwise have been withheld from blacks. In New York City in particular, outside of direct military combat, blacks assisted the British army as spies and informants as well as taking part in foraging campaigns in the outlying New York and New Jersey counties. Black Loyalists also labored in more mundane ways; they helped to build fortifications, and served as cart men, woodcutters, cooks, and military servants. Likewise, black women labored as cooks, washerwomen, domestic servants, and even prostitutes.[66] A careful perusal of runaway advertisements in the *Royal Gazette* attests to the various prospects for employment available to blacks in British-occupied New York City. Of note in the September 9, 1778, *Royal Gazette* was a ten-dollar reward for the return of an unnamed "Negro servant, who ran away about six weeks ago," but who "plays well on a violin, is a very good cook, and very handy about a gentleman." This account offered by the slave owner Richard Williams highlights the fact that in the urban environment of New York City, whites increasingly prized a diverse and highly skilled black population for its labor potential.[67] Reflective of the motley skills possessed by many Black Loyalists, Hector, age 40, was described in an advertisement for an escapee in the *Royal Gazette* of July 25, 1778, as being able to speak English and Dutch.[68] Likewise, Joe, described as a runaway, had supposedly left his master in Charleston, sailed for New York, and apparently plied his trade in the city as a carpenter.[69] Particularly telling was the advertisement in the *Royal Gazette* on February 17, 1779, that managed to combine both the selling of a "strong healthy negro wench, who understands all kinds of housework, and is a good plain cook," with the offer of employment for "a girl, white or black, of about 13 or 14 years old, with a good character, to feed children."[70] In general, these advertisements, despite their intended purpose, suggest the profound ways in which blacks began to shape and develop independent economic means within a unique war-torn urban environment.

Apart from New York City, the garrisoned cities in the South also provided unprecedented prospects for Black Loyalists who wanted to work and earn wages. In Savannah, Black Loyalists were employed as day laborers, cart men, skilled craftsmen, and artisans. According to an advertisement in the *Royal Georgia Gazette*, dated June 21, 1781, the church wardens for the parish vestry of Christ Church gave notice that "all male slaves, free negroes and mulattoes within the town of Savannah, the hamlets of Yamacraw, Ewensburghand the Trustees Gardens," were to appear "with hoes or spades, Monday next to be employed in the clearing of the town common."[71] If such labor was demanded, and often exploited, Black Loyalists nevertheless made the most of such opportunities to earn wages in the emerging self-hire system. Similarly, within British-controlled Charleston, there is compelling evidence that Black Loyalists capitalized on the reduced labor market in ways that expressed their sense of being free loyal subject-citizens of the Empire.

A significant number of blacks worked as spies, scouts, and informers. An analysis of the roster of a company of fifty black laborers assigned to Charleston listed particular information on each man, "such as his knowledge of certain roads and wooded areas." This information suggests that these men were often called upon to carry messages or procure information for the British army. Evidently, black spies and messengers made up a key component of British intelligence operations.[72] Blacks also served onboard naval vessels, mostly as crew members of the armed galleys that protected the inland waterways. When the Patriots captured the galley *Balfour* at the end of September, they found a roster of "blacks on board" that contained the names of two freemen, five slaves, and "Moses a good friend."[73]

Aside from direct military service, blacks were also employed with the Royal Artillery Department. In this instance it was noted that "by October 1781 the Royal Artillery Department employed ninety blacks, eighty-five of them as laborers." It appears that a differentiation in labor existed within the Artillery Department whereby skilled blacks tended to be enslaved persons hired from Loyalist owners whereas Black Loyalist fugitives who had fled to the British performed much of the unskilled labor. For those Black Loyalists possessing a skill and employed by the Artillery Department, it is clear that they faced an unfair labor environment. "White workers received three shillings per day, while blacks received only two, except in the case of sawyers, who were paid two shillings per day regardless of race."[74] Arguably, the differentiation between skilled and unskilled labor indicates the emergence of a group of Black Loyalist artisans whose pay and skill may have been the source of increasing intraracial friction within the black community. Such evidence also demonstrates that despite the fact that skilled blacks were paid less than their white counterparts, their labor was done alongside other artisans in ways that fostered interracial alliances and perhaps even the forging of a common artisan culture.

In addition to establishing a strong economic base, British-garrisoned cities also provided an arena in which Black Loyalists began to see education as a vehicle for self-improvement and greater social and political mobilization. Indeed, the British occupation of New York City provided the means by which religious and educational instruction greatly enhanced and supported the development of black social and political values.[75] Anglican missionaries were the most active in attempting to convert Black Loyalists in New York City. This was borne out by the establishment of an orphan school by the Society for the Propagation of the Gospel (SPG), the missionary arm of the Anglican Church, strategically located across from Trinity Anglican Church. Though both church and school were destroyed by fire in 1776, black refugees were instrumental in rebuilding the church by 1778.[76] The aim of the school was suggested from a close reading of the advertisement provided in the *Royal Gazette*. Although the advertisement makes no mention of the racial makeup of the students, it clearly ascribed in rather pejorative and paternalistic language the central purpose of the school, to inculcate in indigent children virtues as the result of their being "snatched from ignorance and vice, preserved from the influence of bad examples, and . . . qualified to be useful members of society."[77] While whites may have envisioned the school as a philanthropic and benevolent institution for the poor and needy, it provided Black Loyalists the institutional structure and pedagogical tools necessary for developing black leadership and organizational skills. Evidently, Trinity as a congregation had long supported missions to blacks, and with the chaos of war likely assisted an enlarged black community of individuals wishing to be baptized, married, or taught to read.[78] While baptism and marriage services performed by the clergy fulfilled an immediate need for those refugees establishing or reconstituting familial links in British-controlled New York City, the reading and instruction in which they engaged as part of that process would later be invaluable for leading Black Loyalists in their dispersion to various locations in the Atlantic world.[79]

Apart from social and educational institutions, British-garrisoned cities also inculcated a political consciousness among Black Loyalists. These cities provided a discursive arena where Black Loyalists could advance their political rights to freedom under British proclamations. In Saint Augustine, Black Loyalists demonstrated an awareness of their political rights in the way they defended their claims to freedom during the Revolutionary War and the difficult evacuation process. As the oldest Spanish city in North America, Saint Augustine had been ceded to the British in 1763 at the end of the Seven Year War, only to be returned to the Spanish Crown in 1783. For British officials and slave-owning Loyalists, the colony came to symbolize both British protection and the availability of land essential to the reconstruction of a thriving plantation economy.[80] The perspective was far different for enslaved and free persons of color claiming loyalty to the British flag. For them, Florida represented an unmarked, frontier borderland where the idea of freedom from bondage drew inspiration from British proclamations and the legacy of Spanish colonial rule.[81] The dream of freedom was attested to by the reports of large numbers of enslaved fugitives crossing the borders during the Revolutionary War. Patrick Tonyn, governor of East Florida, admitted this much when he noted a "number of fugitives from the neighboring provinces," including a number of "runaway negroes from Georgia." As further evidence of the British commitment to protect those blacks and persons of color who came behind British lines in East Florida, Tonyn remarked that he would keep them protected and supported in the fort until the "unhappy differences [the Revolutionary War] terminate."[82]

Escaping to Florida was neither a secret, nor a random act. Rather, during the Revolutionary Era, blacks demonstrated considerable political acumen by resourcefully following the trail to freedom through swamps and riverways that led to the promised land of East Florida. But this was not the only way in which Black Loyalists acted politically. Once in East Florida, many in fact presented their claims and "liberation papers" that were authenticated by the signature of General MacArthur, the British commanding officer responsible for evacuating East Florida. Included in the claimants were Thomas Mellivery, Michael, and Dick (described as "negroes"), and Samuel Patrick, a mulatto, all of whom had presented papers of liberation from General MacArthur. Additionally, in this list were a number of Black Loyalist women, including Betty and Nanny who appealed as single females; and Phoebe, who along with her children Nancy, Britain, Frank, Peggy, Manny, Kitty, Ned, and Polot applied for freedom. Of particular interest, and reflecting the unique multilinguistic borderlands represented by East Florida, all these documents were written in Spanish, though they were addressed to British military officials and included in the general census documents for the territory. It is also worth noting that while the documents appeared in Spanish, the claimants were fairly diverse, reflecting various ethnic and racial identities as well as places of origin.[83]

Though the claims were unique in being written in Spanish, Black Loyalists in East Florida were not alone in their desire to defend their right to liberty. Indeed, the determination of Black Loyalists to secure their political liberties and livelihood was at the heart of a case brought before the Board of Police in Charleston on July 11, 1780. Apparently, "two free negroes" within the garrisoned city had been prevented from plying their trade as fishermen in the rivers and waterways surrounding the city. One particular man, George Pascott, a pilot, had "violently beat and bruised them, and threatened to run them down in their canoes with his pilot boat for no other causes or provocation," other than they had offered assistance to a master of a schooner from Savannah, who was in need of a pilot. The deposition further stated that the "two free negroes" had been deterred by "Pascott's menaces from following their occupation of fishermen and supplying the town with that commodity of fish." On hearing the complaints, the Board of Police ordered Pascott to appear. Interestingly, on the day Pascott was to appear in court, he "secreted himself to avoid the summons."[84] Unfortunately, the outcome of this case has not been found. Nevertheless, the case underscores two significant elements of black politics. First, it highlights the importance that Black Loyalists placed on being able to work and earn a livelihood free of interference. Second, it underscores the ways that blacks asserted their right to freedom in courts, before boards, and in other public spaces.

In a similar vein, New York City became a theater where claims to freedom by blacks were contested outside the strictures of army or legislature.[85] Thus, enslaved people employed strategies both old and new to achieve their ultimate goal of freedom, including "forging papers, passing themselves off as freemen, or, if light skinned, claiming they were white or painting their faces to enhance their light color."[86] This tactic was evidently clear in the case of an escapee named Pamela described in an advertisement in the *Royal Gazette* as being "very deceitful and given to lying." According to J. Agnew, her master, "Pamela had absconded about a month ago, and says that she is a free Negro, tho' born in my family, and often calls herself Mira, after her sister." Agnew further hinted at the complex web of social relations that may have aided Pamela in her escape when he noted that "as it is imagined some evil disposed persons encourage her in this way, for wicked purposes; all persons therefore, are hereby forewarned, not to harbor, employ, conceal, or carry off said Negro, by land or water."[87] Agnew's commentary suggests the ways in which enslaved blacks took advantage of the wartime urban environment of New York City to increasingly assert their political claims to freedom. It is also evident that this political consciousness was not limited to Black Loyalist men. Clearly, Pamela, like her male counterparts, had gained sufficient political acumen to negotiate and navigate the urban environment of New York, taking on a different name, disguising her identity, and seeking refuge among those willing to harbor her. Evidence of the growing confidence of Black Loyalist women in New York was demonstrated in Dinah Archery's petition to Sir Guy Carleton, Commander in Chief of the British forces in 1783. Apparently, William Farray had attempted to claim Archery as his chattel despite having no bill of sale. When the police vacillated on making a decision on the case, Archery was forced to appeal to Carleton. In the letter, Archery defended her right to freedom, stating that she had come into the city five years earlier and "agreeable to his Excellency General Howe's Proclamation."[88] Most striking in her letter is the fact that Archery appeared knowledgeable of the significance of the British proclamations and was assertive in defending these liberties even as she faced the possibility of re-enslavement.

The process of evacuating black refugees from New York City between April and November 1783 further demonstrates the ways in which Black Loyalists had begun to assert themselves politically. According to the orders establishing the Board of Commissioners on April 15, 1783, three British officers along with three American soldiers were to preside over and superintend embarkations with the additional responsibility of hearing "persons claiming property embarked, or to be embarked."[89] While the establishment of the Board served the purpose of appeasing white Patriot slave owners, it also provided a unique opportunity for blacks to agitate and make claims for their legitimate freedom. An analysis of a number of claims made before the Board suggests that Black Loyalists, whether destined for Nova Scotia, Jamaica, or the Bahamas, were intent on preserving the freedom they had sought during the Revolutionary War. One such case documented in the minutes of the Board of Commissioners on May 30, 1783, involved the Black Loyalist "A. Bartrasm," who defended his daughter Nancy's claim to legitimate freedom against attempts by a slave owner named Henry Rogers to re-enslave her. Not only did Bartrasm contend that his daughter had come within British lines as early as July 1779, but in a show of confidence he actually *demanded* that Rogers release her. The Board ruled in favor of Bartrasm and his daughter Nancy because Rogers failed to produce a clear title of property ownership.[90] How unique was this case? In the ten cases that went before the Board, blacks rarely won. If the owner was a Loyalist, there was no chance of a favorable outcome. As a result, "no British subject could be divested of his property without his consent; rebels could of course, because their slaves were either freed by proclamation or taken as war prizes."[91]

Though Nancy did not defend her rights directly in the court, her case nevertheless highlights the significant presence of Black Loyalist women involved in cases brought before the Board. Indeed, Black Loyalist women appeared to be involved in seven of the ten surviving cases documented. Judith Jackson appeared before the Board claiming that not only had her owner, John Mclean of Norfolk, Virginia, released her from bondage when he left the country, but that she had "gone into the British army, where she washed and ironed for Lord Dunmore, among others." Beyond identifying the gender-specific work normally assigned to Black Loyalist women during the War, Jackson demonstrated considerable political acumen, noting that she had obtained a "certificate from General Birch's office" and was about to go to Nova Scotia when her alleged owner, Jonathan Eilbeck, showed up to "steal me back to Virginia." Although Jackson possessed the necessary documents, the Board decided to defer the case to the commanders and Police of the Garrison. This decision was influenced by the fact that Eilbeck had both a bill of sale dated July 16, 1782, and claimed fidelity to the British flag.[92] In a similar case, "a negro woman named Sally lately embarked to go to Nova Scotia," was brought on shore before the Board for examination. Sally produced a certificate from General Birch, and argued that she came within the British lines under the sanction and "proclamation respecting negroes." However, based on the testimony of her former owner, Thomas Smith, it was revealed that Sally had only arrived in New York in April 1783, and therefore did not qualify under the terms of Sir Guy Carleton's evacuation orders.[93] Overall, while individual cases such as Nancy Bartrasm's highlight the possibility that Black Loyalist women could achieve a favorable ruling before the Board, the majority of cases favored white men as claimants.

Perhaps these gender inequalities explain why Black Loyalist women were less than enthusiastic in filing grievances before the Loyalist Claims Commission convened at various locations throughout the Atlantic world after 1783. Indeed, not a single black woman filed a claim before the Commission. Even in places where white women filed such claims, they did not succeed as well as their male counterparts (unless the claims were filed by an influential man), despite their having similar proof and certificates.[94] Yet the fact that Black Loyalists defended their freedom before the Board provides a powerful example of how deeply rooted revolutionary traditions had been transmitted and transformed by freedom-seeking blacks. Moreover, through their petitions, letters, defiant words, and open defense of their claims to freedom, Black Loyalists in New York City demonstrated the profound ways in which they had become politicized as loyal British subjects.

Such politicization speaks to the fact that the experience of fighting during the Revolutionary War as well as the communities of Black

Loyalists that emerged behind British lines indelibly shaped the contours and context of the emerging black Atlantic. Indeed, in the Bahamas, as was true for other Atlantic sites, Black Loyalists built upon these received traditions, establishing their own communities, black churches, schools, and political organizations. Accordingly, it was in the Bahamas, Nova Scotia, England, and Jamaica and other more far-flung locales throughout the Atlantic world, that Black Loyalists such as George Liele, David George, John Marrant, Joseph Paul, Prince Williams, and Amos Williams not only built on an inherited revolutionary spirit and religiosity that had been engendered during the American War of Independence, but in doing so also extended these ideas beyond the continental boundaries of the United States. Thus a study of the peculiarity of a local host society such as the understudied arena of the Bahamas has great value as it not only sheds light on the peculiar challenges these refugees faced in a nonplantation slaveholding society, but also sharpens our understanding of the commonalities shared by the larger Black Loyalist diaspora in the Atlantic during the Age of Revolutions.

In order to understand the ways in which the inherited traditions of the Great Awakening and the Revolutionary War were transmitted to the Bahamas, it is first necessary to explore the local host environment to which Black Loyalists were evacuated. Before the arrival of the Loyalists, the Bahamas had struggled to survive as a productive British colony. Visiting in 1783 and just prior to the arrival of the Loyalists, Lieutenant John Wilson observed that much of the Bahamian archipelago remained unsettled and uncultivated. The entire population amounted to 4,002 people scattered throughout the seven inhabited islands, with two-thirds residing in the capital of Nassau on the island of New Providence. Of this total, some "800 were slaves and 75 [were] free negroes or mulattoes." Wilson also highlighted the lack of a staple crop, as he reported that the islands were largely uncultivated "owing to the indolence of the inhabitants, who pay no attention to the improvement of their land but content themselves with whatever is produced by nature without being at any trouble to assist it." Finally, even as Wilson blamed the lack of cultivation on the habits of the local inhabitants, he also found the islands to be "rocky and the surface uneven." Thus, Wilson surmised, "it would appear to me that one fifth part of the face of the country is nothing but rock without any soil," and where dirt was "to be found on the surface," in no place does it exceed "twelve or fourteen inches."[95] Though Wilson's account may have exaggerated the habits of the older inhabitants, much of his description of the islands on the eve of Loyalist migration was accurate. Their marginality was evident by the fact that the islands remained remote, scarcely settled, underdeveloped, and poorly defended. Moreover, in contrast to the extremely valuable and productive neighboring sugar islands of Jamaica, Barbados, and Antigua in the Caribbean, the Bahamas had emerged as a nonplantation colony with few commodities worth exporting. Understanding the pre-Loyalist geopolitical and social context will invariably assist in measuring the extent to which the mass exodus of Loyalists—both black and white—led to dramatic transformations of the Bahamian archipelago. The emergence of the Bahamas as a nonplantation slaveholding colony in the pre-Loyalist era indelibly impacted the kind of social institutions and political mobilizations that would occur with the arrival of Black Loyalists after 1783.

One of the unique features of the geography and climate of the Bahamas is its archipelagic nature. In fact, as geographers have noted, the Bahamas is the largest and most expansive Atlantic archipelago, extending southeast from the Manzanilla Bank off Florida some 590 miles to Great Inagua, near Cape Nicholas, Haiti.[96] These general geographic and archipelagic features would figure prominently in deterring European colonization of the Bahamas. Indeed, because of the vast distances between islands, the shallow waters, and the numerous shoals, travel between islands would remain hazardous, even for the best of navigators. The islands themselves were small, generally rocky, and scattered across the Great and Little Bahama Banks. Such physical conditions contrasted with those of the larger islands of the Caribbean and the mainland territories of South America. Indeed, unlike the mountainous islands of the Greater and Lesser Antilles, the Bahamas contained no rich alluvial deposits, no mineral resources, and no freshwater rivers or waterways that could provide natural irrigation systems for farmers or livestock.[97] Instead the entire archipelago consisted of honeycomb rocks and shallow deposits of limestone soil, often too porous for farming. Such conditions explain why the Bahamas remained virtually uninhabited after 1492.[98] Thus, for the better part of a century and a half, the Bahamas remained remote and completely empty of people—either indigenous or European.

Even as the arrival of the Eleutheran Adventurers in 1648 marked the beginning of steady and permanent European colonization of the

Bahamas, the marginality of the islands would remain an enduring legacy. Arriving in the Bahamas by way of Bermuda, these first settlers had hopes of establishing a godly puritan society in which the first one hundred settlers would control commercial enterprises and agricultural activities.[99] From inception, however, their vision for creating a godly community was challenged by the hostile Bahamian environment. In time, the Eleutheran Adventurers discovered that the land in Eleuthera, though possessing a few pockets of good soil, was in general unfit for large-scale husbandry. By 1660, most of the Adventurers had returned to Bermuda, leaving behind in the Bahamas only a handful of poor settlers. Indeed, even William Sayle, who had worked so tirelessly in establishing the colony, eventually gave up and left for Bermuda.[100]

Subsequent efforts to colonize the Bahamas in the pre-Loyalist period reflect a general trend whereby the initial hopes of settlers were dashed by the inability to produce a viable commodity for export. By 1670, the Bahamas officially came under the jurisdiction of the Lord Proprietors of the Carolinas. These six men, all of noble rank, intended to increase their own personal fortunes by investing in the colony and encouraging the lower classes and those disposed toward husbandry to settle in the Bahamas.[101] Unfortunately, not only did the Lord Proprietors fail to provide the kind of investment necessary to produce a thriving colony, but the inhabitants who settled in the Bahamas, like the earlier Eleutheran Adventurers, soon discovered that the small islands and cays and the rocky Bahamian soil were ill-equipped for large-scale farming.

Writing in a time of desperation and depravity, John Darrell, a native of Bermuda, noted that by 1670 there were, on Sayle Island (later known as New Providence), "near 500 inhabitants" besides "about 20 families of Bermudians" thought to be living on Eleuthera and its offshore cays. Interestingly, Darrell still found reason to hope, particularly in his self-promotion of New Providence. As such, Darrell idealistically spoke of the island's potential, claiming New Providence produced "good cotton and tobacco, sugar caines and Indico Weed," the very commodities that were increasingly the foundation of British trade throughout its Atlantic world empire.[102]

Darrell's account was not completely fictitious. Indeed, a few commodities were exported from the colony, including various dyewoods, most commonly braziletto, mahogany, and lignum vitae; salt extracted from various salt ponds in Exuma; and finally ambergris, used to make perfume.[103] These commodities were shipped to the Carolinas and Jamaica, British-controlled colonies in close proximity to the Bahamas. Yet for the most part, early settlers struggled to survive, farming at a subsistence level, using simple slash-and-burn techniques or potholes and caves to grow garden crops. Even John Darrell put the conditions of the Bahamas in perspective when he listed as the chief needs of New Providence, "small arms and ammunitions, a godly minister and a good smith."[104]

By the turn of the eighteenth century, the overall picture of the colony remained troubling. Apart from the inability to produce a genuine export crop like sugar or tobacco, a general lawlessness appeared to permeate society from top governing officials down to the laboring population. Moreover, the Bahamas lacked important institutional structures, including churches and schools, and personnel such as clergy who could perform basic services including marriages and funerals. Added to this was the problem of defense. The Bahamas lacked a fort or garrison, proper ammunition, and even regular troops to defend the expansive archipelago from frequent attacks by the Spanish from Havana, Cuba. Though Fort Nassau was eventually built by 1695, it did not prevent the colony from being attacked by foreign invaders.[105]

Yet even as the Bahamas remained marginalized as a site of European colonization, its location within the Atlantic world would become increasingly important as trade networks expanded. Indeed, large sea vessels carrying gold, spices, and raw products from the Caribbean, South America, and British North America often traveled to their European destinations through the Gulf Stream separating the Bahamas from the Florida Keys. Apart from the Gulf Stream, the less-known sea routes within the archipelago gave daring sea captains a quicker, more direct route to European markets. Evidently, one of the dominant and salient features of the Bahamian pre-Loyalist period was a history defined by maritime or sea-based activities rather than land-based exports.[106]

Of chief importance was the development of the Bahamas as a privateering and pirate base. By the 1690s, and especially after the destruction of Port Royal by earthquake in 1692, Nassau, New Providence, became the center of a dynamic pirate network. Of the total of approximately five thousand men "serving under the Banner of King Death" during piracy's heyday, up to a thousand pirates were constituted into a dozen or so fluctuating crews normally based in the Bahamas. Other records suggest that there were at least twenty pirate captains who used the Bahamas as their main point of attack.[107] In sum, during the Proprietary period from 1660 to 1718, the lack of a stable government and religious institutions provided an excellent opportunity for pirates and other antiauthoritarian elements to prosper in early Bahamian society.[108] Thus, when Royal Government was established in 1718 it was done under the pretext of abolishing piracy and "restoring" law and order.[109]

Though the establishment of Royal Government certainly prevented the spread of piracy, it did not prohibit the expansion of privateering as a significant maritime activity. Indeed, where pirates tended to pillage all vessels laden with treasure or goods, the Bahamian privateers thrived during periods of warfare, when under direct sanction of British officials they would target Spanish and French vessels. By providing letters of marque to Bahamian privateers, the British government tacitly afforded these independent ships the opportunity to police the large expansive waterways and sea routes throughout the Caribbean and British North America. As wars proliferated among European rivals throughout the late-seventeenth and eighteenth centuries, privateering became a steadier, almost reliable way of earning a living. The establishment in Nassau of a Vice-Admiralty Court in 1697 also bolstered this seafaring activity.

If piracy and privateering had not attracted island inhabitants to the sea, then wrecking and fishing certainly would have. Wrecking, by definition, was the legal salvaging of goods from ships that had run aground on the thousands of reefs, shoals, or shallow banks of the Bahamas.[110] The first known wreck was, of course, *The William*, the fateful vessel carrying the Eleutheran Adventurers from Bermuda to Eleuthera. *The William* was not alone. Hundreds of vessels traversing the shallow Bahamian waters were wrecked. Ironically, whereas a wrecked vessel was viewed as a tragic event by its captain and crew, for islanders, such an event provided opportunity—if not a livelihood—in an otherwise harsh Bahamian environment.

Likewise, fishing provided Bahamians with an important livelihood when the land failed to produce. Apart from grouper, snapper, and the larger deep-sea fish such as the blue marlin and tuna, Bahamian fishermen explored the outlying reefs surrounding the islands for conch, turtles, and lobster. Turtling, in particular, was important in providing a source of food. The shells of turtles were also prized for making combs, costume jewelry, and other luxury items. In addition to turtling, Bahamian fishermen during this period could also find various species of whales and monk seals, the oil from which had an export market as fuel and lubricants for sugar mills in Jamaica and Barbados.[111]

Although fishing, wrecking, and other sea-based activities provided viable means of survival for many Bahamians, they also reflected the continued marginal status of the Bahamas within the broader Anglo-Atlantic world. The successful British colonies in North America and the West Indies achieved their status by producing an export staple. Where North American colonies produced tobacco, rice, and indigo, the West Indies produced sugar.[112] The Bahamas, on the other hand, produced no significant exportable staple before the arrival of the Loyalists in 1783. Indeed, in the pre-Loyalist period, the Bahamas most resembled Belize, Bermuda, and the Cayman Islands, territories on the periphery of the British-controlled sugar islands in the Caribbean that survived principally on seafaring economic enterprises such as fishing, wrecking, and turtling. With no staple export crop, local inhabitants in these territories often found resourceful ways to survive, growing subsistence crops such as guinea corn, peas, beans, potatoes, yams, and plantains while also exchanging various dyewoods such as mahogany, madeira, and boxwood for provisions imported from staple-producing Anglo-American colonies.[113]

The failure of the Bahamas to produce a viable export staple also had long-term effects on the development of the islands in the pre-Loyalist period. Much of the archipelago remained virtually uninhabited, with only New Providence, Harbour Island, and mainland Eleuthera holding any significant populations. Accordingly, "economic marginality, and the fact that their populations were small, scattered, transient, fluctuating, poorly integrated and often disreputable," ensured that the Bahamas was regarded as "unimportant in the British imperial scheme."[114] Yet notwithstanding the lack of a plantation system and its general economic marginality, the Bahamas was still considered a slaveholding society, with the first enslaved persons arriving as early as 1648.

As a nonplantation slaveholding society, the Bahamas developed in ways that reflected its unique geopolitical position on the margins of the Anglo-American Atlantic world.[115] To begin with, the Bahamas departed significantly from demographic trends in either the Southern colonies in British North America, the sugar plantation complex established in the larger Caribbean islands, and even the frontier environment of Nova

Scotia. Comparative census data for the mid-eighteenth century reveal the demographic differences between the Bahamas and the larger sugar plantation islands. By 1757, Barbados, the oldest and most established sugar island under British control, had a population heavily skewed toward a slave majority, with 16,772, listed as whites, 63,410 as slaves, and 235 described as free persons of color. Jamaica reflected a similar demographic profile, though with a much larger overall population owing to its position as the most successful sugar island in the Anglophone Caribbean. The 1754 census data for Jamaica listed 12,000 whites, compared with a massive slave population tabulated at 127,881 and a free colored population of 2,119 persons.[116] Significantly, unlike in Barbados, a much larger group of free persons of color had emerged in Jamaica by the mid-eighteenth century. In spite of this difference, both Jamaica and Barbados shared a similar demographic profile whereby the enslaved majority vastly outnumbered both the white and free colored class. This suggests the labor-intensive nature of sugar-dominated islands in which the majority of enslaved persons labored on sugar plantations and the much smaller white population worked mainly as overseers, or in urban settings as accountants, office clerks, and government officials. In this respect, "by the time that Jamaica became a major sugar producer, sometime around 1774; slaves outnumbered the white population by 130,000 to 12,000."[117] Such demographic considerations also resulted in communities of sharply delineated, mutually reinforcing social cleavages.[118] Hence, prior to the arrival of Loyalists, Jamaican planters had created a socially stratified society in which the majority of Jamaica's population consisted of enslaved persons, forced to work within an exploitative labor system.

In contrast, the data for the Bahamas reveal a very different demographic picture. According to the 1745 data, the Bahamas had 1,268 inhabitants listed as whites, 1,145 enslaved, and only 76 persons described as free persons of color. Thus the total population of the Bahamas at mid-century was only 2,486, compared with 142,000 in Jamaica and 80,417 in Barbados.[119] The demographic picture for the Bahamas did not change much over the next twenty years. Indeed, on the eve of the arrival of Loyalists in the Bahamas, the total population amounted to only 4,000 to 5,000 people, most of whom were free. The principal white inhabitants owned very little property, usually consisting of a couple of small vessels and a few enslaved persons.[120] Though remarkably different in demographic profile from the sugar plantation island of Jamaica, the Bahamas was still not quite a newly formed slaveholding environment like Nova Scotia.

A closer analysis of population data for the early and mid-eighteenth century underscores the uniqueness of the Bahamas within the larger Anglo-American Atlantic world. The first accurate tabulation of the Bahamian population occurred in February 1722, shortly after the arrival of Governor Phenney. According to his official census, Phenney listed the Bahamian population as consisting of 427 whites, 233 blacks on New Providence, with an additional 150 whites and 34 blacks on Eleuthera, and 124 whites and 5 blacks on Harbour Island. Of the total of 989 persons, 35 percent were enslaved. It is also worth noting that 67 percent of the entire population in the Bahamas lived in New Providence.[121]

Later census data by Phenney's successors would provide more specific distinctions between free and enslaved populations as well as give a general indication of the demographic uniqueness of the Bahamas as a nonplantation colony. The census conducted by Woodes Rogers in 1731 for the first time gave totals of free men, women, and children, and of enslaved children and adults. It also listed all householders by name, indicating the number of men, women, children, and slaves in each household. According to this census, of the 1,388 people counted, no fewer than 1,042, or 75.1 percent lived in New Providence. Indeed, compared with the 1721 census, the population of New Providence had increased by two-thirds, whereas Harbour Island, with 169 persons, had grown by only a quarter, and mainland Eleuthera, with 177, had not grown at all. Regarding the total adult free population, men outnumbered women, 256 to 190, with the disproportion higher in New Providence (190 to 135), owing to the presence of the small garrison in Nassau and remnants of the pirate community.[122] Significant for understanding the nature of the Bahamas as a nonplantation slaveholding society, 453 persons, or 32.6 percent, were listed as "Negroes"—clearly used as a synonym for slaves. Regarding the enslaved population, the 1731 information is less clear given that gender was not indicated and the only differentiation was between adults and children. However, it is noteworthy that since at least a third of the enslaved had been imported in the early 1720s, perhaps as many as half were African-born, and their average age was higher than that of whites and free coloreds, with a disproportion of adult males to adult females about the same as for whites in New Providence.[123] These demographic figures indicate the emergence of a diverse community in which a substantial

African-influenced population existed alongside other creole-born enslaved persons and a small majority white population.

The 1734 census also highlights the demographic anomaly that the Bahamas represents in relation to other Atlantic world slave societies. Remarkably, for the first time the households and families of free mulattoes
and blacks were distinguished from those of white freemen, thus allowing
an initial analysis of a group that would eventually grow in size and importance with the arrival of Black Loyalists after 1783. Due to an epidemic,
the overall population showed a slight decline from 1,388 to 1,378. Despite
the decline of the overall population, the enslaved population increased
from 453 to 491. The proportion of enslaved thus had risen from 32.6 to
35.6 percent since 1731—with an additional 5.6 percent of the population
registered as coloreds—neither enslaved nor fully free. The majority of
this newly listed cohort of free coloreds and blacks lived in 16 nuclear-
family households, averaging 2.5 children per family. The trend toward
nucleated households was also evident in the organization of slave units,
where fewer enslaved persons were listed as living singly. Such social arrangements reflect a unique maritime society in which small free white
and black households and slave units almost certainly existed side by side.
The growth of more nucleated households was also a result of the gender
balance in the white population, reflected in a ratio of 108 men to 100
women.[124]

In broader terms what is most significant about this 1734 census data
is the size of the white population in relation to that of the enslaved and
free black population. In fact, the demographic balance whereby whites
only slightly outnumbered blacks was not changed until the arrival of the
Loyalists. This unique demographic feature is borne out by a report by
Thomas Shirley in 1772. Shirley reported that Nassau, New Providence,
had 1,024 whites and 1,800 "reputed blacks," Harbour Island had 410
whites and 90 blacks, Eleuthera had 509 whites and 237 blacks, and Exuma, a scarcely settled island, had 6 whites and 24 blacks. It is worth noting that while whites outnumbered blacks 60 to 40 percent in the overall
tabulation, the figures for New Providence were far different from those
for the other inhabited islands. Thus in the colonial capital, enslaved and
free blacks emerged as a significant majority.[125]

Because of the failure to establish an export crop, labor conditions were
also very different for enslaved Bahamians in relation to their contemporaries around the Atlantic basin. Many worked alongside their owners on

small vessels or dinghies. Others worked in domestic roles as housekeepers, cooks, and artisans. Such work environments dictated close working relations with their owners, negating the need for overseers or managers. The case of John Stead is illustrative of the kinds of work and familial relationships that emerged between the slave owner and the enslaved in the pre-Loyalist period. Analyzing Stead's will provides details about his material conditions as well as his relations with both free and enslaved persons. Stead's modest possessions, all worth less than 500 pieces of eight, were bequeathed to three women, most likely his sisters. Interestingly, "more than half of his estate consisted of four slaves, together valued at 270 pieces of eight: two women called Ruth and Kate, and two children," identified as Dick and Moll—the latter listed as a mulatto.[126] Stead appears to have lived among the lowest stratum of Bahamian society with relatives who were both black and white. In addition to the very real possibility that Moll was his child, Stead's "three female beneficiaries were married to men called Sims, closely related to each other," and all defined in the 1734 census as either free black or coloreds.[127] John Stead's relative Benjamin Sims, who wrote a will and testament within a year of Stead's final testimony, also exemplified this complex maritime cultural and social world. From Sims's will, it appears that he was a mariner, most likely a privateer or possibly even a former pirate. As a freeman of color, Sims apparently lived in a fluid multiracial society, as evidenced by the fact that in his will, his beneficiaries were whites as well as Moses and Aaron Sims, his cousins and several other persons listed as free blacks or mulattoes in 1734.[128] Living most of his life at sea, Sims nevertheless owned nine enslaved persons along with half-shares in the sloop *Two Brothers,* which he bequeathed to his brother Aaron Sims. Significantly, at his death, Benjamin Sims manumitted all those enslaved to him, noting that all should be "made free and . . . be no longer slaves to any person whatsoever." Remarkably, Sims's two executors were John Howell, once acting Governor for the colony, and Benjamin Watkins, both planters and substantial slave owners.[129] In general, the intersecting lives of John Stead and Benjamin Sims and their enslaved and other black and white relatives, suggest a dynamic and diverse slaveholding society. Moreover, as sailors and sea captains, these men would have deployed their chattel in maritime activities and domestic chores that were markedly different from the work of enslaved persons living in Caribbean slave societies. Indeed, in most venues where labor was performed, it was not as labor intensive as the gang system that increasingly dominated the Southern colonies in British North America and the sugar islands of the Caribbean.

Instead, in the pre-Loyalist period in the Bahamas, a labor system emerged that resembled the task system prevalent in the Lowcountry of South Carolina. Unlike the gang system associated with the sugar plantation complex, the Lowcountry rice economy created material conditions that allowed enslaved persons greater flexibility and autonomy in their time away from plantation labor. As such, the task system allowed enslaved persons the latitude to apportion their own day, to work intensively at an assigned task and then have the balance of their time for themselves.[130] Now free to labor outside the plantation complex, enslaved persons working within the task system were able to grow a variety of subsistence crops that could augment their regular provisions and provide a more balanced diet.

However, it is evident that while the pre-Loyalist period in the Bahamas reflected many of the characteristics of the Lowcountry region of South Carolina, there were significant differences. Unlike South Carolina, throughout much of the eighteenth century, the Bahamas remained underdeveloped with no staple crop such as rice or sugar, and with a substantially smaller enslaved population working in an urban-maritime economy characterized by diversification. Apparently, as a slaveholding society, the Bahamas had enslaved persons who labored in a diverse but constricted maritime environment, employed as domestics or engaged in seafaring activities, often working alongside their masters.[131]

Yet it is significant that elements of the task system were beginning to emerge in the Bahamas by the mid-eighteenth century. Particularly important was the 1767 Act that forbade enslaved persons to engage in planting except on the lands of their owners.[132] This indicates that enslaved persons were already accustomed to organizing and planting provisional grounds, most likely during time allotted to them after completing their daily tasks. This provided the enslaved Bahamian population with subsistence crops they could either sell or use to supplement the provisions furnished by their owners.[133] Like those held in bondage in areas of the Chesapeake where tobacco could no longer be profitably grown as a staple crop, enslaved Bahamians cultivated food crops as part of their estate labor, as well as outside their required duties.[134] In the end, before the arrival of the Loyalists, they existed in an economic environment in which the absence of a major export staple created the conditions for the development of a task system.[135] Such a system stood in direct counter-point to the labor-intensive gang system that prevailed in Jamaica and the other sugar islands of the British Caribbean.

Despite these differences, there were significant ways in which the Ba-hamas, as a nonplantation society of slaves, did reflect many features com-mon to British Caribbean slave societies. First and foremost, as the en-slaved population within the Bahamas expanded, slave codes were passed to better control and regulate their movement and freedom. Though slav-ery was established with the arrival of the Eleutheran Adventurers in 1648, the first major importation occurred in 1721, under the direction of Gov-ernor George Phenney. The 295 Negroes were transported in the *Bahama Galley* from the Guinea Coast in West Africa. Apart from owning shares in the slave vessel, Phenney was directly involved in attempting to estab-lish a plantation system in the Bahamas. "With these slaves a handful of plantations were established in New Providence, including the governor's own," built about five leagues west of the town of Nassau, at an area called Old Fort Bay.[136] With the growth of the enslaved population, the first sub-stantial slave laws were passed in 1723. Included in the laws were pro-visions to prevent enslaved persons from assembling in groups of more than five or six at night, as well as the requirement that those in bondage traveling beyond the confines of their owners' homes needed to have in their possession a passbook, signed by their masters. Additionally, the slave regulations decreed by Phenney's council in 1726 enjoined masters and mistresses to set an example and discourage "Oaths and unseemly discourses" among their enslaved. Later laws passed in the pre-Loyalist period reflect a trend toward greater policing and punishment, particu-larly in respect to enslaved persons' participation in activities beyond the immediate gaze of their owners. Such laws were in fact modeled after similar legislation passed in Barbados and other Anglo-American colo-nies where enslaved persons were increasingly defined as chattel property, "fit to be bought, sold, and bequeathed, and thus not capable of owning property themselves."[137]

Apart from the actual slave codes, Bahamian slaveholders held many of the same attitudes toward enslaved persons and free blacks that were emerging in the late-eighteenth-century Anglo-American world. Evi-dence of a racialized attitude toward enslaved persons in the Bahamas can be discerned in the various laws passed during this period. These laws sought to distance and separate African practices from European norms and behavior. Blacks were seen as uncivilized, ignorant, and "suspect."[138] Consequently, their practices were viewed as dangerous, pagan, and subversive to the establishment of law and order. Ultimately, the socioeconomic and political environment faced by enslaved persons in the pre-Loyalist period in the Bahamas was thus marked by continuities in laws, values, and practices upheld by whites throughout the Atlantic world. Inconsistencies existed in terms of demography, labor arrangements, relations between free blacks and whites, and the types of commodities produced.

These salient features of pre-Loyalist Bahamian society would be indelibly altered with the arrival of black refugees from British-occupied ports at the end of the Revolutionary War. Yet these transformations were complex and not always one-sided. Indeed, even as these black newcomers espoused rights in courts, erected buildings, and established important social institutions, they also creatively adapted to the exigencies of a geopolitical terrain that had long existed on the margins of the British Empire. In this respect, Black Loyalists, similar to their white counterparts, were as much catalysts of transformation as they were subjects to be transformed by the unique political space they entered after 1783. Added to this complexity was the fact that Black Loyalists as a group were extremely diverse, particularly in terms of their place of domicile, their experiences during the war, their material resources, and their routes to the Bahamas from British seaports in America.

The first 250 settlers departing New York in August 1783 on two vessels—*The William* and *The Nautilus*—arrived in Abaco with far fewer material resources than their counterparts who would later migrate from Saint Augustine. Augmenting this first group of 250 black and white Loyalists were two contingents that left New York City onboard the *Charlotte* in September and the *Hope* in October. In total, 941 refugees (of whom at least the 403 counted as "servants" were blacks), embarked from New York for Abaco.[139] In addition to the 403 counted as blacks, the total white Loyalist population leaving New York was tabulated as "217 men, 118 women, 203 children, (108 under the age of ten)."[140] Apart from these New York refugees, 650 white Loyalists and their enslaved arrived in Abaco via Saint Augustine by the end of 1783. Unlike the group from New York, the Loyalists from Saint Augustine settled on the southern part of the mainland near Spencer's Bight and Eight Mile Way.[141] The composition of the two groups was remarkably different. The southern group appears to have consisted of would-be planters and their enslaved, whereas the northern group "consisted of modest white families with very few slaves and a high proportion of blacks of equivocal status."[142]

In contrast to Abaco, the more prosperous planters and merchants who entered the Bahamas from Saint Augustine dominated the Loyalist migration to Nassau. The white émigrés totaled just over three hundred families, of whom more than a hundred owned ten or more enslaved persons. Of these migrants, more than half of the whites stayed on New Providence, while two-thirds of the enslaved ended up on previously undeveloped Out Islands in the central Bahamas.[143] Another descriptive source related to the cohort of Loyalists that settled in New Providence is given by Johann David Schoepf, who noted that "the real planters, but of lesser consequence live near to the town on their estates."[144] Missing from all these records is a tabulation of free blacks who would have comprised those considered Black Loyalists. Fortunately, C. F. Pascoe's descriptive ecclesiastical history titled *Two Hundred Years of the SPG: An Historical Account of the Society for the Propagation of the Gospel in Foreign Parts, 1701–1900*, provides a useful source not only for tabulating the number of free blacks counted as Loyalists, but also for supplying a more general demographic picture of the changes brought to New Providence as a result of the Loyalist migration. According to Pascoe, in a report submitted by the Society to the English government, the overall white population had doubled from 1,750 in 1784 to 3,500 in 1791. During this same span of time, the black population, including coloreds (presumably enslaved and free), had trebled from 2,300 to 6,500. Pascoe also commented on the free population of blacks residing in New Providence when he remarked, "some 500 were free negroes," who by escapes and "other fortuitous circumstances were disentangled from the disgraceful shackles of slavery."[145] In addition to Pascoe's account, William Wylly provides useful demographic figures related to the free black and colored population. In his *Short Account,* Wylly estimated the population of Nassau in 1788 as 1,264 new slaves and 165 new white household heads.[146] Moreover, according to Wylly, 500 persons of color lived in the islands, in addition to 350 black persons arriving from America who were "either free or pretending to be so."[147] Unlike Pascoe's tabulation, Wylly's account makes a distinction between preexisting free blacks and coloreds and those more recently arriving from America who would fit the criteria of Black Loyalists. Overall the total free black and colored population (including both Black Loyalists and the preexisting free black and colored population) numbered 850 persons. Notably, while most of the Black Loyalists entering Abaco came from New York City, in Nassau the port of embarkation appears to have been Saint Augustine.[148]

Such demographic data suggest that the Loyalist migration to the Bahamas was far from monolithic. Indeed, it is important that distinctions be made between those Loyalists who arrived in Abaco from New York, and "those who came more or less directly from southern plantations," entering the Bahamas from Saint Augustine, and eventually settling in "either Nassau, the colonial capital or (far more numerously) shipped out to set up plantations or work the saltpans in the Bahamas Out Islands, a half dozen of which were previously unpopulated."[149]

If Loyalists disembarking in the Bahamas were a heterogeneous and polyglot group, equally complex were the landscapes and physical environments they encountered in the Bahamas. Those Black Loyalists entering the urban space of Nassau, New Providence, found a small town marked by seafaring activities and meager subsistence agriculture. In time, the new arrivals—both black and white—would establish thriving businesses, build stone buildings and expand roads and public works. The expanding town afforded Black Loyalists opportunities to labor in diverse jobs, often utilizing their varied skills in ways that might have been advantageous to living as free men and women. However, though Nassau as an urban space provided opportunities for newly arrived Black Loyalists, they entered a world in which newly arrived white Loyalist merchants, lawyers, and professionals were attempting to transform the sleepy town into a thriving plantation slave society. Such efforts required political and economic initiatives that often conflicted with the habits and lifeways of older inhabitants and newly arriving Black Loyalists. Thus, Nassau was to be transformed by a new and more assertive white merchant Loyalist class, ascending to political positions in the House of Assembly, holding various public offices, and eventually passing regulatory measures that would ultimately undermine the efforts of Black Loyalists to extend their newfound liberties to New Providence.

Black Loyalists in Abaco fared little better. Those black émigrés settling in Abaco, like their white counterparts, encountered an uninhabited and uncultivated island environment. Though initial reports of the island indicated favorable conditions for establishing thriving plantations, a later, more accurate report, provided by Lieutenant John Wilson, described

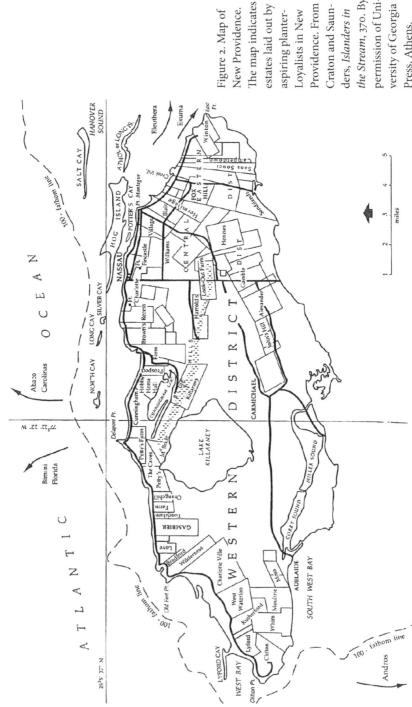

Figure 2. Map of New Providence. The map indicates estates laid out by aspiring planter-Loyalists in New Providence. From Craton and Saunders, *Islanders in the Stream*, 370. By permission of University of Georgia Press, Athens.

Abaco as having "no extensive tracts of land and . . . the soil was composed of nothing more than vegetable bodies rotted on the surface of the rocks."[150] Arguably, the raw and hostile terrain of Abaco had a great leveling effect in that both black and white Loyalists faced the same day-to-day challenges of surviving in a frontier environment. Yet in many respects blacks faced more formidable obstacles as they were entering a society not as unequivocally free persons, but rather as persons of color living in a world marked by racial slavery. Such notions would invariably influence how life and freedom would be worked out in the swampy frontier environment of Abaco as well as the urban environment of Nassau.

Though this chapter has focused primarily on the roots and routes of Black Loyalists settling in the Bahamas, it is important to place that experience within the larger black Atlantic and Black Loyalist diaspora. Indeed, just as individuals such as Prince Williams and Joseph Paul entered a hostile racial environment in the Bahamas, others such as Moses Wilkinson, Boston King, and David George faced their own unique barriers to freedom. All entered societies where their claims to freedom, land, and political liberty were questioned, challenged, and often denied. Yet even as their liberty was constrained and circumvented, Black Loyalists, as culturally conversant individuals, navigated the new terrain by using tools they had inherited—ideas and values rooted in the Revolutionary War—and the experiences of the revivalism associated with the Great Awakening.

Yet this chapter has made a case for the distinctive place the Bahamas holds within the larger Black Loyalist diaspora. Arguably, Black Loyalists entering the Bahamas made their claims to freedom against the backdrop of a unique nonplantation slaveholding society on the margins of the British Empire. It was in this unparalleled geopolitical space that Black Loyalists extended their efforts to redefine and reclaim freedom against white Loyalists bent on re-enslaving them. Beyond possible re-enslavement, Black Loyalists in the Bahamas arrived as disenfranchised subjects in that they could not participate in formal politics, nor could they freely engage in trade and conduct business transactions without encountering legal encumbrances.[151] Though these legal impediments made attaining liberty far more difficult and costly, Black Loyalists brought before the courts in the Bahamas remained committed to advocating for change. Thus Black Loyalists were forced to defend their certificates of freedom and fight to have their property rights acknowledged before courts and attorneys, and when denied opportunities to preach, teach, or earn a living, they appealed to the appropriate authorities.

In the end, Black Loyalists in the Bahamas were imbued with a strong desire to see their dreams of liberty extended to their new host society. Consequently, they defended their claim to freedom, greater political liberty, and economic opportunities by invoking their right to be considered free subjects of the British imperial government. Though Black Loyalists had gained protection and civil status by allying with the British during the Revolutionary War, the host society they entered shaped their peculiar politics in important and lasting ways. The subsequent chapter investigates the specific ways in which Black Loyalists in the Bahamas applied the lessons of the American Revolution to advance their own desire for freedom from bondage. Put another way, it was in the Bahamas, a marginalized British territory, that aspiring planters and freedom-seeking Black Loyalists fought over the question of whether Black Loyalist freedom would be extended or denied.

2

THEIR STRUGGLE WITH
FREEDOM FROM BONDAGE

On April 14, 1788, "a negro woman calling herself Sarah Moultrie" and her child appeared before Dunmore's Negro Court where the receiver-general and two other magistrates pronounced them free. This decision is remarkable given the fact that John Martin Struder, a white Loyalist claimant, had appeared and given testimony that challenged Sarah's claim. In his affidavit, Struder revealed the long, hard struggle that Sarah faced as a black woman attempting to claim freedom in Dunmore's Negro Court in the Bahamas. According to Struder's testimony, Sarah "at the time of the evacuation of Charleston South Carolina by his majesty's troops in 1782" was carried to "Saint Augustine by Ann Nelson as her lawful property." On moving to the Bahamas, Ann Nelson brought the "said woman with her." Sarah was eventually given to Struder as a "free gift" shortly before Ann Nelson embarked for England.[1] Attempting to make a profit from his newly acquired property, Struder in turn sold Sarah to Hugh Dean, a notorious slave auctioneer in New Providence.

Undoubtedly Sarah's brief appearance in the court and her own life story is shrouded by the fact that it is told from the perspective of Struder, a white privileged male. To recapture Sarah's struggle it is necessary to work against the grain of this official narrative and unpack the gender and racial assumptions embedded in this historical record. Sarah's story was tragic from the start. We can imagine she most likely entered into the official narrative once she fled to the British lines in Charleston. Despite the likelihood that she possessed a certificate of freedom, she was illegally re-enslaved (most likely claimed as confiscated property) and evacuated by Ann Nelson to Saint Augustine by 1782. In this instance, Sarah Moultrie's story bears a remarkable similarity to those of Mary Postell and thousands of other blacks who arrived in Saint Augustine claiming freedom but were cheated out of their liberty by whites who falsified claims of ownership at the state house presided over by Governor Patrick Tonyn. In other words, royal refugees such as Sarah Moultrie and Mary Postell were made vulnerable by a legal status marked by ambivalence rather than clarity, in which any scrap of official documentation was valuable—both to persons claiming freedom and to persons claiming ownership.[2]

Sarah's struggles were compounded by the fact that upon her forced removal to the Bahamas with Ann Nelson, she was once again sold as a chattel, first to Struder and later to Hugh Dean. Neither of these slave owners would have thought much about Sarah. She was a "free gift," property, and chattel, to be exchanged and removed at their convenience. Yet in escaping from bondage in the Bahamas, Sarah's actions proved she was far more than chattel. Ironically, Struder's account betrays his own efforts to portray Sarah as a contented chattel slave. Apparently, Sarah not only escaped from Hugh Dean's plantation but also sought refuge with Lord Dunmore at his plantation, where she worked as a cook until her case could be brought before the courts. Even before an official trial date was established, Struder made numerous applications to have Sarah removed, by force or persuasion, from Dunmore's plantation. Yet, in every instance Sarah appeared determined to be free. Struder confessed this much when he noted that on one occasion when he visited Dunmore he was told, "Sarah says she was free."[3]

Sarah's personal struggle for self-determination had significant bearing on the Black Loyalist quest for freedom in the Bahamas. First, it demonstrates the ways in which Black Loyalists used Dunmore's Negro Court and other venues to advance their claims to freedom. Though Sarah's actual testimony was never recorded, and despite never penning a petition, her actions before the trial and her presence in the courtroom indicate a person who was acutely aware of her right to freedom. Like other Black Loyalists, Sarah used her recently acquired status as a British subject to demand that her case be heard before the court of law. Indeed, seeking refuge on Dunmore's plantation and utilizing the court and legal system underscore the fact that Sarah was cognizant of the limits and opportunities offered by such contested spaces. Sarah's struggle for freedom was also shaped by overriding gender assumptions regarding the efficacy of a woman's testimony in a court of law. While the presence of women in courts throughout New England was progressively rare, the appearance of Sarah and other women in Nassau's courtrooms suggested a political opening that flowed against the tide of legal practices in the Anglo-American world.[4] Although courts in New England and across the Eastern seaboard of the United States were foreclosing participation of black women and other nonwhites in courtrooms, it appears that in other locales across the Atlantic world—inclusive of Spanish Florida, Cuba, and British host societies where Loyalists were evacuated—judicial space expanded or at least continued to be accessible to black men and women.[5] As such, courtrooms in Shelburne, Nova Scotia; London, England (where the Loyalist Claims Commission was initially established); and Saint Augustine remained viable spaces where access to courts for blacks not only "granted them a moral and juridical personality" but also the opportunities to claim rights as subject-citizens within a monarchical and imperial legal tradition.[6]

Sarah Moultrie's case also demonstrates the global dimensions of the Black Loyalists' struggle for freedom. Sarah herself had been born in South Carolina, but moved to Charleston during the British occupation. Eventually, she was evacuated to Saint Augustine by 1782, before finally arriving in the Bahamas after 1783. Sarah's trans-Atlantic trek to the slave-holding society of the Bahamas was not unlike that of countless other Black Loyalists entering the Bahamas at the end of the Revolutionary War. Yet the migration of people tells only part of the story. Black Loyalists such as Sarah Moultrie were in fact transmitters of a revolutionary ideology that imbued them with a strong sense of their rights as loyal subjects to the British Crown. Black Loyalists began to see themselves as loyal subjects, protected and recognized by the imperial state during and immediately following the Revolution. Such recognition engendered a political consciousness whereby blacks not only acted as loyal subjects, but also brought specific grievances directly to the British government.[7]

Notwithstanding their sense of being loyal subjects of the British Empire, Black Loyalists' political thought was also shaped as much by gender, class, and religious proclivities as by local circumstances in Nassau and Abaco. In spite of the differences between the rural environment of

Abaco and the urban environment of Nassau, Black Loyalists entering both had much in common based on their desire to extend their liberty to the Bahamas and to defend these claims in courtrooms and other contested political spaces. This chapter seeks to explore the specific element of black activism that was related to the question of freedom from bondage, a claim that was tenuously held by Black Loyalists settling in both Abaco and New Providence. Such claims to freedom reflected a broad spectrum of political activity that crossed class, religious, and gender lines. Significantly, it will be demonstrated that even before disembarking in 1783, Black Loyalists who settled in Abaco and New Providence showed a determined effort to hold onto the liberty they had been promised during the Revolutionary War. Ultimately, Black Loyalists throughout the archipelago confronted and confounded Bahamian society with the central issue of whether freedom would be either extended or denied to them.

On embarking from New York and Saint Augustine for the Bahamas, Black Loyalists faced the grim reality that despite certificates of freedom and other official documents in their possession, custom and law considered them unequal to the white passengers who had departed with them. White Loyalists were given free transportation by the British government, allotted six months of provisions, and offered forty acres of free land for each head, in addition to twenty acres for each dependent or enslaved person. Additionally, though an exhaustive survey of lands had not been made upon their arrival, white Loyalists were promised a ten-year exemption from quit rent (a rent paid by freemen in lieu of services required by feudal custom) from the date of the making of such grants.[8] In contrast, Black Loyalists faced an uncertain future because their legal status as free persons was ambiguously defined.

The difference between black and white Loyalists was most clearly evident in the case of the passengers listed on *The William* and *The Nautilus*, two vessels departing for Abaco from New York on August 21 and 22, 1783. Though the passengers of these two ships shared a common fate as Loyalists forced to evacuate British North America at the end of the Revolutionary War, their collective identities and individual experiences differed greatly. Of the 250 evacuees, the majority consisted of white families identified as "former soldiers, townsfolk, and farmers" of mostly humble origins, and who generally possessed fewer enslaved persons and dependents than their southern counterparts.[9] Additionally, among the passengers were 95 Black Loyalists varying in age, sex, skills, place of origin, and time of service to the British military. Indeed, a profile of the Black Loyalist cohort on these two ships suggests an eclectic group of individuals possessing a single common identifier: all either claimed to be free or were legally and customarily qualified as free, based on British proclamations issued throughout the Revolutionary War. The majority were listed as "formerly the property of," denoting specific owners—many from the plantation colonies, especially South Carolina and Virginia. A large portion had migrated from other Atlantic world ports to New York at a much earlier time. The random nature of this particular group is illustrated by the fact that they derived from eleven of the former mainland colonies, with other individuals from Bermuda, Barbados, Jamaica, and Haiti. Taken together, the passengers on *The William* and *The Nautilus* shared the common experience of being on the losing end of the Revolutionary conflict; yet their racial, ethnic, and gendered identities reflected manifold differences that would ultimately be the source of discord upon settlement in Abaco.

On looking more closely at the ship registers for *The William* and *The Nautilus*, it is evident that the black refugees were described in ways that suggest their position as free men and women was tenuous if not ambiguously defined from the inception of their sea voyage to the Bahamas. Indeed, next to the name of each Black Loyalist leaving New York for the Bahamas was the name of a white Loyalist *"in whose possession they are now."* Not only was this term unique to those Black Loyalists forced to evacuate to the British Caribbean, but it also suggests an uncertain legal status that could be manipulated to the advantage of those whites deemed the possessor of a black passenger. Arguably, the term "in whose possession they are now," was intended to establish a form of apprenticeship whereby former masters would continue to extract work and other responsibilities at the expense of the formerly enslaved.[10]

The efforts to establish a form of servitude or apprenticeship from the labor of blacks in their possession not only reflected the widely held "custom of the country," but it was also legally sanctioned.[11] In fact, the legal authority may have been a product of the larger issues brought about by the Somerset ruling of June 1772. While the ruling appeared to establish the legal precedent for ending slavery in England, the decision by Lord Mansfield was much more narrowly and ambiguously defined. As such, the verdict established certain protections once enslaved persons landed in England, but this did not completely sever master-slave relationships. Rather, it meant that the master's right to a formerly enslaved person's service could possibly continue in a form similar to apprenticeship. In this context, servants generally labored without the expectation of wages, although other obligations including room, board, and provisions were normally provided.[12]

Ultimately, the Somerset ruling had implications for white Loyalists entering slaveholding societies like the Bahamas. It effectively provided the legal grounds to justify extending a form of apprenticeship or other bonded labor to the black passengers headed for the Bahamas. Put another way, the Somerset ruling legitimized the efforts of whites to move blacks to a "foreign country" while retaining customary and legal rights of servitude among those "in whose possession they are now."[13] Such a rereading of the Somerset case runs contrary to scholarship that sees in the ruling an early humanitarian impulse that would eventually culminate in the abolition of the slave trade (1808) and slavery (1834) in the British Empire. Indeed, it could as easily be argued that across the Atlantic world, blacks of undefined status faced greater uncertainty and less protection under the law as a result of Lord Mansfield's ruling.

The ripple effect of Lord Mansfield's ruling was particularly amplified in communities in the North Atlantic such as Nova Scotia, where slavery had only recently been established with the founding of Halifax in 1749. Despite the newness of slavery in the Maritime province and the fact that it never evolved into a dominant or numerically significant means of labor production, Black Loyalists arriving en masse in 1783 still experienced the crude traits of a slaveholding society particularly in terms of restrictions on provisions, land, and their ability to labor freely.[14] More pointedly, black people entering Halifax at the end of the American Revolution, no matter their legal or apparent status, faced the danger of being sold as slaves and transported to an area where persons of African descent were assumed to be enslaved—and where they were more valuable as chattel than as free or enslaved workers in Nova Scotia. The case of Nova Scotia reveals the inescapable truth that regardless of prewar status or wartime service, Black Loyalists would face impediments to their quest for freedom simply because they lived in an age of African-based slavery.[15]

Nevertheless, Nova Scotia was not the only place where one's prewar status or service could be reversed or revoked. Indeed, the fragility of freedom for Black Loyalists was most definitely borne out in the case of the passengers destined for Abaco onboard *The William* and *The Nautilus*. In this respect, it would appear that slave owners and colonial officials had much leverage in interpreting the claims of those purportedly "in possession of" enslaved persons and the claims of the enslaved persons themselves to absolute freedom. Such an interpretation would obviously be detrimental to the aspirations of Black Loyalists intent on exercising their freedom. Accordingly, thirty-one white masters were listed for the ninety-five blacks on board *The William* and *The Nautilus*. Of these masters, twenty "possessed" only one or two blacks, but a few controlled small gangs. Perhaps more disturbing and suggestive of the true motives behind the appellation, in ten cases the white person listed as possessing the black was also listed as the former owner, even purchaser of that individual.[16] In any event, where the white person "in possession" of a Black Loyalist had made an actual financial investment, or where the formerly enslaved person had been inherited, the "possessor" had sufficient incentive to reduce the black to a state of absolute bondage.[17]

If the term "in whose possession they are now" put limits on their unequivocal right to freedom from bondage, the black passengers embarking from New York for Abaco were certainly not quiescent in claiming their rightful status as free persons. A careful analysis of the black passenger list of *The William* and *The Nautilus* reveals the subtle ways in which Black Loyalists by the end of the war had already begun to assert their rights as free persons. It is in the "remarks" column of the ship's registry that the voices of blacks such as Joseph Scott surface in unintended expressions of political consciousness. Scott was described by the ship's clerk as a stout fellow, aged 40, and in the possession of a white Loyalist named Alexander Dean. The clerk noted that "he says he is free, lived in Charleston, a carpenter." Similar expressions were given for John Jackson, who apart from being described as a 27-year-old stout fellow, was also reported as saying "he is free, lived with Tom Hutchinson of Charleston, left him 5 year agoe." Finally, there was the case of George, described as a 20-year-old stout fellow who had come "from Jamaica where he says he was born free."[18]

Black Loyalist men were not alone in having their quest for freedom noted in the ships' registers. Indeed, while men constituted the majority of the adult passengers on both *The William* and *The Nautilus* (50), it is worth noting the significant number of female passengers (29), both single and married, and the unique remarks transcribed by the clerks relative to their claims of being free persons. Particularly revealing was the description of Betsy, the sole case of a female Black Loyalist whose remarks were daringly transcribed as [she] "says she is free." However, unlike her male counterparts, Betsy was also described as an "idiot."[19] Why such an appellation? It may be that her singular effort to assertively claim she was free made her the target of such a pejorative remark. Though not as overtly assertive as Betsy's claims, other Black Loyalist women listed on these two vessels did, however, have their fight for freedom recorded. Take for instance Daphae Rivers, described by the clerk as "a stout wench, age 22," who had escaped from her owner, Samuel Fulton of Charleston, four years before and thus qualified for free status by the time she was evacuated from New York in 1783. Likewise, Hester Scott, described as "a stout mulatto wench," had qualified for her freedom "per Governor Bull's Certificate" (most likely issued in Georgia), before embarking for the Bahamas from New York. There was also Kate Johnson, recorded by the clerk as "a 37 year old stout wench" who had left her master "Andrew Johnson 2 years agoe" and sought freedom with the British in Charleston.[20] All these women had in common the fact that they were negatively characterized as "wenches," a term increasingly associated with black women.[21] Equally telling were the inscribed comments pertaining to their pattern of flight, reflecting their hard-fought struggle to secure freedom and sanctuary behind British lines. Such comments suggest the complex ways in which Black Loyalists destined for the Bahamas attempted to gain rights by taking advantage of the unique circumstances of the Revolutionary War. This self-assertiveness on the part of Black Loyalists highlights the kind of underlying social tensions that likely existed during the sea voyage and then surfaced as explosive political contests upon their arrival in Abaco.

The first signs of social tension appeared in early September 1783 at the outset of their establishment of a settlement called Carleton, located in Northern Abaco.[22] These tensions were inevitable given the fact that Black Loyalists' status on disembarkation remained ambivalent. Indeed, such conditions engendered divisions within the group, although ironically not immediately between black and white Loyalists. In a letter to Lord Sydney in London dated March 1, 1784, Brigadier General McArthur noted on taking over the command of the Bahama Islands that:

I am sorry to inform your Lordship I found matters in a very different state at the island of Abaco, where the Colony of Refugees sent
in September last from New York has settled; they had been but few
days on shore when dissention got among them, which by degrees
rose to such a height they were on the point of taking arms against
each other.[23]

Although McArthur's comments encapsulated the prevailing tension
within the group, he did not conclude that the conflict was between black
and white Loyalists. Instead he argued that the root cause was actually between various white Loyalists who refused to work at the provisional store
that was apparently operated collectively by the group.[24] It appears that
this initial discord on Abaco stemmed not from race relations but from
disappointment with the island's resources and the system of martial law
imposed on the first settlement. Apparently, the settlers had no immediate
plans, or even authority, for land distribution.[25]

Further aggravating the conflict and exposing the fissure between the
settlers at Carleton was Captain Stephens of the Pennsylvania Loyalists, who had been chosen as the agent for the settlers before they left
New York. Stephens, according to McArthur, apparently did not act with
"much prudence or temper having withheld the Commissions of two militia officers and assumed the entire command, in which the Militia Officers acquiesced, supposing he had a commission, as he ordered the court
of enquiry and approved of the sentence." What is most revealing about
Stephens' actions, however, is that, fearing his own safety, he armed "his
servants and negroes and seized two reputable inhabitants keeping them
prisoners at night in his house."[26] Evidently, the prisoners were eventually released by order of McArthur himself. The immediate effect of the
conflict was that many of the Loyalists who had supported the prisoners established a rival settlement eighteen miles southeast of Carleton,
christened Maxwell Town, after the recently returned governor of the Bahamas.[27] Nevertheless, the disturbance suggests a number of underlying
issues that reflect the ways in which whites ascribed value to and con-
ferred value on Black Loyalists. On the surface, Stephens' decision to arm
his servants and "negroes" made sense given the context of the recently
concluded Revolutionary War. Yet Stephens clearly went beyond the traditional use of power not only because he had not been commissioned to
do so, but also because he was arming Black Loyalists during peacetime.

In the end, this case demonstrates ways in which white Loyalists began to circumvent the laws to further their own self-interests. This established a pattern that would be both perpetuated by whites and contested by blacks in future conflicts.

Invariably the arrival of black and white Loyalists in Nassau in 1783 created social and racial cleavages that mirrored the conflicts that had already surfaced in Abaco. Governor Maxwell observed the growing hostility between the two groups of Loyalists when he pointed out the practice of white Loyalists going beyond the limits of the law in order to assert the servitude of Black Loyalists if not their absolute bondage. In a message to the General Assembly on August 29, 1784, Governor Maxwell noted how many of the blacks had initially been given protection by "our general" (referring to Carleton in New York) but unfortunately "masters deceive them and produce a bill of sale for them on landing."[28] More telling of the uneasy tension between black and white Loyalists was Maxwell's comment in his correspondence with Lord Sydney dated October 15, 1784. Maxwell perceptively remarked that "there are several indictments for riots—as also demands upon sundry people who have lately arrived on account of Negroes in their possession."[29] Interestingly, Maxwell seems to have appealed to the white Loyalists to honor the proclamations and orders that established the legitimacy of Black Loyalist claims when he wrote, "I have remonstrated to them, that their detaining them may be attended with bad consequences, their answer thanks, the courts are competent."[30] While Maxwell certainly defended the claims of the Black Loyalists, his position stemmed less from an allegiance to their desire for freedom than to his status as a British official determined to uphold the letter of the law and maintain order within the colony.

Where Maxwell's comments reflected his personal views as the governor, it was also clear that he had support from other appointed officials in the government. In a letter to the governor dated June 30, 1786, G. Barry expressed his growing concern about the ways that blacks were being treated at the hands of white Loyalists:

> It is with great pain of Mind that I every day see the negroes, who came here from America with the British general's free papers, treated with unheard of cruelty by men who call themselves Loyalists. These unhappy people after being drawn from their master by promises of Freedom, and the king's protection, are every day stolen

away from these islands, shipped and disposed of to the French at Hispaniola, notwithstanding my utmost endeavor to prevent such barbarity.[31]

Barry's letter is significant for underscoring the ways in which Black Loyalists' legitimate claims to freedom under British proclamations could be obstructed or creatively ignored by unscrupulous white slave owners. Barry would later be appointed receiver-general and chief magistrate of Dunmore's Negro Court, established in November of 1787. Though it might be tempting to read into his comments an early abolitionist sentiment, a closer analysis of Barry's comments suggests a man who was likely concerned with the illegality of the trade with British foreign powers, particularly with the French sugar colony of St. Domingue. Quite possibly Barry's comments were also informed by a larger debate within British imperial circles emanating from the Mansfield ruling of 1772. This ruling asserted that freed blacks could no longer legally be forced into servitude or sold as chattel to a foreign power according to British common law and the rights of habeas corpus.[32] Beyond the legal jurisdictional issues, perhaps Barry also echoed the sentiments of Mansfield in determining that slavery, or re-enslavement in this instance at the hands of opportunistic white Loyalists, was an "odious offense" that ran against the natural law of civil societies.[33] Like Mansfield and many other British officials living in the Age of Humanitarianism, Barry was both a loyal servant of the Crown and a friend of justice. As such, his views regarding the ill-treatment of Black Loyalists being sold to French traders may well have reflected an effort to balance the rule of law as a royal official of the Crown while also demonstrating his acute sense of the rights of free blacks to have "access to the courts to protect against unlawful imprisonment or abuse, and freedom from chattel slavery."[34] Regardless of his intentions, his letter demonstrates the fact that even before the arrival of Lord Dunmore in 1787, the question of freedom from bondage was a central issue dividing black and white Loyalists.

Such tensions beset the political and social climate of Bahamian society throughout the early period of Loyalist migration (1783–1785), particularly in Abaco, where the original social arrangements remained contentious. For many of the wealthier white Loyalists, particularly those who had settled near Spencer's Bight, the immediate solution was to migrate with their slaves to New Providence, other Bahamian islands (particularly

Long Island and the Caicos), or elsewhere in the British Caribbean. The destitute conditions of those white Loyalists who remained in Abaco was accentuated by the removal of some of the blacks whose labor they had anticipated would support their aspirations to become planters. The granting of lands to Loyalists after September 1785 was a decided relief for Abaco whites, but because of the scarcity of slave labor in Abaco, these new landowners continued to try to coerce the free black population.[35] As a result, incidents of unrest persisted throughout the mid-1780s. In 1785, for example, Cornelius Blanchard, listed in the *Book of Negroes* as a white in possession of a number of Black Loyalists, informed Governor Powell that no sooner had the people begun to "make a trial of the land," and start "to reap the fruits of their industry, than a number of Negroes had taken to the wood, and have robbed the places, that they have now no support left."[36] Blanchard's comments reveal the frustrations typical of white Abaconians whose aspirations to establishing plantations were dashed by the unwillingness of Black Loyalists to submit to exploitative labor conditions.

Likewise, in Nassau, the dominant urban center and seat of colonial government, a political contest emerged by 1785 between those whites willing to exploit and coerce black labor and many self-determined Black Loyalists who assertively defended their rightful claims to freedom. The case of a "certain negro man named Romeo" is particularly important for understanding the contested terrain that developed in Nassau between black and white Loyalists. Romeo had apparently been claimed as an enslaved person by the administration of "one George Eden, deceased." His case was eventually brought before magistrates in Nassau, who pronounced on September 27, 1786, that Romeo "is a free man."[37] Though there is no record as to whether Romeo had come to Nassau as a Black Loyalist, his trial was lumped together with other cases that clearly concerned Black Loyalists who had emigrated from the thirteen colonies to the Bahamas as free persons. Another case, involving Jenny, provides more explicit connections with Black Loyalist experiences during the American Revolutionary War as well as the challenges they faced on arrival in Nassau. During her trial, the testimony of William Jebbs, most likely a free black, revealed that the "said wench Jenny," had taken "protection within the British lines at Charleston and afterwards at St. John's." Jebbs' testimony further indicated that he saw Jenny receive "her free pass signed by Doctor Frazier and one by Major Frasier, town mayor of Charles town." Given Jebbs' convincing firsthand testimony, the justices ruled that Jenny, "together with her four children named Lydia, Bethy, Pally, and Bristol, are free."[38] This case underscores a number of important facets of the Black Loyalist struggle in the Bahamas. First, it reveals through Jebbs' testimony the ways in which free blacks may have forged important partnerships with other Black Loyalists in order to advance their claims to freedom. This pattern of forging alliances with other Black Loyalists to advance particular legal cases was also found in Nova Scotia.[39] In the case of Mary Postell's 1791 court trial in Shelburne, Nova Scotia, her strongest evidence came from the testimony of Scripio and Dinah Wearing, who attested to her free status as a Loyalist doing construction work for the British military engineers in Charleston from 1780 to 1782. Likewise, in the 1791 case of the orphaned boy Stephen George, a number of Black Loyalist witnesses appeared in the Shelburne, Nova Scotia, court records testifying to his parents' free status as Loyalist laborers in British service.[40] In line with these court cases, Jenny evidently sought Jebbs' support to provide testimony of the time she spent behind British lines and to verify the certificates of protection she possessed, signed by two British officials during the Revolutionary War.[41]

Second, Jenny's case also highlights an important gendered dimension, since enslaved persons and women were two populations generally excluded from active politics, including voting, bearing witness in criminal and civil cases, and holding political office during this period.[42] Finally, this case underscores the significant opposition that Black Loyalists faced, even when they carried appropriate certificates of freedom. Though the initial opposition to Black Loyalists' claims occurred during the course of British evacuation from seaports such as New York, Charleston, and Savannah, such contestations were eventually extended to host societies across the Atlantic, inclusive of East Florida, Nova Scotia, and most certainly the Bahamas. Two cases drawn from Spanish Florida and Nova Scotia illustrate the great lengths to which whites often went to undermine the legitimate claims made by blacks such as Jenny through the courts. Major Henry Williams and his brother William Williams had tried for years to reclaim three escapees who had run away in 1784 as they prepared to evacuate their slaves from East Florida to Nassau, New Providence. Yet from the testimony of Hector, Sam, and Reyna, the three allegedly enslaved persons, it was clear that they had arrived in East Florida as free persons as a consequence of their military service. By the time the Williams brothers initiated a suit to recover Hector, Sam, and Reyna in 1788, all three had hired themselves as free laborers to a Spanish plantation owner. Interestingly, despite numerous appeals by the Williams brothers, Governor Zespedes upheld the claims to freedom of the three blacks.[43]

Of a similar nature was the 1785 case of James Singletary brought before the courts in Shelburne, Nova Scotia. According to Singletary's affidavit, Samuel Andrews had illegally claimed him as a slave despite the fact that he arrived in East Florida and later Nova Scotia as a free person. In court, Andrews opposed Singletary's testimony, arguing that he had "paid fifty pounds for said Negro James" but had lost the bill of sale. Apart from his own testimony, Andrews received additional assistance from John Fanning, who attested to the circumstances by which the Negro John was always "considered as the property of Mr. Andrews." Tragically, the courts ruled that Andrews would be given a year to get his documents together while Singletary and his wife and child would remain within the household of Andrews ostensibly as "servants."[44] In this instance, the notion of race-blind justice was clearly aborted, as white Loyalists were not only assured that their property would not be moved, but also given time to locate the requisite documents needed to counterbalance the legitimate "free pass" or certificate of protection that blacks had dutifully brought to court. Singletary's case was far from an isolated instance of courts' inequitable and biased handling of witness testimony and evidence. As evidenced by affidavits and legal documents, countless other Black Loyalists found their way into Nova Scotia courts where they challenged efforts by white Loyalists to re-enslave them. These cases reflect a common pattern extending from Loyalist evacuation centers such as New York and Saint Augustine whereby forged bills of sale and white witnesses giving false testimony stood up against the legitimate assertions and even legal documents produced by blacks in court.[45] Thus, from a broader comparative perspective, Jenny's case in the Bahamas, much like those of her contemporaries in Nova Scotia and East Florida, reflects the tenuous and fleeting nature of black liberation that emerged in courtrooms in exiled communities across the Atlantic.

A similar case involving William and Hester Willis, passengers onboard *The William*, suggests that even where Black Loyalists had appropriate documentation to prove their legitimate claim to freedom, they could still be forced into servitude against their will. Evidently, William

Armstrong, one of the commissioners inspecting *The William*, had written a certificate of freedom for both refugees that contained the remarks: "The Bearers, William Willis and Hester his wife, both free negroes, are inspected and passed." Yet, in spite of their claims and the possession of a certificate signed by the inspector, both William and Hester were forced to fight the efforts of John Cameron to assert absolute control over their status later in Abaco. In fact, Hester was forced to serve an indentured contract to Cameron. The indenture did not last however, as William, at great financial sacrifice, was able to repurchase his wife from Cameron for 25 pounds in 1784.[46]

The case of William and Hester Willis reflects the widespread problem of illegal indenture contracts that emerged out of the tensions between black and white Loyalists in the Bahamas. It was in this increasingly hostile political environment that the 1784 Negro Act was passed. This act made it lawful for the receiver-general and any two magistrates "to examine the manumissions or passes of any negroe, mulatto, mustee or Indian pretending to be free," which placed the burden of proof on Black Loyalists rather than on whites. Incidentally, the law also stipulated that all illegal indentured contracts or other forms of servitude were to be made void and of no effect, with the offending white person expected to pay to the treasury the sum of thirty pounds. This last clause suggests that the indenturing of black labor was a common practice that had emerged in the Bahamas at this time. Yet even as the 1784 Act attempted to regulate the widespread practice of illegal indenture contracts, it is evident that such labor relations continued.[47] It is worth noting that the uneasy friction between black and white Loyalists in the Bahamas mirrored labor conditions in the frontier environment of Nova Scotia and the plantation colony of Jamaica. In each host society where black refugees were transported with white households (usually on the same vessel) they were eventually forced into various kinds of servile relationships, either serving out formal indentured contracts, as in the case of George Liele, or more often than not initially listed as "servants" or dependents of whites, as was John Singletary in Nova Scotia.[48] In the end, the 1784 Act reflected the uneasy tensions that had gripped the Bahamas as a consequence of the influx of black and white Loyalists.

Lord Dunmore arrived in this explosive environment as governor on October 26, 1787. A decade earlier, as Virginia's last royal governor, John Murray, the fourth earl of Dunmore, had ignited an unintended social revolution by arming able-bodied enslaved persons owned by rebels as potential agents of British imperial power. Now on entering the Bahamas, Dunmore would face a situation where he had to defend the very claims of Black Loyalists that had been set in motion by his infamous declaration at the outset of the Revolutionary War.[49] From the moment he arrived as governor of the colony, Dunmore was faced with a serious dilemma regarding the efforts of whites to claim control over the labor of blacks, while attempting, at least publicly, to honor the commitment made by the British to protect Black Loyalist claims. Reports of disturbances across the islands reached Dunmore within his first month of office. The widespread nature of these disturbances and the willingness of blacks to take up arms were reflected in Dunmore's correspondence with Lord Sydney dated November 28, 1787:

> I arrived here the 26th. . . . It having been represented to me that a number of negroes had for sometime absented themselves from their owners or employers, and were plundering and committing outrages upon the inhabitants of this and several of the other islands. I thought proper to issue the enclosed proclamation: no 1 & 2 offering His Majesty's free pardon to such of the said negroes as should surrender themselves.[50]

Such comments reflect on the one hand the tacit assumption that Black Loyalists were guilty of committing outrages against white inhabitants, while also revealing the conciliatory political strategy employed by Dunmore in order to get blacks to surrender. This method, according to Dunmore, had led a number of blacks to come in, claiming "their freedom under the Proclamations issued by the Commander in Chief of His Majesty's forces in America during the late war."[51] With the mounting social crisis weighing heavily on his mind, Dunmore acted decisively to establish by proclamation a special court to inquire into "the nature of their claims agreeable to Act of Assembly."[52] But rather than allaying the conflict between white and black Loyalists, Dunmore's "Negro Court" exacerbated the local situation.

From the white elite's perspective, Dunmore's Negro Court was viewed as unconstitutional—a legal anomaly that breached traditional societal and judicial assumptions regarding race, class, and gender by empowering enslaved and free blacks to testify in courts of law normally reserved for white men. For this reason, many slave-owning elites argued vehemently

Figure 3. Lord John Murray, Fourth Earl of Dunmore. The iconic and infamous Lord Dunmore distinctively served both as last Royal Governor of Virginia and as Governor of the Bahamas from 1787 to 1797. The original painting is housed in the Scottish National Gallery. From Craton and Saunders, *Islanders in the Stream*, 233. By permission of University of Georgia Press, Athens.

against its proceedings. Most notable was William Wylly, the transplanted Loyalist from New Brunswick who served as the solicitor-general for the Bahamas from 1788 to 1804. Having resided in Virginia up to the outbreak of hostilities, Wylly undoubtedly was familiar with Dunmore's inflammatory November 7, 1775, proclamation and the social upheavals that ensued when large numbers of enslaved persons escaped Patriot masters to serve the British cause. Mindful of how such upheavals had the unintended consequence of dissolving the social order of colonial society, Wylly likely surmised that Dunmore, as liberator, was bent on repeating such offenses, and thus saw in the Negro Court a nefarious harbinger of moral decay, if not revolutionary design. Writing self-consciously as an advocate for the Bahamian slaveholding class in 1789, Wylly argued that the Negro Court was "instituted under the most specious pretexts" with its intended purpose being to "harass the new inhabitants."[53] As an educated man familiar with the law, Wylly further undermined the legitimacy of the Negro Court by pointing out:

> the trial by Jury is unnecessarily and wantonly taken from the subject; that, in lieu of it, an unconstitutional tribunal, consisting of three persons nominated by the Governor, chiefly pro hoc vice, and removable at his pleasure, is substituted to decide upon all questions of Negro property, which in the Bahama Islands is the principal property of the people; that the most improper persons have, from time to time, been appointed to put this act to force; that they proceed upon no established principles, and that their practice is governed by no certain or known rules.[54]

Not only did Wylly provide details asserting the impropriety and illegality of this court, but he also defended the property-owning class and their right to appropriate the labor of blacks in the colony. Wylly further expanded on this latter point when he argued, "the Planter has, in some instances, been robbed of his property, by arbitrary decisions, to which he has not been made a party by any previous process, or notice of trial." Wylly ended his vitriolic condemnation of the Negro Court by noting,

> The slaves in the Bahama Islands (who greatly outnumber the whites) encouraged by this Act, by this court, by proclamations, and by other means, have broke out into some acts of open rebellion; and that the town of Nassau is actually overawed by a considerable body of runaway and other Negroes, collected and kept together in the neighborhood of Government House, and fort Charlotte, in open and flagrant violation of the laws of the colony, and in the face of repeated presentments solemnly made by the Grand Inquest of those Islands.[55]

In general, Wylly's comments regarding the defects of the Negro Court reflected the mercantile elite's fears of the potential for insurrection,

particularly given the opportunity for blacks to claim rights. Yet Bahamian slaveholders and those supporting their interests in the Bahamas
were not alone in their fear of the repercussions associated with arming
black persons with certain inalienable rights. Indeed, work by African dia-
sporic and Atlantic world scholars suggests that during the Age of Revolutions, slaveholders were increasingly concerned about how the contagion
of revolutionary ideas—ignited by movements in British North America,
Spanish America, and particularly Saint Domingue would spread to black
populations throughout the Atlantic littoral. From Gabriel Prosser's call
for Death or Liberty in Richmond, Virginia, to Toussaint Louverture's
unique rearticulation of the Rights of Man, black radicals increasingly
were viewed as tangible threats, with their insurgent activities symbolically hovering like a blood-stained ghost over slaveholding societies in the
Americas.[56] Despite these real or imagined fears, slaveholders throughout
the Atlantic maintained a conflicted duality—on the one hand showing
increasing concern or trepidation about plots and insurgent activity, while
simultaneously passing more punitive slave laws and continuing to engage
in the trade and expansion of slavery within their local districts. This was
true in the Bahamas, where despite Wylly's condemnation of the Negro
Court, Dunmore and his executive council, along with countless other
slave-owning Loyalists, saw in the Negro Courts an occasion to acquire
additional chattel slaves who would invariably serve as the foundation of
a thriving plantation labor force.[57] Thus, whites often demonstrated am-
biguity toward the Negro Courts: on the one hand questioning the court's
legality, particularly where it gave blacks unprecedented legal rights, while
at the same time tacitly supporting its decisions when it worked to uphold
slaveholding interests in the colony. Indeed, a favorable ruling for a slave
owner could return a free Black Loyalist to a lifetime of servitude, despite
the fact that in some instances the claimants possessed documentation
to prove they were free. In the end, Dunmore's Negro Court served very
different purposes. For whites it represented a source of bitter contention
even while it bolstered their hegemonic grip over the colony. In contrast,
for Black Loyalists throughout the colony, the Negro Court initially held
the promise of freedom and provided a political opening that would have
far-reaching consequences for the colony.

Perhaps with this in mind, Black Loyalists in Abaco in late November
of 1787 moved beyond simply demanding change; in a moment of collective consciousness, they absconded from their plantations and began to

revolt. The news of their actions eventually reached Nassau, where Lord Dunmore relayed his growing concern to Lord Sydney:

> I am just now informed from the island of Abaco that members of the outlaying negroes went about with muskets and fixed bayonets, robbing and plundering, that the white inhabitants had collected themselves in a body, and having come up with the negroes had killed, wounded and taken most of them prisoners, three of the latter they immediately executed. Since this my Proclamation reached them, and some of those that escaped have surrendered themselves, and I hope the rest will follow their example.[58]

Dunmore revealed his ultimate allegiance to planter interest by depicting Black Loyalists as insurgents, guilty of robbing and plundering, whereas the white Loyalists were sanitized in a way that ignored their brutal execution of three of the "offending" blacks. Additionally, it appears that the proclamation served as a mechanism for restoring order rather than as a means of addressing the social injustice at the heart of Black Loyalist claims. Dunmore's conservatism was confirmed by the actual proclamation, dated November 7, 1787, in which he appears to be most concerned with maintaining the proper social order rather than subverting it. In this context, the preface to the proclamation assumes the guilt of Black Loyalists in advance of an enquiry:

> It has been represented to me, in Council, that a Number of Negroes have for a considerable time past absented themselves from their owners or employers, and have committed felonies and other crimes, to the great detriment of the community, as well in the island of New-Providence, as in the Out Islands.[59]

The remaining portion of the proclamation reflected a mix of British paternalism and Dunmore's own unique rhetoric employed to counterbalance both white demands for employable bondservants and the claims of "unruly" Black Loyalist insurrectionists. Hence, Dunmore composed a purposely ambiguous and paternalistic message when he remarked,

> Whereas it is thought fit, by and with the advice of his Majesty's Honourable Council, to issue this my Proclamation, offering, and I do hereby offer, his Majesty's most gracious and free pardon to each

and every of the said Negroes, under the above description, who shall surrender themselves to any of His Majesty's Justices of the peace, in the town of Nassau, or any Justice of the peace in any of the Out Islands on or before Saturday the third day of November next for those on the island of New Providence and in eight days after this proclamation shall be published in the several districts of the Out Islands. And I do hereby command and require each and every of his Majesty's said Justices of the peace to whom such surrender shall be made, forthwith to transmit to me a certificate thereof, under his hand and seal, with the name or names of such negro or negroes, and a description of their owners or employers, in order that they may receive the full benefit of this proclamation.[60]

Upon closer scrutiny, the proclamation served to establish a method of controlling the free black and enslaved population by ensuring they were listed and certified in a bound relationship either to a slave owner or to an employer. In this context, the proclamation reinforced and codified the very power relations that white Loyalists had begun to assert over Black Loyalists. In essence, by accepting the pardon offered, Black Loyalists were forced to agree to greater surveillance by both Justice of the Peace and employer, to whom they were expected to show gratitude for receiving the full benefits of the proclamation.

Significantly, although the proclamation favored white Loyalists, it did not prevent the Bahamian legislature from passing draconian measures in an effort to police and regulate black claims to freedom. An act passed on November 27, 1787, stated that

Whereas many inconveniences have arisen from the method of trying negroes, mulattoes, muskees and Indians claims of freedom, at the courts of Quarter sessions only, be it hereby enacted that from and after the publication of this Act it may at any time be lawful for the receiver general and any two magistrates to examine the manumissions or passes of any Negro, Mulatto, Muskee or Indian pretending to be free and if they should be forged or otherwise insufficient or producing no satisfactory proof of their being free, then he, she or they are to be forthwith committed to the common gaols and such negroes, mulattoes, muskees or Indians shall remain there not longer than one month when the Provost Marshall is required after giving three days public notice, to cause the said Negroes, Mulattos, Muskees or Indians to be sold by public auction and the money aris- ing from the sale . . . be paid to the public treasury.[61]

The 1787 Act was clearly intended to put into place a regulatory system that would impede, through a protracted bureaucratic process, the efforts of blacks to claim their rights. In this case, two magistrates in addition to the receiver-general were required as witnesses for each claim made by a black. If that were not enough, the legislators clearly assumed that blacks were guilty of criminal acts in advance of their inquiry, implying that they were pretending to be free and forging documents to make their claims seem legitimate. Nevertheless, the legislators did include the provision that if any claimant proved to have bona fide free status, such individuals would be "warned and ordered by the magistrate to depart this govern- ment in three months under the penalty of losing his or her freedom un- less he or she gives security to pay ninety pounds into the treasury at the end of three months."[62]

Interestingly, while the punishment for a black person found guilty of fraudulently claiming freedom was imprisonment in the public jail for up to one month and the forfeiture of their previously claimed freedom, for a white Loyalist illegally in possession of a black as a servant or chat- tel, the punishment was simply a fine of "thirty pounds to be paid into the public treasury of these islands."[63] Even where the Black Loyalist was found to possess the legitimate documents, under scrutiny, he was still subject to a security bond of ninety pounds as a form of collateral to the public treasury, failure to comply with which would result in deportation. Though not explicitly stated by the legislators, it appears that the bond security regulation functioned as a way of impeding the unconditional access to liberty envisioned by Black Loyalists. No doubt, the tremendous financial risk required of all claimants discouraged some Black Loyalists who were unwilling or unable to acquire the necessary ninety pounds as security bond. But not all were discouraged. Indeed, despite the efforts of whites to create such legal impediments, it is clear that a number of Black Loyalists rejected docile acquiescence and chose instead the path of self- determination opened by Dunmore's proclamation.

In Nassau in particular, Dunmore's proclamation had an immediate impact, with a substantial number of Black Loyalists coming forward publicly to declare their intention to have their status determined once and for all in his Negro Court. Within a few days of Dunmore's proclamation, a Black Loyalist named Thomas Smith appeared before three magistrates to have his case for freedom heard. Remarkably, despite the fact that a white claimant, Henry Stiles, provided evidence to support his claim to ownership of "the said Negro," Thomas Smith was deemed "absolutely and to all intents and purposes free, and acquitted from all obligation of slavery and servitude."[64] Smith certainly was not the only Black Loyalist to assert a claim to freedom in Dunmore's Negro Court and achieve a favorable outcome. In January 1788, Hannah, a "negro woman formerly the property of George Galphin of South Carolina," was adjudged to be free after the magistrates presiding over her case had "perused and considered her papers and other proofs," to which no objections had been made. Unlike Smith's case, Hannah's trial did not involve any objections from white claimants. In this case her favorable ruling appeared to be based on the fact that she had ample documentary proof of her claims.[65] Another favorable ruling worth considering was the case involving a "negro fellow named Matthias." This case is significant because apart from the records related to the actual ruling in the case, there is an additional letter written by one of the magistrates requesting William Green, the alleged slave owner, to attend the trial. According to the summons written by Justice O'Halleran dated October 31, 1787:

> Sir, a negro fellow named Matthias who calls himself free, has this day applied to me for protection, he having as he affirms, been taken by his majesty's troops during the late rebellion and is of consequence included in the description of Negroes, declared by the King's Proclamation to be free. As the laws of these islands direct that in all cases where the freedom of any Negro shall be in contestation the same shall be determined by the Receiver General for the time being and two magistrates; and it appearing to me that this fellows' presentations to freedom are well grounded I am desired that you will attend at the Court House on Friday next at twelve o'clock to show cause good and sufficient, why the abovementioned negro, should not obtain a certificate of freedom, agreeable to His Majesty's Proclamation and to the said Act.[66]

O'Halleran's letter is significant for a number of reasons. First, it indicates the unique openings that Dunmore's Court created for blacks, allowing them to seek protection in the law against potential slave owners. Second, the letter also clearly indicates Mathias' initiative in actively seeking freedom from enslavement. In the end, the trial transcripts dated February 8, 1788, declare Mathias "free and acquitted and released from all obligations of slavery or servitude to the said William Green or any other person or persons."[67]

Public notices published in the *Bahama Gazette* often served to reify the expectations of freedom sought by Black Loyalists in Dunmore's Negro Courts. In an official notice provided in the February 21, 1789, edition of the *Bahama Gazette,* the Commissioner, William Gramble, reported, "whereas George, alias George Brown, a negro man, gave in some time ago, pretensions to freedom; he is hereby required to attend at the courthouse with his proofs on Tuesday next."[68] Though such statements suggest that Black Loyalists were pretending to be free or had pretentions of freedom, for George and others such as Joseph Pearis, mentioned in the same notice, such language validated their claims by demanding they prove it with relevant documents and certificates in a court of law. Thus on entering Dunmore's Negro Courts, Black Loyalists were empowered with the necessary weapons—their certificates, letters, affidavits, and other legal documents that could be marshaled in their fight for freedom. Beyond legal documents, the testimony of other witnesses and the legal proceedings themselves functioned as a form of public legitimization for Black Loyalists wanting to finalize their claim to freedom once and for all. Similar to the way the Catholic Church and canon law were instrumental in sanctioning the private lives of enslaved and free blacks in Colonial Mexico, so too the courts in the Bahamas afforded Black Loyalists a space where they could legitimize their personhood as subjects of the British Empire.[69] The case of James Kelly is illustrative of this point. The court ruled Kelly was in fact free based on "the testimony of good and credible men, inhabitants of the said islands." Kelly's certificate of freedom was signed by Governor Dunmore with the attached notation reading, "the bearer hereof, James Kelly (a Negro) is a free man, and came from New York as such upwards of five years ago."[70] Such language speaks to the ways in which certificates of freedom issued by Dunmore's Negro Court in Nassau provided public authentication of freedom for the claimant.[71]

Yet in many ways it was in the frontier environment of Abaco that the true efficacy of Dunmore's Negro Court would be challenged. It was in fact the alarming news that another insurrection had erupted on the island of Abaco that compelled Dunmore to quickly establish a special tribunal at Marsh Harbour—the very epicenter of the revolt. The various accounts of the event demonstrate both the complicity of Dunmore in causing it, as well as the familiar tensions that continued to exist between black and white Loyalists. In a memorial appealing to Dunmore to intervene in the ongoing conflict with blacks, the local white Loyalists in Abaco reminded Dunmore that not only had they "abandoned their connections and possessions" in North America, preferring an "obscure life under British government," but they had also "brought with them a number of slaves, whom they had legally purchased, by whose labor they have hitherto been able to support themselves with the necessities of life." Central to the petitioners' argument was the assertion of their rightful claim to the labor of the blacks that had accompanied them from North America. In furthering the legitimacy of their right to possess the "Negroes" as their property, the petitioners noted that

On the return of Captain Mackay [master of the Governor's yacht] from New Providence on Sunday the 4th instant, many of their slaves (through the encouragement of Mackay or his people) came in open day before your Memorialist faces, and put their baggage on board said Mackay's boat, saying that Mackay had declared to them he came with your Excellency's authority to take away all the rebel property Negroes, as the annexed affidavits will sufficiently prove.[72]

In addition to revealing the ways in which the white Loyalists attempted to establish authority over Black Loyalists as masters, the petitioners implicated Dunmore in the affair. Indeed, within the narrative of the Abaco insurrection is a carefully constructed account that attempted to exonerate Dunmore directly from the event, even though it appears that it was in his boat that Mackay sailed to Abaco, and it was almost certainly on his orders that Mackay encouraged Black Loyalists to leave that island.

The account offered by the petitioners was corroborated by a private letter written by Richard Pearis, a white Loyalist in Abaco who had previously served in various Loyalist provincial corps in South Carolina, where he had also been a substantial landowner.[73] In the letter, Pearis disclosed to a friend in Nassau that "this man [Mackay] has likewise spread such confusion among our Negroes that some of my neighbors are left without their house servants, and all have gone in the woods." Pearis further mentioned that

> Those who have been retaken or come in uniformly declare that they were misled by Captain Mackay and his crew who told them he had the Governor's authority to carry them to Nassau, and that all the rebel property Negroes would be made free.[74]

Pearis' comments clearly cast aspersions on Dunmore's Negro Court, a source of friction and animosity for most white slave owners. Yet in the end, Pearis and the other petitioners appealed to Dunmore to intervene personally, realizing that the possibility of insurrection was far more dangerous than their petty issues with Dunmore's illegally constituted court.[75]

Not surprisingly, then, when in May of 1788 Dunmore elected to hold his Negro Court in Abaco to quell the widespread spirit of insurrection, he received very different responses.[76] News of the impending court elicited a highly favorable response from white Loyalists in Abaco. The glowing endorsement of Dunmore's Court was evident in a letter attached to Wylly's report. The signatories of the letter expressed their "extreme gratitude" to the governor for the "happy consequences of your arrival among us." Unlike Wylly, who took issue with the way in which the court apparently was illegally constituted, the Abaconian whites argued that

> The salutary effects which are likely to ensue from the fair, candid, and impartial trials which have been afforded our runaway slaves, and the quiet and peaceful restoration of most of them to their lawful owners are events for which we cannot be sufficiently thankful to your Lordship and the gentlemen composing the court.[77]

Such sentiments must be equivocally framed, reflecting the anticipated ruling that would allow white Loyalists to achieve their planter aspirations at the expense of the dreams of freedom envisioned by Black Loyalists. The response of blacks reflected a great deal of apathy and reluctance. This was borne out by the fact that only thirty blacks were willing to come forward to claim their freedom. Black reluctance reflects both the antipathy of blacks toward a system that was never intended to function as a dispenser of race-blind justice and also their fear of the possible consequences of a ruling against them. Unfortunately, there are no records of the names of those thirty who did come forward, nor is it possible to determine whether the thirty claimants included passengers from *The William* and

The Nautilus. It is important to note that one of the eleven signatories included in the original petition, J. M. Moore, was one of the white Loyalists named "in possession of" a Black Loyalist on *The William.*[78]

The actual details of this particular Negro Court session and its proceedings are sketchy. From Wylly's earlier remarks concerning the legality of the court as it was constituted in Nassau, it is clear that "the present mode of trying the freedom of Negroes by three men," was the order of the day. However, it is also clear from Wylly's account that the nascent revolt in Abaco and the desperate pleas of the white inhabitants required the appearance of the Governor. Thus with the Black Loyalists "having taken up arms," the governor went in person, and "carried with him the judges of a court illegally constituted, and gave a general invitation [to slaves] to come in and claim their freedom; to which their owners made no opposition." Wylly also noted the outcome of the proceedings when he remarked, "Yet, upon that occasion only thirty claimants appeared; of whom twenty-nine were adjudged to be slaves, even by this court, held under the Governor's immediate inspection."[79] Clearly, Wylly believed that despite the illegality of the court, justice was still served by a ruling that overwhelmingly favored slave-owning interests. Dunmore described the outcome in even more glowing language. He noted that "upon our arrival at Abaco all the outlying Negroes came in except five or six who are supposed to have gotten off the island." Ignoring the fact that only one of thirty claimants was adjudicated as free, Dunmore boasted that "those that were entitled to their freedom were declared so."[80] Dunmore's rather sanguine assessment was most likely driven by a desire to present a tranquil image of the colony in which order and good governance had been restored as a consequence of his actions.

Even as Dunmore managed to quell the immediate maelstrom of discontent on the island, the Abaco insurrection of 1788 had far-reaching consequences for the Bahamas. From Dunmore and his executive council's perspective, the revolt and the subsequent tribunal held in Abaco demonstrated the effectiveness of his Negro Court. Dunmore was thus determined that greater power be vested in these courts in order to establish more firmly the rule of law throughout the archipelago. With this in mind, Dunmore pushed to have amendments made to the previous acts of 1784 and 1787. The end result was the passing of a new act on July 25, 1788.[81] Though very similar to the 1784 and 1787 Acts, a number of significant changes tended to exacerbate existing social tensions. To begin with, the receiver-general and two other magistrates were now expected to meet more regularly, "on the first Monday of every month in every year between the hours of nine and three." More importantly, the magistrates were empowered, when the need arose, "to meet from time to time to any other day or days as they shall think fit." Apparently, the magistrates interpreted this clause rather loosely to mean that they could not only meet more frequently, but also that the court itself could be moved to other sites of conflict when necessary. This latter clause was the source of great friction among leading whites such as Wylly and the provost marshall, William Baylis, who alleged that the magistrates would at times adjudge cases involving "negroes" in the "hut of the Receiver-General."[82] As much as this clause angered leading whites, it was the wide and discretionary power allocated to the governor that created far greater opposition. According to the act, if "a negro was determined free," the magistrates were to report "their determination under their hands and seal to the Governor who would provide certificates of freedom."[83] These certificates would then be registered with the public secretary for the colony, and provide the authentic and final proof that the claimant was truly free. For slave owners in the Bahamas, not only did this clause provide the governor with exceeding power beyond that which was customarily expected, but it empowered blacks with a document that could not be challenged in any other court of law by whites. Wylly summarized the sentiments of many white Loyalists regarding the impropriety of this law when he remarked,

> Such certificates shall be considered as a full 'proof of the freedom.' In all other cases and in all other courts, every party in interest must be brought into court, or at least service with some process or notice before judgment can be given against him—but neither by the possession of this Act, nor by the practice of the Judges under it, is any such process or notice required—it is therefore the simplest thing in the world for a negroe to elope from the service of his master, and claim his freedom, go next day to trial, and obtain a decision in his favor, which (unless appealed from within two months by his owner who perhaps has heard nothing of the business) will bar the right of all persons whatever whether absentees, married women, minors or other person laboring under disabilities—but why the governor give the certificate? Could not the justices grant it and with more propriety?[84]

THEIR STRUGGLE WITH FREEDOM FROM BONDAGE · 89

At the heart of Wylly's opposition to the 1788 Act was the fact that in unprecedented fashion, Dunmore's Court and the certificate of freedom issued by him empowered Black Loyalists with political rights at the expense of white Loyalist claimants. Accordingly, where blacks were given the right to testify in a court, whites were restricted to appeals within two months of the trial date.

More than simply the issue of empowering blacks to testify, Wylly also questioned the kind of evidence that the 1788 Act allowed Black Loyalists to use in the court. Wylly in fact noted the way in which the court admitted as evidence "a certificate, a ticket (of the authenticity of which, or whether the person granting it was an officer or commander or not, no proof is required) from any person," claiming to be an "officer from a commander in chief down to corporal." According to Wylly, such evidence was suspicious and subject to forgery given that the bearers of the certificate often were not described adequately to "ascertain the identity of the persons, nor did it actually indicate when they came within the British lines during the war." Such evidence, Wylly believed, reflected the overall inadequacy of proof that was held "as sufficient to entitle a negroe to his freedom, against the best established title on the part of his American master or any other person claiming under him."[85] Overall, at issue for Wylly was the fact that by allowing such evidence in the Negro Court, the burden of proof shifted from slave owners to Black Loyalists. While Wylly's claims may have been exaggerated, it is clear that within the broader Atlantic world context, blacks were slowly gaining access to courts and leveraging the legal systems to their advantage.[86] Take for instance Black Loyalists in Nova Scotia, where despite the burden of proof continuing to rest decidedly in favor of slaveholders, Black Loyalists could at least garner the cooperation of individual magistrates in getting the challenges to court, underscoring "the availability of British justice for persons claiming to be illegally enslaved."[87]

A more general erosion of the slaveholder's legal power seemed to be occurring across the English-speaking world. In particular, in Britain, abolitionism seemed to be accelerating since the foundation of the Society for Effecting the Abolition of the Slave Trade in 1787. Two years later, in August 1789, the *Bahama Gazette* carried a special supplement covering the parliamentary debate on the slave trade, where white and black Loyalists could read that Wilberforce had delivered "one of the most animated, perspicuous, methodical and ably argued speeches ever heard on a copious and comprehensive subject."[88] Undoubtedly, in a nonplantation slaveholding society such as the Bahamas, such news or that of the Mansfield ruling seven years earlier might instill fear among enslavers that even on the periphery of Empire their judicial and legal authority could be undermined by law.

Perhaps these circumstances explain why Wylly essentially became a crusader for the rights of Loyalist slaveholders in the Bahamas, actually traveling to England in 1788 to lobby the Pitt government and Anthony Stokes, the colonial agent for the Bahamas, with a comprehensive statement of grievances against Lord Dunmore. As a highly effective polemical publicist, Wylly set out in his *Short Account* a systematic effort to demonstrate how the Negro Court not only undermined the very foundation of slaveholder rights but was also "perceived as a dangerous departure from Colonial Customs and Laws."[89]

In the *Short Account*, Wylly also offered an interesting gendered argument for why the 1788 Act was inimical to the elitist social order. He noted that even if the proclamations had the force and legality of an Act of Parliament they were only intended "to bring troops to the British standard, and applied only to men slaves—yet the justices have in various instances most liberally extended them to women and children."[90] In fact, Wylly inaccurately interpreted British proclamations during the war. While Dunmore's proclamation of November 7, 1785 was limited to enslaved males owned by Patriots, the Philipsburg Proclamation of 1781 and even Sir Guy Carleton's April 15, 1783 evacuation orders were expansive enough to include men, women, and children found behind British lines.[91] Despite the fact that Wylly misconstrued the implications of these later proclamations, his comments are particularly revealing for the masculinist assumptions built into his argument. Most notably, his argument reflects the growing concern of white men regarding the status of black women and children, as seen in the cases of Sarah Moultrie, Hannah, and Jenny, who took it upon themselves to appear before a public hearing to agitate for freedom in the Bahamas. Wylly in fact posited the view that by liberally extending the right to women and children to have a voice and assert their claims in a court, these women were subverting the very authority and traditions upon which parliament was founded. Thus echoing the separate-spheres ideology of his contemporaries, Wylly saw the inclusion of women and children in a public space as an affront to British custom and a challenge to paternalistic values considered normative for late-eighteenth-century Anglo-American societies.[92] Indeed, Wylly's sentiments paralleled the ideas emerging in the United States, where in the decades following the American Revolution the issue of women's rights and political participation was so explosive that "after a brief moment of receptivity, American women and men chose to foreclose the debate rather than pursue it to its logical conclusion."[93]

Wylly also took offense at the segment of the 1788 Act related to the payment of fees by those the Negro Court deemed free. According to this clause, instead of paying the ninety pounds that had been required under the 1784 Act, those receiving a favorable ruling were required to pay only twelve shillings and to register the certificate of freedom with the Public Secretary. As Wylly succinctly noted, "by the present Act [1788] the American negroes are exempted from those penalties [ninety pounds] which still remain in force against free negroes of any other description."[94] Wylly's critique of the 1788 Act went beyond simply pointing out the illegality of the court, construed as it was without a jury and in contradiction to parliamentary proceedings. Arguably his cause was the defense of slavery and the rights of slaveholders throughout the Atlantic world. In this light, Dunmore's actions in Nassau were tied to a broader antislavery image of the governor dating back to his 1775 proclamation in Virginia. As such, Wylly cast Dunmore in the role of the great liberator when he noted that

> much confusion has existed by this Act among a part of the slaves in the Bahama islands as was occasioned in the year 1775 by the proclamation of a certain Commander in Virginia—for every Negroe in the Bahamas now thinks himself entitled to his freedom, who happened at any period of the war to be employed about any of the works or departments of our army, without enquiring how he happened to be employed, or whether his master was a rebel or a loyalist.[95]

While Wylly's remarks can be read as a clear indictment of Dunmore and his self-proclaimed Negro Court, it is important to understand that in the wake of the Abaco insurrection of 1788, the legal edifice created by this particular act had far different implications for Black Loyalists. The Negro Courts initially inspired blacks to believe that the promises made by Dunmore and other British officials during the Revolutionary War would be upheld in the court of law in the Bahamas. Yet, in many respects, Black

Loyalists had also gained important lessons from the Abaco insurrection and subsequent tribunal established by Dunmore. Their claims to freedom, though verified and legitimated through various proclamations and codified by laws, did not always mean that liberty was to be extended to them. The Abaco insurrection and ensuing legal proceedings served to remind Black Loyalists of the inevitable contradictions and limits of British imperial justice. In other words, Black Loyalists were cognizant of the fact that their freedom from bondage would be continually contested given Dunmore's general concern for retaining law and order in a society of slaves and the contempt of slave owners for those seeking greater political liberty. Thus, after 1788, new strategies and tactics would need to be deployed to ensure that their liberty was extended to the Bahamas.

In fact it was in Nassau that Black Loyalists employed a range of strategies and plans in order to stake their claim for freedom. Cato Lynch's case was significant given the fact that he actually appealed to the governor to have his unfavorable ruling overturned. According to the notice posted in the May 29, 1792, edition of the *Bahama Gazette*, "the appeal of the negro man Cato Lynch to the governor and council from the adjudication of the Receiver-General and justices by which he was declared to be a slave, will be heard" on July 3, 1792.[96] While the outcome of this case is unknown, it is evident that Cato had become sufficiently informed that he appealed to the highest official in the colony for redress. Several other cases are recorded in which Black Loyalists clearly used their political acumen to appeal to the courts, request hearings, and publish notices of their cases in the *Bahama Gazette*. In a notice appearing in the *Bahama Gazette* of August 31, 1790, a group of Black Loyalists "presented their pretensions to freedom, including Ben, Grace and their boy George, late the possession of Cap't Lyford." This case is instructive for understanding the complex social and familial networks that existed among Black Loyalists as well as their willingness to plead collectively for freedom.[97] In fact, apart from the aforementioned family, the notice posted by the receiver-general also included Jack, Sam, and Titus, all allegedly owned by different white Loyalists. Such collective action hints at the growing political consciousness of blacks, and their willingness to mobilize en masse. Unfortunately, there is no indication that these Black Loyalists' claims to freedom were upheld in Dunmore's Negro Court.

While the outcome of the legal proceedings of Cato, Ben, Grace, and the boy George is uncertain, there were in fact a number of cases in which the judgment of the Negro Court clearly did not favor Black Loyalists. Thelma Peters notes that while the antigovernment white Loyalists charged that Dunmore was partial to the blacks and tended to declare them free on the slimmest of evidence, the decisions did not always favor Black Loyalists. At one such trial, a "Negro and his wife" produced a document apparently signed by Patrick Tonyn, the former governor of East Florida, to show they were free. Unfortunately, the court held that the document was a forgery and the two were punished for "false evidence."[98] Similarly, the case of a woman called Binah illustrates the devastating consequences of an unfavorable ruling for Black Loyalists in the Bahamas. In February 1788, Binah had applied to the receiver-general's office for freedom "under the British General's Proclamations in America."[99] However, once her case was taken to court, Thomas Ross, a slave owner, contested it. In an affidavit submitted on behalf of his father, John Graham Ross claimed that Binah had "absconded from the house and service" of his father in Nassau about "three or four months ago." Later, while "riding past Lord Dunmore's country house to the eastward of Nassau," he saw "the negroe woman sitting upon the steps of the front door of the house." While Dunmore apparently provided Binah a momentary haven from her enslavement, his motives were far from altruistic. Indeed, in his affidavit, John Ross revealed that Dunmore had in fact offered to purchase Binah, after he discovered that her current owner resided in Cat Island. Later, John Ross noted that Dunmore "pretended she was free," and only after "several months during which time Binah continued in any sense of the word in Lord Dunmore's possession," was she finally brought to trial.[100] At the trial it was determined that she was in fact enslaved to Thomas Ross. Remarkably, the judges ruled that despite belonging to Thomas Ross, she should be sold to Dunmore.

Evidently, when Black Loyalists failed to have their claims to freedom upheld in Dunmore's Negro Court, escaping and hiding among the growing free black community in Nassau became a viable option. A number of escapee advertisements demonstrate the resourcefulness and creativity deployed by Black Loyalists in order to escape from bondage. In an advertisement in the *Bahama Gazette,* a "negro wench named Nancy," was claimed to be the property of Dr. Allan. Most revealing, the subscriber noted that Nancy "speaks good English has worked about town these two years past, under the name of free Nancy, has been lately adjudged a slave by the Court appointed to ascertain the freedom of negroes." Though

Nancy had been "adjudged a slave," it is evident from the subscriber's comments that she had exercised a degree of self-determination, escaping from her alleged owner, and plying her labor in the urban environment of Nassau.[101] Of similar importance is the escapee advertisement posted in the *Bahama Gazette*, dated November 21, 1789, and signed by Alexander Inglis, Queen Street, Charleston. According to Inglis, a "negro woman named Dymba, but calling herself Bella, of the Angola Country," had made attempts "to pass for a free woman—having many acquaintances in Georgia and New Providence." Interestingly, Inglis, suspecting she was being harbored within the expanding social network in Nassau, offered a ten-pound reward for information provided by any white person, and a five-pound reward to any black person with information, on conviction of the offender.[102] This case and others highlight the role played by free Black Loyalist communities in harboring black claimants.

Black Loyalists at times also resorted to petit marronage, hiding out in the interior of the island of New Providence, much as their counterparts had hidden in the woods in Abaco.[103] By definition, petit marronage was the flight of enslaved persons from their masters, either singly or in groups for a finite period of time. Though common throughout the Americas, it was particularly manifested in locations in the Caribbean where large uncultivated lands or mountainous terrain made escaping detection more probable. There were several factors that converged to make the scale of petit marronage in the Bahamas during the 1780s a serious problem for slave owners and the government. Particularly troubling was the emergence of a distinct nonwhite district in Nassau, located behind the hospital to the south of the town center.[104] This largely uncultivated terrain in the area stretching southward toward what is now known as Blue Hills was increasingly a vexing problem for the governor. On January 6, 1792, Lord Dunmore issued a proclamation published in the *Bahama Gazette* relative to the "considerable body of negroes . . . collected together in the interior parts of this island," many of whom had "for some time past, absented themselves from their owners or employers and have committed felonies and other crimes to the great detriment of the community."[105] Dunmore's concerns were echoed by the House of Assembly on more than one occasion. In the 1784 and 1788 Negro Acts, the legislators recognized that it was "notorious that runaway slaves have been often harboured, employed and protected," often for great lengths of time, "by slaves inhabiting and planting on the south side of and other remote parts of the island."[106] The presence of such semipermanent maroon communities certainly created ample reasons for the legislators to include in the act a clause whereby masters were "ordered to inspect and check on their slaves."[107] Even where petit marronage was not explicitly indicated, it was evident that the congregation of large numbers of free blacks or enslaved persons created a great deal of anxiety for slaveholders. This was most evident in a list of grievances presented by the Grand Jury to the Governor and published in the *Bahama Gazette* on February 24, 1789. The Grand Jury presented as a particular grievance the "want of proper laws and regulations for the government of free Negroes; and we consider these people being permitted to harbor in prodigious numbers behind government house and elsewhere as a great nuisance."[108] Remarkably, within the same list was a more troubling concern, reportedly due to "the law lately passed empowering one or more commissioners to try and determine cases relative to negro property without the intervention of a jury." This according to the Grand Jury was not only "subversive to the rights of British subjects, but also contrary to the spirit of the law."[109] Ultimately, in coupling the threat of unregulated black communities with the establishment of Dunmore's Negro Court, leading whites provided a clear articulation of the extent to which Bahamian society had become fundamentally divided.

In the final analysis, it appears that the initial underlying tensions that had undoubtedly existed between black and white Loyalists arriving in the Bahamas in the early 1780s became more explicit and more troublesome by the time Lord Dunmore left the Bahamas in 1796. Was Dunmore to be blamed for such uneasy tensions? Certainly the establishment of a Negro Court exacerbated the tensions between black and white Loyalists. In this respect, it was during his tenure as governor that the receiver-general and two magistrates presided over the largest number of cases of freedom. In fact, between 1783 and 1787, eleven enslaved persons gained freedom by this process; during the next nine years while Dunmore was governor, forty-one achieved freedom in a similar fashion. After Lord Dunmore left the Bahamas in 1796, the number of cases of claims to freedom brought before the receiver-general diminished greatly, with only seven gaining freedom by proclamation. The peak period for gaining freedom by proclamation had come during Lord Dunmore's tenure as governor.[110]

By utilizing the *Register of Negro Freedoms* and *Registry Office Books*, one can expand and more accurately calculate the manumission figures for the early period of Loyalist settlement. Of the 451 individuals manumitted between 1782 and 1799, 237 were directly linked to the intervention of British officials in their varying capacities during the Revolutionary War.[111] However, the 54 manumission entries ascribed to "Certificates of Justices" suggest that these individuals were Black Loyalists who successfully claimed their freedom in the Negro Court in the Bahamas. Perhaps more telling of the involvement of Lord Dunmore in black liberation were the cases between 1788 and 1793, where 95 were by "Governor Certificate." Notably, Dunmore signed all of them except for three occurring prior to 1788, when an Act of Parliament established the Governor's Certificate formulation. After 1793, when the Loyalist opposition finally wrested control of colonial finances from the governor, the level of manumissions fell off dramatically, signifying the involvement of Dunmore. Thus, "after an annual peak of 47 in 1793, just 8 are recorded for the following two years."[112]

Dunmore, as governor of the Bahamas through most of this period, headed a "state-mandated manumission system" that was decidedly unusual for the Atlantic world. Indeed, in most sites of Atlantic slavery, manumission was in the first instance a private matter. Owners made decisions to free enslaved people, most commonly the illegitimate children of slaveholders by enslaved women, but also other enslaved persons "for whom owners felt particular regard, affection or gratitude." Some slave societies also permitted enslaved persons to purchase themselves from amenable enslavers, but manumission was normally the prerogative of individual slaveholders.[113] But Dunmore's direct involvement in the Negro Courts appears at odds with these trends. Most likely, Dunmore did not act out of altruistic motives or as an ardent abolitionist. Rather his proclamations and policies were driven by a peculiar mix of British authoritarianism—a concern for the rule of law and regulations—and a kind of paternalistic sentiment that led him to protect the "poor" and "delinquent" free black subjects of the Empire.[114] Thus, Dunmore's formulation represents a peculiar moment in Atlantic world history in which "blackness could be partially disassociated from slavery via the operation of an authoritarian but benevolent paternalism." Yet, it was a view that was becoming obsolete even as it came into being, "as the rise of the antislavery movement raised the more ambitious prospect of an Atlantic without slavery."[115] Certainly, Dunmore was no abolitionist, nor did he envisage a world of racial equality. He was an enslaver who owned dozens of enslaved persons in

Virginia, and upon arriving in the Bahamas, expanded his plantation designs by adding more enslaved persons to his personal property.[116]

Thus, it would be simplistic to attribute the political actions of Black Loyalists to Lord Dunmore and the establishment of his courts. As this chapter has demonstrated, Black Loyalists were protagonists in the unfolding drama during this early settlement period. Black Loyalists showed an unequivocal determination to seek freedom from bondage, even while facing the virulent and often violent efforts of whites to coerce them or to co-opt their lives and their labor. Such instances of individual agency were evident in the responses of William Willis and Sarah Moultrie. More powerful, though, were the instances of collective resistance in Abaco and Nassau, including refusing to work, running away, and actually engaging in armed revolts, as in Abaco in 1788. It is worth pausing to assess the magnitude of the latter insurrection. Arguably, the 1788 insurrection stands as a turning point in the Black Loyalist struggle for freedom in the Bahamas. Dunmore's intervention invariably left slaveholders in Abaco and throughout the rest of the archipelago feeling that their property rights and the legality of slavery itself had been upheld—even if by a governor who appeared infected by the spirit of liberty and humanitarianism. Black Loyalists saw things differently. The insurrection had raised the expectation that the liberties and freedom for which they had fought during the Revolution would be secured through the very governor who had initiated the clarion call by official proclamation. Yet in the immediate aftermath of the 1788 insurrection and court ruling, Black Loyalists, though disenchanted, did not simply acquiesce to relations of bonded servitude with white Loyalists. As has been demonstrated in this chapter, Black Loyalists during this formative settlement stage extended their liberty by seeking out like-minded persons to harbor and conceal them, and sometimes by appealing to the courts collectively. Such activity underscores the ways in which Black Loyalists in the Bahamas were self-consciously aware of both the limits and the possibilities of their political status within the British Empire. Yet such demands for freedom from bondage were only part of a multifaceted struggle for liberty in the Bahamas. In extending liberty to the Bahamas, Black Loyalists would also have to build sacred and secular institutional structures, develop autonomous businesses and commercial interests outside of white interference, fight for access to land, and continue to advocate for greater inclusion in civil society.

3

SETTING THEIR FEET DOWN

In 1817, William Dowson, a white missionary returning from his mission field in the Bahamas, published a journal in which the work of the Black Loyalist Joseph Paul surfaced in the footnotes.[1] In the journal, Joseph Paul is described as a "black man" from America who "came to Nassau from Abaco in the time of Lord Dunmore." Evidently, once in Nassau, Paul had formed a class where he taught five persons in a schoolroom. Equally important is Dowson's description of one of the students taught by Joseph Paul. According to Dowson, "Old Mrs. Wallace" was a leader in the Methodist society and "one of the first who met in class with Paul." Though Mrs. Wallace's maiden name was Faulkner, Dowson reveals that she had in fact been born among the "Ebo in Africa." From West African origins, Wallace had traversed the Atlantic, being "first brought to Jamaica, then to Pensacola, then to Charleston, then to St. Augustine and then to Nassau."[2] It was in this small classroom, in a building located on the corner of Augusta and Heathfield streets, that Joseph Paul, as teacher, and Mrs. Wallace, as pupil, converged to establish what would be the first school open to free blacks in the colony of the Bahamas.[3]

Though colored by Dowson's own paternalistic attitude, his account of this school provides tantalizing details of the kind of institutional structures that emerged with the arrival of Black Loyalists in the Bahamas. Beyond the immediate need to fight for freedom, Black Loyalists established churches and schools that eventually became important centers of black community activity. The significance of the Black Loyalist impact on social institutions in the Bahamas can be measured by the fact that almost all the denominational churches established between 1784 and 1800 were either founded or led by black itinerant preachers who came to the Bahamas from the thirteen colonies in America. Much like their counterparts in Nova Scotia and Jamaica, Black Loyalists exiled to the Bahamas not only established the first Baptist and Methodist churches, but also transmitted a unique brand of evangelical Christianity based on the revivalism of the Great Awakening.

Additionally, the lived experience of Joseph Paul and Mrs. Wallace speak to the complex ways in which black kin and familial relations reflect the global dimension of the Black Loyalist diaspora. Though Mrs. Wallace's travels were sufficiently traced by Dowson, it is worth noting that as an Atlantic Creole, her transatlantic travels involved multiple destinations. This experience likely shaped her various crosscutting identities. Accordingly, even as Wallace eventually took on the maiden name of Faulkner and clearly became integrated into a creolized community in Nassau, she was still known by her African ethnic identity, evident in Dowson's reference to her Ebo origins. Such interwoven identities underscore the ways in which Black Loyalists navigated complex worlds based on relationships with other Africans, African Americans, and even whites of varying classes and social strata. Moreover, Wallace's various nomenclatures suggest that the process of acculturation was far from linear or one-dimensional, but rather, often involved complex multidirectional transmutations emanating from African, European, and Anglo-American traditions. Even as acculturation was often expressed in Caribbean and Atlantic world environments as multidimensional and multifarious, it was also expressed differentially in relation to colonial power structures. Indeed, Wallace, as an Ebo woman, would have traversed various host societies where, despite her nominal education, her "blackness" would have undoubtedly consigned her to a racially subordinate position, particularly as she encountered white slaveholders in various Atlantic world seaports.

Wallace and other African-descended persons experienced two realms of acculturation in the Bahamas and across the black Atlantic. One represented a unique African-based invisible institution that emerged as a hidden transcript—the veiled dissemblance and cultural practices of blacks unobserved by elite whites.[4] The other, a public and official image, was shaped by unequal interracial encounters prevalent in a slaveholding society. American scholars have used this theoretical approach to explore the ways in which hidden transcripts underscore tensions and resistance within working-class black culture, as well as the public performances that surface in conflict with Jim Crow laws and values.[5] Applying this formulation to the Bahamian colonial world is significant given the growth of a small white "agro-commercial oligarchy" that by the first decades of the nineteenth century dominated the local House of Assembly and imposed, through slave codes and courts, a stratified vision of Bahamian society.[6]

Building on this blueprint, I explore various public sites where intra- and interracial tension and conflict existed. Such sites include, but are not exclusive to churches, schools, taverns, and public recreational grounds. Understanding the nature of intra- and interracial tensions in relation to the Bahamian Black Loyalist experience has two important dimensions. First, it suggests that far from constituting a monolithic group, Black Loyalist settlements were in fact polyglot, heterogeneous communities reflecting ethnic, class, and gendered differences. These manifold differences were often expressed in conflict over land titles, access to buildings of worship, and the contentious question of who was considered fit for a respectable education.[7] Second, from the interracial perspective, blacks and whites often opposed one another regarding whether Black Loyalists ought to have the right to live in self-contained communities or even be allowed to establish black schools and churches. Yet even as such public spaces often created tension, anxiety, and even open conflict, there were also moments when such venues provided opportunities for alliances to be forged, either with sympathetic whites or with blacks of different socioeconomic backgrounds. In essence, this chapter highlights the complex intra- and interracial encounters that occurred among the enslaved, free blacks, and whites within the city of Nassau.

The arrival of Black Loyalists in the Bahamas after 1783 had a profound impact on the development of black social and religious institutions. Black Loyalists were in fact in the "vanguard of the movement to build churches and schools" that eventually would serve as the focal points for free black communities located throughout the island of New Providence.[8] Chief among the Black Loyalist religious leaders who founded congregations in the Bahamas were Joseph Paul, Anthony Wallace, Sambo Scriven, Frank Spence, Amos Williams, and Prince Williams. Where Paul and Wallace were important figures who laid the foundation of Methodism in the Bahamas, Sambo Scriven, Frank Spence, Amos Williams, and Prince

Williams were instrumental in establishing the Baptist denomination in the Bahamas. It is significant that although these men were affiliated with various Christian denominations, they held in common some important features: all were American born; all lived in the South Carolina and Georgia backcountry; and all experienced their initial foray into Christian religiosity by way of the evangelical revivals associated with the Great Awakening.

Once established in the Bahamas, these leading religious figures erected chapels or meetinghouses, often located within or in the vicinity of free black communities. Of central importance would be the work of the black evangelical Joseph Paul, loyal refugee evacuated from New York who had previously lived in Abaco. While the exact date of Paul's arrival in Nassau is not known, it is evident that sometime between 1790 and 1793 a small chapel was erected and reportedly used by the master [Joseph Paul] "to read prayers and instruct the Negroes."[9] The chapel was described as a "solid stone structure which could seat three hundred people."[10] Even though the majority of the congregation comprised free blacks and enslaved persons during this period, there is evidence that a few members were identified as poor whites. In a report for the Society for the Propagation of the Gospel, John Richards noted on May 12, 1795, that the Methodist preachers met with no encouragement "except from a few of the very lowest class of whites and a few Negroes from whom they collect money three or four times every week when they preach."[11] Though Paul's evangelical efforts initially produced large interracial followings, it also appears that by 1795 those numbers had greatly diminished. What caused this reduction? Various accounts written by foreign missionaries attributed the decline in membership to the work of three missionaries who had arrived from Charleston, South Carolina, between 1794 and 1797. These men may have been initially encouraged to embark on the Bahamian mission field through their tangential links with William Hammett, a white resident of Charleston who had accidentally stumbled upon the rich mission field of Jamaica a few years earlier. Hammett himself was both slaveholder and transient preacher who had little genuine interest in the spiritual welfare of the blacks in the Bahamas beyond the desire to see his own brand of Primitive Methodism expanded to the islands.[12] Consequently, the men he sent at the request of Paul lacked the kind of character needed for mission work in the Bahamas. Indeed, the men Hammett sent out proved "unworthy of that confidence which they had obtained."[13] It appears that all three of these men were of such ill repute that they created dissension among the members gathered under Paul's leadership.[14] While the first was likely considered an "unwanted intruder" because he was a free black Methodist preaching a radical theology to enslaved persons, the latter two were sent packing for issues pertaining to their character. One had a wife of "alleged inconstant chastity and considerable strength"; the other, also a free black exhorter, was removed because he was an "abusive alcoholic who repeatedly beat his parishioners."[15] It is plausible that the turmoil that emerged with the arrival of the missionaries from South Carolina reduced the number of those blacks that professed the Methodist creed. Indeed, Thomas Coke lamented that the society had been reduced to merely sixty members as a consequence of these "deplorable transactions."[16]

Such dissension may also account for Paul's gravitation toward Anglicanism sometime between 1793 and 1794. In a letter dated June 12, 1794, John Richards, the Anglican missionary stationed in Nassau, reported that "I have agreeable to Mr. Lylleton's request establish[ed] a school for the instruction of Negroes, the master is black, [a] very diligent and constant attendant of the church, and the children improve very fast."[17] Richards' letter reveals much about the work of Paul and the esteem in which he was held both by the Black Loyalist community and by white missionaries. Tellingly, John Richards' account also highlights the fact that Paul had shifted from Methodism toward Anglicanism, forging an alliance with the Society for the Propagation of the Gospel as a religious instructor or catechist as well as a schoolmaster connected with Dr. Bray's Associates, an Anglican-based educational enterprise with headquarters in London, England. Paul's stewardship of Dr. Bray's Associates School has been corroborated by documents supporting the fact that the institution officially opened in March 1793. However, Paul likely had already begun teaching in the chapel before the official invitation was extended by Dr. Bray's Associates to establish this fee-paying school for free blacks. His competence was evident in the fact that his students comprised "twenty-four or twenty-five free children of blacks from America," who paid tuition of "twelve pence per annum to attend class and receive instruction in reading, writing and arithmetic."[18]

However, Paul's shift to Anglicanism also created divisions within the small congregation, with a number of the members gathered as a small Methodist society under the leadership of a free black named Anthony

Wallace (?–1830).[19] The division between Wallace and Paul is mentioned by Dowson when he notes that "it appears there had been a small society raised by Mr. Hammett's preachers, but from their bad conduct a division took place and part went with a Mr. Paul, a black man, and part with a Mr. Wallace, another black man."[20] Although this division between Paul and Wallace persisted, it appears that both men were able to develop strong, devoted followers, drawing mainly from the free black community congregating in the western suburbs of the town of Nassau. Paul, for his part, continued to be employed as a teacher associated with Dr. Bray's Associates, but also serving as a lay preacher to his congregation. Accordingly, Paul taught in the school for nearly a decade before he died in April 1802.[21] Joseph Paul Jr., his older son, eventually emerged as an equally competent instructor, hired by Dr. Bray's Associates to continue his father's work.[22] It appears that Joseph Paul Jr. did an outstanding job, teaching a much larger class of seventy scholars—only thirty of whom were funded by Dr. Bray's Associates.[23] In 1806, after visiting the school, Richard Roberts, a white, reported to the Society for the Propagation of the Gospel (SPG) that "the scholars shewed a readiness in writing and ciphering beyond my expectation."[24] Similarly, when John Stephen, rector of Christ Church, visited the school around 1810, he "found it was a rule to exercise them [scholars] once every day on the church catechism and to explain it to them from *Lewis' Exposition*." Stephen further observed that the "scholars read a portion of New Testament with great readiness and correctness and their writing books and cyphering books, likewise, in point of neatness, regularity, and correctness very far exceeded his expectation."[25]

When Joseph Paul Jr. died in 1811, his brother, William Paul, succeeded him. William Paul's tenure as master of Dr. Bray's Associates School was much shorter, as he died on August 23, 1813. The Pauls, as a family, effectively controlled the school, the first of its kind in the Bahamas, from as early as 1793 to 1813—a period spanning twenty years. How do we explain this long-standing commitment to education on the part of the Pauls? Quite possibly, for the Pauls and for many other Black Loyalists, formal education was a way to achieve status and respectability. This view was often reluctantly acknowledged by mercantile elites, who generally viewed all persons of color as ignorant and misled by strange doctrines. White missionaries and visitors to the Caribbean often perpetuated the notion that blacks were generally ignorant and unlearned. Edward Bean Underhill, the leading historian of the Baptist Missionary Society, maintained that "the [black] leaders of the so called Baptist churches were illiterate men—only one could read. The people who followed them indulged in many superstitious practices, and paid scant regard to the moral precepts of the gospel."[26]

Underhill was not alone in depicting black preachers as illiterate and uneducated. Such views were evident in a report by D. W. Rose, a white Anglican missionary stationed on Exuma in 1803. Rose noted that he had encountered difficulty in converting many of these blacks to the Anglican faith, owing to the fact that they were misguided, ignorant, "poor creatures."[27] More subtle examples of British condescension were reflected in the two reports connected to Dr. Bray's Associate School operated by the Pauls. In the reports for both 1806 and 1810, the missionaries noted that the learning and conduct of the students "exceeded their expectations." It appears that from the missionaries' perspective, they expected little to come from a group of free black students only recently removed from the barbarism of slavery. If missionaries observing the school had less than great expectations for its pupils, it is equally telling that the large number of students who flocked to the school for instruction, read, counted, and wrote with "great readiness."[28] It is probable that for these students, education represented far more than merely reading and writing.

The value of education as a vehicle for social change was reflected across the Anglophone Caribbean. In Antigua the presence of Methodist missionaries from the 1770s had led to the development and expansion of an educational system that focused on religious instruction and reading lessons to enslaved persons. Spurred by a desire to ameliorate slavery, free black evangelicals such as Anne and Elizabeth Hart were instrumental in initially opening a Sunday School in 1809 to slave and free children and then later expanding this work to a full day school in 1813. By 1815 a special all-female school was opened and dedicated to the instruction and moral education of enslaved women. For the Harts and other black evangelicals, education had a reformist goal in rescuing the sinning slave from the vices of enslavement in order to elevate and improve her moral standing in society.[29] This was also true of Baptist education in Jamaica, where "through education, men were formed who were able to assert qualities of leadership and organizational talents and to express acceptable and negotiable verbal and written skills."[30] It is worth noting that in the Jamaican case, George Liele actually "employed a teacher to instruct the children both of free parents and of slaves," with the goal of expanding his evangelistic efforts on plantations surrounding the city of Kingston. Such efforts were undoubtedly met with resistance from whites who charged Liele with sedition, a clear sign that his efforts at education and evangelism were too potent a combination for the liking of Jamaican slaveholders.[31] Though slaveholders attempted to curtail the preaching and teaching of black evangelicals through the restrictive 1805 Licensing Act, the expansion of both under the leadership of Liele and Moses Baker suggests the continued efficacy of such efforts in Jamaica. This was also the case in Nova Scotia and Sierra Leone, where Black Loyalist preachers such as Boston King, David George, and John Marrant transmitted the twin pillars of Christianity and education.[32]

Thus, it is not surprising that Black Loyalists in the Bahamas viewed education as an important tool that allowed them, as adults, to more effectively navigate the social world of Bahamian society.[33] In essence, Black Loyalists, in creating schools and opening their doors to black and colored children, facilitated the perpetuation of future generations of free black leadership rooted in a good English education.[34] In reference to Dr. Bray's Associates School, out of a total population of roughly 850 free blacks and coloreds, the school provided an educational foundation for as many as 70 students by 1802.[35] Yet even as Joseph Paul's association with Dr. Bray's Associates School provided unprecedented opportunities for free blacks to pursue educational goals, it did not appear to service the larger number of blacks that constituted the enslaved majority. Indeed the school was established as a fee-paying institution, making it nearly impossible for enslaved persons to attend.

Where Paul moved toward Anglicanism and its associated educational system, Anthony Wallace became a leading figure in the development of Methodism, particularly at a time when the small society appeared to be challenged by the inappropriate conduct of white missionaries sent from abroad. Though Wallace, a free black and husband of Old Mrs. Wallace, likely arrived in New Providence from South Carolina as part of the Loyalist migration, his name appears only after the American missionaries were forced out of the colony.[36] However, by 1800, it was apparent that Wallace had taken over the leadership of the small society of Methodists. Arguably, it was in fact Anthony Wallace and not Joseph Paul who should be credited with establishing Methodism in the Bahamas. It was Wallace who initially wrote to Thomas Coke in England requesting a Wesleyan missionary be sent to the Bahamas after William Hammett's men proved inadequate. Equally important is the fact that Wallace remained a staunch Methodist, working within the free black community in the western suburbs. The leading role Wallace continued to hold within this community is evident in his opposition to an act to control the licensing of sectarian preachers, passed on December 31, 1816, and a Police Act passed on January 1, 1817.[37] Though the political implications of this petition will be addressed in chapter 5, it is worth noting that Wallace, as late as 1817, remained an ardent supporter and leader of the black Methodists in Nassau.

Although Wallace remained a pivotal figure in Methodism, the arrival in 1800 of William Turton, a mulatto missionary from Antigua, ushered in a new phase in which leading blacks worked alongside white missionaries sponsored by the home society in England.[38] Upon arrival, Turton recorded that "Mr. Wallace came to my house, as soon as it was known I had arrived, and fearful of offending, enquired if I intended to teach a school?" When Turton communicated his desire to preach the gospel as soon as he was able, Wallace then "made known who he was" and promptly invited Turton "to his house."[39] It appears that Turton in fact rented a home from Wallace that also served as the initial meetinghouse of the small society of Methodists gathered in the town. Later, as the house once again became too small, Turton appealed to Wallace to enlarge the edifice. This was agreed upon apparently only after Turton promised Anthony Wallace, in good faith, to continue in the work that Wallace had started. Wallace, in consequence, enlarged the house to ten feet by thirty.[40] At this point, the expanding congregation comprised eighty members, including blacks and a few whites willing to rent pews built for them.[41] Even after enlarging the building in the West, Turton found that the congregation was still too large for the structure. Thus, Turton established a second chapel in order to service "a multitude of poor people, who manifested an earnest desire that the gospel be preached to them."[42]

While perhaps unintended, Turton's establishment of a second congregation in the Eastern district in November 1801 would change the racial dynamics of Methodist congregations in the Bahamas. Interestingly, though the racial composition of the group is not given, leading white planters with Methodist leanings, including Thomas Forbes, John Kelsall, and Richard Hunt, financed and supported this church in the East. Equally important, a "serious white woman was placed in charge of this group in the East to hold prayers."[43] Though not mentioned by name, reportedly this white woman was also "employed in teaching and instructing and

Figure 4. Ebenezer Methodist Church. The current church building as shown was built in 1841; however, the roots of this "eastern" congregation date back to the work of William Turton, who assisted in establishing a second Methodist church in New Providence in November 1801. Photo by the University of the Bahamas student Clethra Dean.

keeping a school."[44] Such anecdotal evidence underscores the fact that the school and chapel functioned as important sites of interracial activity—with black and white members attending. This source also highlights the prospects that potentially opened to an educated white woman in a desperately underdeveloped British colony. Despite the establishment of both chapel and school in the Eastern district, by 1802 it was reported that the number of individuals gathered there totaled only 17. On the other hand, the church in the Western district, with a majority of black congregants, comprised a total of 83 members.[45] The demographic difference between the two Methodist churches in New Providence is further supported by Turton's 1804 report indicating that the church located in Delancey Town in the Western District had "10 whites, 10 colored people, and 147 blacks." By contrast, Turton noted that the chapel erected in the Eastern district had so prospered that the membership for the month of May amounted to 71.[46] Though Turton failed to analyze the demographic profile of the Eastern congregation in the way he did for the West, it is possible to conclude that because of the support garnered by leading whites and the presence of a white teacher, this congregation differed markedly from the one in the West. In general, it appears that during the period 1800–1804, when Turton served as the major missionary in New Providence, two congregations emerged—one with a majority black membership and the other supported and possibly dominated by whites.

The 1804 arrival in New Providence of Mr. Rutledge, a second white missionary, led to the development of racially segregated congregations that would remain a central feature of Methodist schools and churches well into the twentieth century. Indeed, before Rev. Rutledge introduced a segregated school into New Providence in 1806, Methodists had actually maintained integrated schools and churches throughout the Bahamas. Additionally, in starting this segregated school, Rutledge laid the foundation for racial division within the Methodist church in the Bahamas.[47] But while Rutledge certainly deserves some of the blame for the establishment of segregated institutions within Methodism in the Bahamas, he was not alone in this endeavor. Indeed, Rutledge and subsequent missionaries had the support of the leading whites in Nassau, who gradually were converting to Methodism. The growing racial division within Methodism was expressed in the fact that not only were schools and churches segregated, but even in death, whites and blacks were to be buried in separate burial grounds. In a letter dated June 16, 1812, Dowson observed that

> We have had an excellent offer of an eligible spot for a burying ground [in the west end of Nassau], of which we are much in want, but as one place will not do for both whites and blacks (for they will not sleep in the dust side by side, or both together) it was agreed upon in the Leaders and Trustees Meetings, to purchase it for the internment of our colored and black people. This excited the watchful jealousy of our Circuit Steward, a white man but a crooked and obstinate stick.[48]

As Dowson's comments suggest, white congregants endeavored to segregate churches, and even burial sites, a clear sign of a society that increasingly demarcated its population along racial lines.

If white congregants displayed open hostility toward their fellow black Methodists, it was also true that black Methodists continued to ally themselves with the teachings of John Wesley. Indeed, evidence of the growth of separate Afro-Bahamian Methodist churches can be gleaned from Dowson's journal. In recording a letter written by James Jones and dated

August 1, 1814, Dowson described James Jones as a "leader and exhorter in our society in New Providence, who had arrived in the Bahamas from America with the Loyalists or refugees."[49] It appears that Dowson's unique relationship with Jones was cemented through their leading roles in advancing Methodism in the Bahamas: Jones as a leader of black Methodists, and Dowson, commissioned to the "new field of Harbour Island" where he served segregated white and black congregants.[50] Despite having to work within a segregated system, Dowson seems to have admired Jones for his religious zeal. This is evident in the fact that not only did Dowson describe Jones as "one of the most pious, zealous, active, steady and affectionate men, I ever knew," but in a more tangible way lent him a book for his own edification.[51] Such exchanges, while significant for highlighting interesting interracial encounters, nevertheless worked against the grain of segregated congregations that marked Methodism as different from the growth of the Baptist denomination in the Bahamas.[52]

Like the founding of Methodism in the Bahamas, the establishment of the Baptist movement in the Bahamas was spearheaded by Black Loyalists who arrived in the Bahamas after 1783. These men were imbued with strong Afro-Christian beliefs that grew out of their experiences living in colonial America as well as from West African traditions transmitted via the transatlantic slave trade. Once in the Bahamas, the black Baptists continued their ministry without interference from white Baptist missionaries until 1833. Edward Underhill, historian of the Baptist Missionary Society, mistakenly tracked the beginning of black Baptist activities in the Bahamas to the ending of the War of 1812. According to his account, a number of persons "calling themselves Baptists . . . , traced their religious beliefs to the exertions of black men, brought from the United States at the close of the war in 1813."[53] Yet, according to the records of the SPG Anglican missionaries, black Baptists had entered the Bahamas at a much earlier date. Thus, the Rev. John Richards as early as 1791 noted that a "society of Anabaptists numbering around 300 or 400" had established itself in Nassau with "several black preachers delegated here by a society of Anabaptists in the United States." He added that "they daily increase."[54] Tellingly, Richards' comments suggest not only the presence of Baptists at an earlier date than Underhill stated, but also an Anglo-American connection between Baptists in the United States and the Bahamas.

Other sources suggest an even earlier date than Richards' account of Baptist activity in the Bahamas. Possibly, Frank Spence was the one who initiated Baptist work in the Bahamas, since he had arrived as early as 1780 as an enslaved person with a group of British Loyalists from East Florida and South Carolina. Alexander McCullough (the grandson of Frank Spence), noted that after arriving in the Bahamas, Spence went to Long Island where he earned enough by working overtime to purchase his freedom.[55] An account by D. L. Rose, an SPG missionary, verifies the presence of a sect of Anabaptists that had been firmly established on Long Island by the turn of the nineteenth century. While Spence is not mentioned directly by Rose, the corroborating evidence provided by McCullough suggests that Spence's removal to Long Island afforded him the opportunity to establish an Afro-Baptist congregation that remained intact after he moved to New Providence. After earning enough money to purchase the freedom of his wife, who had been living in Florida, Spence moved with her to Nassau and established a place of worship on the south side of Fort Fincastle.[56] It was here that by 1806 Spence had purchased land and built a chapel. In time, Frank Spence's congregation had a membership of blacks numbering more than nine hundred.[57] Though these figures may be overstated, it is clear that the congregation consisted entirely of blacks, both free and enslaved. Apparently Spence's congregation outgrew this initial building, and in 1827 he erected a new church on Spence Street.[58] Spence served as pastor of this church until his death in 1846.[59]

An analysis of Spence's 1846 will and testament provides additional insight into his religious and material world. Frank Spence apparently purchased a "lot of land" in the "southern districts of the town of Nassau," on which a "commodious building was subsequently erected by me at my own individual expense." The building apparently had been used "for some years since [by] a number of the inhabitants of the island of New Providence" who had "associated themselves together as a worshipping assembly of Christians." Most revealing of the role of religious figure played by Spence was the fact that the congregation had "for their spiritual improvement and instruction, recommended and elected me their religious pastor, teacher and leader." Demonstrating his pastoral concern for the flock he presided over for so many years, Spence included a provision in the will that would allow the building to be "dedicated and set apart for the exclusive use and occupation of the members and followers of the said society," so that they could perform "religious duties, services and exercises." Spence directed that the group be known as "John the Baptist

Christ Church."[60] This appellation indicates that Frank Spence nominally subscribed to the tenets of the Baptist faith.

Besides Frank Spence, Amos Williams and Sambo Scriven, Black Loyalists who had arrived in the Bahamas by the late 1780s, also assisted in disseminating the Baptist faith throughout the urban world of Nassau, New Providence. Although Williams and Scriven are reported to have arrived in the Bahamas in 1788, they may have been in New Providence a few years earlier.[61] In this report, Sambo Scriven is described as an enslaved black runaway from Saint Augustine who arrived in New Providence in late 1784 and most likely began preaching shortly afterward. Significantly, Scriven's story reflects the general struggles faced by many Black Loyalists upon settlement in the Bahamas. In 1790 he is reported to have acquired official freedom by way of a favorable ruling in the Commissioner of Claims Court held in Nassau.[62] This ruling enhanced his ability to function as an itinerant preacher for two reasons. First, by being defined as a free person, Scriven instantly became more mobile, able to move about without a pass or permission from a slave owner. Second, as a free person, he was no longer bound and constrained by the restrictive legislation that prohibited enslaved persons from meeting or congregating at night. Such freedom was of particular importance given that by 1790, Sambo Scriven had collaborated with black itinerant preachers Amos Williams and Prince Williams in order to found a Baptist society.

Much like that of Sambo Scriven, Amos Williams' early life as an itinerant preacher was shaped by his experiences with revivalism in the lowcountry area outside Savannah, Georgia. Though the exact date of his arrival in the Bahamas is unknown, circumstantial evidence places his evangelical activities in Nassau in the early 1780s. Indeed, according to Samuel Kelly, a sailor who visited Nassau in 1784, "a man of color frequently preached to the eastward of the town under a large spreading tree."[63] Though Amos Williams is not identified specifically, there is additional evidence that suggests he was engaged in evangelical work in New Providence during the mid- to late 1780s. Communications between Amos Williams and George Liele not only place him in New Providence in the 1780s, but also suggest that he was highly effective in attracting Black Loyalists to the Baptist cause. Accordingly, Amos Williams in Nassau wrote to Liele in Jamaica indicating that from an initial society of forty members his congregation had grown rapidly to over three hundred members by 1791.[64] Beyond placing his work in the Bahamas in the late 1780s, Williams' correspondence with Liele underscores the fact that far from being ignorant profaners of the gospel, black Baptist leaders in the Bahamas were articulate, self-educated men who actively maintained ties with other like-minded men throughout the Black Loyalist diaspora.[65]

Apart from developing social networks across the Atlantic, it appears that Amos Williams also maintained relations with other aspiring leaders of the Baptist denomination within the Bahamas. Of particular significance is the relationship that emerged between Amos Williams, Sambo Scriven, and Prince Williams, all of whom were directly involved in the congregation established by 1790–1791 in the Western suburbs of Nassau. Evidently, since Sambo Scriven "was not directly associated with George Liele he doubtless came under the influence of brother Amos, either in East Florida or upon arriving in the Bahamas."[66] It was most likely in Nassau that both men also joined forces with Prince Williams.

Though portrayed initially as the assistant to Sambo Scriven during the formative period of black Baptist activity, Prince Williams would eventually emerge as an important leader. As such, his early work alongside that of Scriven and Amos Williams is documented in a petition he wrote to the governor in 1826. In his petition, Williams revealed that he had, "together with a certain John Williams and with those of the said Society," met in August 1801 in order to "buy two lots in Delancey Town in the Southern suburb of the town of Nassau for the use of the said society." Clearly, Williams, "as a free man of color," was intimately involved in the land purchase that enabled the congregation to erect a place of worship. Indeed, Prince Williams further noted that he, along with John Williams, paid Benjamin Lord, esquire, the sum of two hundred and forty five dollars on September 24, 1801. Prince Williams' involvement went beyond handling financial transactions, as he noted that he was also "by the congregation appointed as assistant to their then preacher Sambo Scriven," who he "occasionally assisted in his functions aforesaid until he intermarried with a certain Peggy Wilson in about the year 1812."[67] Overall, it appears that the birth of the Baptist denomination in the Bahamas can be traced back to the efforts of leading Black Loyalist men, who by the early nineteenth century had purchased lots on which chapels were eventually erected. Particularly revealing is the fact that Amos Williams, Prince Williams, and Sambo Scriven chose for the location of their new edifice a site on Meeting Street, on the south side of Delancey Town and within the same free black community in which Anthony Wallace and Joseph Paul lived and worked. Taken together, these leading black men, of both Baptist and Methodist persuasion, serviced an enlarged community, including many Black Loyalist refugees, arriving in the urban environment of Nassau after the Revolutionary War.

While both the Methodist and Baptist faiths shared a similar foundation based on the work of Black Loyalist evangelicals, their historical trajectories were also marked by significant differences. Unlike Methodism, by the turn of the nineteenth century it was clear that the Baptist denomination in the Bahamas comprised exclusively black preachers, ministering to entirely black congregations. The presence of such autonomous and independent institutions ultimately led elite whites to construct a narrative that pejoratively stigmatized black Baptist preachers and their followers in ways that set them apart from white-led Methodist congregations. In an 1805 report offered by Henry Jenkins, an Anglican missionary, he noted that there were some "sectaries among us, chiefly people of color, of which the Baptists, as they call themselves will not come near me." Jenkins' account reveals the extent to which the Baptists were racially identified as black, as well as suggesting that they could be demarcated as different from both Anglicans and Methodists. In the same account Jenkins alludes to two Methodists who had lately come from the missionary society at home and who at times would join him "at the table."[68] Apparently, the presence of white Methodists leading segregated congregations was more tolerable to leading whites and Anglican missionaries than the presence of a largely autonomous institution under the charge of black preachers from America whose congregants included free and enslaved blacks.

Perhaps one of the reasons white missionaries felt threatened by the growth of black sacred institutions in the Bahamas was that their religious traditions drew on practices inimical to the interest of slaveholders. Congregating at night (despite laws that prohibited it), black Baptists orchestrated lively emotive sermons that emphasized participatory and personal religiosity expressed through trances, spirit possession, and prophetic visions rather than the staid and formulaic orthodoxy normally associated with the established church and the white oligarchy.[69] These night visions, trances, and spirit possession reflected elements of African religion that were intensified by the experience of enslavement. Thus black evangelicals were imbued with strong Afro-Christian beliefs that grew out of their experiences living in colonial America as well as their knowledge of West African traditions transmitted via the transatlantic slave trade. As such, certain discernible traditions and practices including "perceptions of time, in esthetics, in approaches to ecstatic religious experiences and to the understanding the Holy Spirit, in ideas of the after world and of the proper ways to honor the spirits of the dead, African influence was deep and far-reaching."[70]

If such African practices were indeed "deep and far-reaching," they were also tempered by and refracted through contact with the Anglo-American colonies where Christian principles and religious institutions dominated the cultural landscape. Ritual practices that may have reflected habits originating in West Africa were not simply remapped completely intact onto a new North American environment. Rather, spirit worship, rituals of adult initiation, emotive dancing, and singing that suggest general West African antecedents were reinterpreted and refashioned by Africans and their descendants to fit the realities of a colonial world where increasingly slavery and inequality shaped their daily lives. During the late eighteenth century, evangelical and revival-based Christianity provided African-descended people with a mnemonic picture that harkened back to their customs and practices in West Africa.[71] Thus, it is reasonable to assume that many Black Loyalists caught up in the revolutionary fervor of war and spiritual awakening recognized in water baptism, emotive sermons, night visions, and trances, experiences that were not at all foreign to their established cognitive way of thinking. Once in the Bahamas, black evangelicals particularly of the Baptist persuasion transmitted these religious traditions to a receptive audience of enslaved and free blacks, many already in thrall to the revivalism with which they had become familiar in colonial America.

Similarly, as transmitters of a revivalism associated with the Great Awakening in colonial America, Black Loyalist evangelicals also espoused in both theory and praxis an egalitarian religious experience. As such, participants and exhorters alike were united as a community of believers who emphasized a spiritual brotherhood of relative equals rather than the hierarchical ecclesiology of the Anglican Church, which held a virtual monopoly on religious instruction in the Bahamas until the arrival of Loyalists in 1783.[72] Obviously, Baptist religious practice had important repercussions in the Bahamas. First, it led to greater religious receptivity among enslaved and free populations settled in New Providence and the more remote islands of the Bahamas. Second, it engendered fear and trepidation among slaveholders and missionaries located throughout the archipelago. Both these themes were echoed in a report submitted by D. W. Rose, stationed at Long Island as an Anglican missionary in 1799. According to Rose's report, the "negroes . . . have been misled by strange doctrines, but I hope that they will in time be converted to the true faith."[73] Elaborating more specifically on the believers he encountered on Long Island, Rose noted that

> They call themselves Baptists, the followers of St. John and were not so happy and contented, as in other parts of the West Indies, though every indulgence and humanity were exercised towards them by their masters. Their preachers, black men, were artful and design-ing making a merchandize of religion. One of them was so impious as to proclaim that he had "Had a familiar conversation with the Almighty," and to point out the place where he had seen Him.[74]

In describing the practices of black Baptist preachers as "artful and de-signing," Rose conspicuously stigmatized these men as ignorant and backward—lacking the kind of orthodox religious approach found in the rituals of the Church of England. Rose in fact questioned the veracity of the claims that a black preacher had actually engaged in a conversation with the Almighty.

Though Rose dismissed such practices as a reflection of the ignorance and misguided conduct of their preachers, for enslaved and free blacks, such trances, visions, and ecstatic experiences remained a powerful mne-monic reminder of the melding of African and European practices asso-ciated with Great Awakening revivalism.[75] It may be that these practices were not entirely foreign to whites living in the Anglo-American world. Indeed, white Baptists and Methodists caught up in the memorizing rou-tines of the Great Awakening could experience such visions. But it was more common for these religious experiences to be identified with en-slaved and free persons of color in colonial America precisely because they appealed to a communal, egalitarian religious ethos in which all members partook in the ecstatic and emotive religious observances as equals—whether black or white, enslaved or free.[76] In addition to provid-ing evidence of visions and trances, Rose's account identified the practice of water baptism. According to Rose, "at certain times in the year the black preachers used to drive numbers of negroes into the sea and dip them by way of baptism, for which they extorted a dollar, or stolen goods."

Though his report is colored by his own condescending attitude toward the black preachers, it still remains a useful source for accessing the practices of black Baptists. In this case, the fact that "numbers of negroes" were driven annually to the sea for baptism suggests the importance of this rite for early Baptists in the Bahamas.

Beyond documenting the religious practices of Baptists in Long Island, Rose's account also reveals the ways in which their nighttime services were seen as a threat by white missionaries and slave owners alike. Accordingly, Rose noted that

> He collects hundreds of negroes together generally on Saturday Nights and if there Nocturnal assemblies are not dispersed, our lives and properties are in great danger—mild language from me has been adopted, but I must apply to the magistrates to prohibit them preaching and illegal combinations. One of their tenets is, as they work for their masters they may rob their masters.[77]

Not only does Rose hint at the explicit threat black Baptists presented in the form of nocturnal meetings, but he equates such assemblies to a real and tangible hazard to the lives and properties of slave owners on the island.

Nevertheless, Rose was not alone in his general concern regarding the spread of a black Baptist faith throughout the archipelago. In Nassau, the migration of large numbers of Black Loyalists and the subsequent establishment of free black communities created opportunities to build autonomous religious institutions. Glimpses into the religious world of Black Loyalists appear in various reports written by missionaries aligned with the Anglican Church. Worthy of mention is the account provided by Rev. H. Groombridge in Nassau, dated July 9, 1802. Groombridge notes that one of the "more sensible negroes" had come to him upon hearing his preaching, saying that he was very unhappy. Apparently, the cause of his discontent was the fact that the two Methodist preachers "had put an evil spirit into him and he could not get rid of it." Groombridge further relays through his black witness the inner workings of the revival meetings whereby "when they met—they prayed, groaned and preached—and afterwards spend most of the night in singing and dancing and other diversions very bad, for they were all shut together."[78] Such commentary illustrates a number of significant features of black evangelical religious traditions. The ecstatic experience of singing, dancing, and groaning no doubt echoed the communal and expressive religious experience found in the revivalism that had swept across Anglo-American societies.

Finally, in articulating the idea that he had been possessed by an evil spirit, the "sensible negro" described by Groombridge was in fact harkening back to the ethos of revival meetings in which an active spirit world and spirit possession were commonplace. In this respect, black leaders in the Bahamas held much in common with their contemporaries in North America such as Murphy Stiel and John Marrant, who articulated notions of a lively spirit world and a direct experience with the Almighty, often leading to physical pain and sickness, trances, or prophetic visions.[79] Such religious expressions were clearly perceived by Groombridge and other white church leaders in the Bahamas as not only strange but also inimical to the established church and political order. This may explain why Groombridge added a final refrain in which he remarked, "if we do our duty as we ought agreeable to the rites and ceremonies of your Church, there will be no occasion for these imposters."[80]

Apart from Groombridge's polemical report, there were other, more subtle accounts of syncretic religious practices occurring in Nassau that surfaced in public transcripts. Of particular significance is the travel journal of P. Townsend, a doctor who visited New Providence in 1823. Apart from recording perhaps the first foreigner's description of a Junkanoo parade in Nassau, Townsend also provides a vivid account of a religious procession in which "several hundred blacks" returning from a baptism service paraded under a white banner into town. A similar parade was observed at a funeral in which blacks "carried lanterns" used in case "night should come before the service is over."[81] Though perhaps ignorant of the syncretism of Afro-Caribbean religious practices, Townsend nevertheless provides a hint at the expressive and celebratory nature of funeral processions by which the dearly departed was sent off to meet the ancestors in the next life.[82] Townsend further observed that "the negroes like to go to funerals. It seems as rich a treat for them as they were to the poor crazy Lord Portsmouth."[83] Such brief impressions by Townsend set in sharp relief the lively religiosity of blacks compared with the formulaic and "awkward sleepy tone" of white preachers he heard at the two Anglican churches he attended, St. Matthew's and Christchurch.[84]

Where Townsend viewed the practices of black preachers and congregants as mere entertainment or a respite from the monotony of daily living in Nassau, local elites were far more critical. In a list of grievances presented by the Grand Jury and published in the March 9, 1790, edition of the *Bahama Gazette*, the jurors made mention of the "frequent and disorderly meetings of Negroes at unreasonable hours in the night, particularly at one Tabb's and Jack Howell's to the great annoyance and disturbance of the inhabitants."[85] Echoing the sentiments of D. Rose in Long Island, it appears that the presence of enslaved and free blacks congregating at night and in close proximity to white inhabitants in Nassau was viewed as anathema to the kind of social order envisioned by those self-identified as "respectable" slave-owning whites. Equally important, such a discursive script implicitly suggests the kinds of expressive culture that occurred behind the closed doors of these urban dwelling houses. The grand jurors advanced on February 28, 1794, a more specific concern related to the work of black itinerants. Their grievance was that

> unlicensed and ignorant preachers . . . convene[d] a number of black coloured people in and about town, to the annoyance of His Majesty's subjects, poisoning, instead of improving the minds of the people . . . which tend to the injury of the community at large.[86]

These sentiments indicate that increasingly elite whites were preoccupied with both the message that black preachers presented and the medium they used. The concern for "poisoning the minds" was a particularly pressing issue given the fact that the adherents were drawn from the free and enslaved populations. For blacks, the syncretism of evangelical revivalism, celebrated at nocturnal meetings, provided a powerful counterpoint to white slaveholding social and religious values.

If a dynamic evangelical religious experience reflected a powerful countercultural force, equally threatening to white elites was the presence of a strong, vigorous black community in close proximity to the town of Nassau and within view of government house. The development of Delancey Town and other free black enclaves located to the west and south of the town of Nassau reflected the significance of social networks and the development of self-reliant communities inaugurated by Black Loyalists. Such self-contained communities were invariably viewed as antithetical to the kind of stratified slave society that leading white Loyalists attempted to graft onto the Bahamian sociopolitical landscape. William Wylly poignantly noted both the location and perceived threat of such a community when he remarked in his *Short Account*:

A considerable village has lately been built by freed and runaway negroes behind government house. It is an asylum for runaways and Negro offenders of every description, and no white person dares make his appearance within it, but at the risk of his life. Many have been assaulted, and nearly destroyed there; and though several of the offenders have been prosecuted to conviction, the governor has interposed and protected them [the perpetrators] from punishment.[87]

Wylly's account not only reveals the location of the "considerable village" but also suggests that the community posed a threat to whites venturing into it. From his vantage point, many whites had been assaulted at the hands of these blacks and despite legal actions, a sympathetic governor essentially protected the perpetrators. Though Wylly's account provides an important descriptive account of Delancey Town, left to be accounted for are a number of important factors, including the overall size of the community; its demographic composition relative to African-born and American-born Black Loyalists; and the extent to which it functioned as a site of intraracial class, gender, and ethnic differences. Various travel accounts written by Europeans give a glimpse into the possible size and demographic profile of this free black community. C. F. Pascoe, for instance, noted that by the commencement of 1790 in New Providence, "there were 500 free negroes"[88]; however, these figures do not include the 350 Black Loyalists "arriving from America" that Wylly included in his calculations.[89] It is also important to note that probably not all of these people resided in the area to the west and south of Government House, later referred to as Delancey Town. In Johann David Schoepf's account he observed a village located several miles to the east of town, "called New Guinea," an area later identified as Fox Hill.[90] Significantly, Schoepf's account makes specific reference to African ethnic groups, namely people from the Guinea Coast. By combining all three contemporaneous accounts, we can ascertain that the 850 free blacks comprised both African- and American-born groups, the majority likely settling in Delancey Town in the western suburbs, with smaller numbers settling in enclaves to the east or south of the city limits.

Over the next two decades (1790–1810) the size of the free black and colored populations clustered in these communities grew steadily. In 1801 Nassau had 1,599 whites, and 752 persons listed as free people of color, and 3,861 enslaved persons. However, in 1805 when Governor Cameron ordered a new census to be taken of free people of color and the enslaved, the census takers counted a total free colored population of 972, comprising 356 men, 334 women, and 302 children. In this same 1805 census the overall enslaved population is given as 3,556, less than the figure for 1801. The continued growth of the free black population is evident in the 1810 figures: 1,720 whites, 1,074 free blacks, and 3,190 enslaved persons.[91] These figures reflect the demographic revolution brought about by the arrival of the Loyalists in the Bahamas. Indeed, the transformation of the urban landscape of Nassau, New Providence, was marked by a diminishing white and enslaved population combined with an increasing free black population, many of whom gained freedom either through favorable court proceedings or by manumission.

The arrival of the Loyalists spurred greater concern for racial separation, and the establishment of an environment in which the urban landscape of Nassau was gradually segregated. Free blacks and even enslaved persons no longer lived beside their employers or owners, but in two distinct areas "just over the hill," on either side of the southward-stretching grounds of the governor's house. Some free persons of color congregated on the southern slopes of Society Hill, later Fort Fincastle; this would include Frank Spence and his congregants. However, it was the stretch of former bush "behind the hospital" on West Hill Street, later called Delancey Town, that caused the greatest concern among the white establishment. For in this area there were not only many newly enslaved persons, but also most of the Black Loyalists who claimed their freedom.[92] These two communities of blacks had much in common: both appeared to include enslaved and free blacks; both were symbolically and perhaps strategically located in close proximity to Government House (where many whites claimed they received protection and legal redress from the governor), and both were located south of the ridge that spatially and racially divided whites living on top of the hill from those deemed inferior, residing "over the hill."

If Delancey Town and the area behind Society Hill were increasingly viewed as a threat to the established order by whites, for blacks they represented something else. These communities became the centers of Black Loyalist institutional development, where black churches provided not only inspiration and solace for those oppressed by slavery and exploitative labor conditions, but also, more practically, a meeting place where

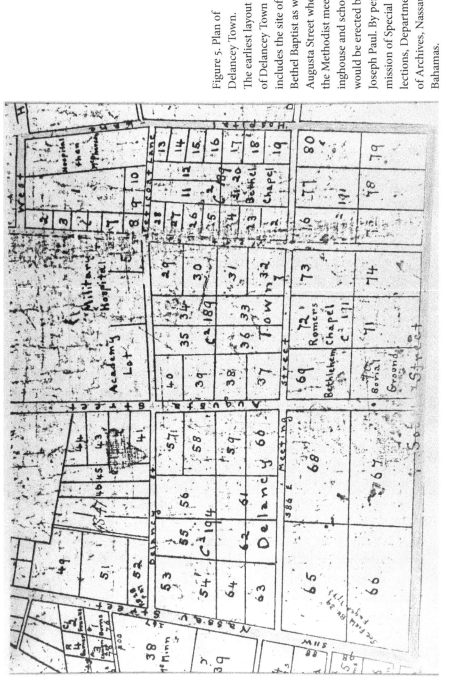

Figure 5. Plan of Delancey Town. The earliest layout of Delancey Town includes the site of Bethel Baptist as well as Augusta Street where the Methodist meetinghouse and school would be erected by Joseph Paul. By permission of Special Collections, Department of Archives, Nassau, Bahamas.

families, fictive kin groups, and extended social networks flourished. An escapee advertisement in the July 25, 1789, edition of the *Bahama Gazette* notes that "Prince, guinea born was seen about the Negro Huts at back of the hospital."[93] This particular advertisement highlights the fact that Prince was most likely African-born, from the catchment area of the Guinea Coast. His effort to hide among the Negro huts not only speaks to the ways in which the community provided sanctuary for escapees, but its location most certainly suggests a reference to Delancey Town or Grants Town—two communities that to this day border Government House. If this is the case, both communities emerged by the 1830s as polyglot in nature: composed of free and enslaved blacks—African-born, American-born, and Bahamian-born; and of men and women of varying social and economic classes. Such differences were often expressed in intraracial tensions and the multiple crosscutting identities that existed in a diverse community.

Ironically, although Delancey Town often functioned as a haven for escapees such as the aforementioned Prince, it is significant that some of the wealthier members of this free black community were themselves slaveholders. Based on circumstantial evidence, it is possible that Anthony Wallace was a slaveholder. In his will, Wallace manumitted at least six enslaved persons, including Alexander, a male child, whose owner remained absent from the record.[94] John Williams likely was a slaveholder as well. John Williams surfaces in the historical record as a leading member of the Bethel Baptist congregation, mentioned in particular by Prince Williams in his narrative of the events in the early life of the congregation.[95] His connection with Prince and other known Black Loyalists makes John a likely candidate for being a Black Loyalist. In any event, by the time of his death in 1818, John Williams owned three enslaved persons.[96] Other cases provide a clearer link between Black Loyalists and slave ownership. Notably, John Simms, described as a carpenter and free black, apparently used his skills to join the ranks of slaveholder. He was listed as owning lot number sixty-seven in Delancey Town along with four enslaved—three males, whom he may have also trained as carpenters to work in his expanding business, and one female.[97] More telling perhaps of the crosscutting identities that surfaced within black communities in Nassau is the case of Timothy Cox, a free black who was also a successful ship's carpenter and slave owner. Cox had in his household employ a liberated African apprenticed to serve an eight-year apprenticeship. Cox was further described as an Anglican who apparently had made it a practice to baptize several of his enslaved into that faith. One of these was a ship's carpenter named Dick, whom Cox hired out on his own time. Notably, within Cox's household, therefore, was a mixture of the three groups of nonwhites in the Bahama Islands: free persons, Liberated Africans (also called recaptives who were legally free but expected to serve as apprentices in bound relations to an employer), and enslaved persons.[98]

At first glance the presence of free blacks as slaveholders seems inimical to the aspirations of Black Loyalists, who held freedom from bondage as an important goal; however, this apparent paradox can be explained in a number of ways. For one, the presence of slave-owning Black Loyalists may speak to the diverse crosscutting interests of this particular community, a polyglot community in which disparities were not only expressed in relation to gender, class, and ethnicity, but perhaps not surprisingly, also in differences regarding political strategies. In many instances individuals rejected the Zionist collective vision of Black Loyalists as a chosen people that had been expressed by black Nova Scotians Boston King and John Marrant. These individuals pragmatically and opportunistically mimicked white values and beliefs in an effort to gain entry into the planter world of status, rank, and slaveholding privilege.[99] Still others seemed to self-identify with a more radical vision in which slaveholding and the trappings of plantation life were seen as antithetical to their notions of freedom and liberty. In general, the question regarding the kind of liberty that could be extended to the Bahamas—either collective and radical or individualized and self-seeking—speaks to the ways in which Black Loyalist politics generated competing understandings of black displacement, enslavement, racism, and inequalities that were echoed throughout the broader Atlantic world.[100] In notable comparison to Gabriel's failed insurrection in Virginia, black communities were often riven by crosscutting identities that shaped their various responses to freedom: some choosing collective insurrection; others seeking freedom by escaping alone at night; still others choosing personal freedom at the expense of others—betraying the plans of their co-conspirators in exchange for the freedom promised by colonial authorities.[101]

Yet another way of reconciling the dilemma of slave ownership by Black Loyalists is to locate this practice within the broader Caribbean perspective. Indeed, it must be noted that the practice of free blacks owning enslaved persons was not unique to the Bahamas or to Black Loyalists but actually occurred in other urban environments throughout the Anglo-Caribbean. In urban environments, free coloreds and blacks often owned enslaved persons, affording them more flexible and less harsh working conditions, and thus providing the means by which the enslaved would eventually be able to purchase their freedom through manumission.[102]It should be noted that the efforts of Black Loyalists to manumit enslaved persons was not an unusual phenomena, but rather reflected a common practice of slaveholders throughout the Atlantic world. Nevertheless, what made their liberation agenda unusual was that most if not all those who were freed by Black Loyalists were family members. Accordingly, by applying his trade as a stonemason, Frank Spence was able to purchase the freedom of his wife, who was still living in East Florida at the time.[103] Similarly, Booby Hall, a free black of New Providence, provided proof of his efforts to manumit his family members when he left a notation that he purchased his daughter's freedom in 1784. Booby added in the Registry Office records, "for and in consideration of the love and affection which I have and bear unto my daughter Sarah."[104] The case of Spence and Booby Hall highlights the fact that much of the pattern of manumissions spearheaded by Black Loyalists appears to have targeted family members and close relatives. This trend is supported in the urban environment of Bridgetown, Barbados, where blacks who were slaveholders often procured enslaved persons as a way of providing protection for kith and kin, with the ultimate goal of securing their manumission.[105] Within the Bahamian context, while there was no single reason for persons of color to be slaveholders, many manumitted their enslaved after the death of a wife, husband, or relative connected to the enslaved. This may indicate that free blacks and persons of color did not hold to the notion of perpetual slavery. It is plausible that slave-owning free blacks and coloreds thought of their enslaved as persons, and thus their engagement in the slave market was simply an effort to capitalize on market conditions at the moment, rather than support a fixed racial caste system that defined enslaved persons and their progenitors as chattel.[106] It is also important to note that the practice of manumitting relatives evident in these cases was also an extension of an earlier custom that had emerged during the Black Loyalist struggles for freedom in colonial seaports during the American Revolution. Indeed, it must be remembered that the leading evangelical and Black Loyalist, Joseph Paul, while in New York City, did in fact manumit his wife and three children before eventually embarking for the Bahamas.

Slave ownership was just one of the many ways in which the black community of Delancey Town reflected complex and multifarious intraracial tensions. Arguably, Cox's efforts to baptize several of his enslaved into the Anglican faith suggest that some of the leading Black Loyalists such as Joseph Paul gravitated toward Anglicanism as a means of garnering a greater degree of respectability and even acceptance by whites while distancing themselves from the lower sort of uneducated and unskilled black masses. In the case of Paul, his building on Augusta and Heathfield streets eventually took on a certain duality; eventually named Saint Paul, it was also adopted as a chapel-at-ease aligned with Nassau's Christchurch cathedral.[107] This duality speaks to the ways in which Paul had firmly aligned himself with Anglicanism while simultaneously remaining a significant fixture within the black community.

Intraracial differences were also played out in the contentious issues over the ownership of land and buildings in the western suburbs of Nassau. This was most strikingly evident in the conflict over the meeting-house that developed between Joseph Paul and Anthony Wallace in the late 1790s. Although the initial split between Paul and Wallace may have been caused by the apostasy of the three American missionaries sent from Charleston, it is also clear that the rivalry between these two Black Loyalists endured for much longer. Even as Rev. Thomas Coke made mention of Hammett's men as the root cause of the split in the Methodist society, he still reserved rather harsh and caustic remarks for Joseph Paul and his defection to the Anglican cause. According to Coke's account, Paul was able to "take possession" of the building from Wallace, and he effectively split the congregation in two when he "joined himself to the minister of the [Anglican] parish, under whose sanction he acted."[108] Most fascinating however, is the fact that Paul and Wallace remained neighbors, residing on property adjoining each other. This fact is borne out by Joseph Paul's last will and testament, dated April 19, 1802, in which he not only ensured that the chapel and land were bequeathed to his wife and two sons "to be shared equally for future improvements," but also passed on to his daughter Mary a second lot adjoining the property of Anthony Wallace, the very man who had fought Paul for control of the church building.[109]

One can speculate that in spite of the initial antagonisms caused by the church split, the men shared common ground: as leading religious figures serving a Black Loyalist community; as property holders and members of a striving elite; and finally as men occupying a privileged public space denied to black women. In essence, Joseph Paul and Anthony Wallace represented the upper crust of Black Loyalists in the Delancey Town community who shared space, land, and buildings with other aspiring elites. Arguably, land ownership became a source of intraracial tension, a social marker for aspiring elites, who attempted to set themselves off from the poorer landless sort who lived within the very same community. Such intraracial tensions were also played out between Prince Williams and the trustees of Bethel Baptist Church in the early 1820s. Though the political implications of this issue will be discussed in chapter 5, it is worth noting that the trustees effectively barred Williams from preaching in the building by appealing to the governor to have his license to preach revoked. The elders also denied Williams and his congregation access to the building by placing custody of the keys in the hands of the governor.[110] In both these cases the issue of access to land and buildings became the source of division and contention within the Black Loyalist community of Delancey Town. Such evidence demonstrates the ways in which black communities were replete with ruptures and class cleavages as well as being held together by common assumptions about white prejudice and privilege.

In the end, it is clear that Delancey Town and other black enclaves established on the periphery of the town of Nassau became important centers of black community activity. It was in fact in both Delancey Town and the area behind Society Hill that the first all-black Baptist churches were founded by leading Black Loyalists. It was also in Delancey Town that leading Black Loyalists established an evangelical revivalism that drew upon the experiences of the Great Awakening and on traditional West African practices. Contrary to the views of most of the Bahamian elites and white missionaries, the black Baptist and Methodist customs comprised Afro-Christian beliefs that were far from misguided or based on ignorance and superstition. Rather, in establishing sacred institutions, Black Loyalists in the Bahamas disseminated a unique brand of evangelical Christianity that reflected elements of both African religious traditions and Euro-American practices. Building on their experience with American revivalism, Black Loyalist preachers of both Baptist and Methodist persuasion employed an array of rhetorical strategies to convey a powerful message that resonated with their listening audiences. Leading religious figures often held camp meetings at night in the open air where their oratory was combined with expressive and emotive sermons intended to prick the hearts of their followers. In general, black Methodist and Baptist preachers brought with them a form of religious observance that was charismatic in its style and centered on the preacher, but which also required fervent participation by the congregation.

Such religious institutions provided tangible evidence of the ways in which acculturation functioned on two levels, providing a site of intraracial affirmation and support while also expressing itself in relation to the unequal power structures that permeated a slaveholding society such as the Bahamas. In establishing viable churches and social institutions based on evangelical Christianity, Black Loyalists in the Bahamas joined in a chorus of black reform traditions that echoed across the Atlantic world from disparate sites such as Philadelphia, Nova Scotia, and Sierra Leone. Accordingly, black activism as manifested in self-reliant social institutions were spearheaded by patriotic blacks such as Richard Allen and Absalom Jones in Philadelphia, Black Loyalists in the figures of Boston King and David George in Nova Scotia, and loyal blacks in the Bahamas embodied in the likes of Joseph Paul, Frank Spence, and Amos Williams.[111] Equally important, though, were the actual religious and cultural practices that Black Loyalists carried with them to the Bahamas and other destinations in the Atlantic basin. Black expressive culture (singing, dancing, and spirit possession) functioned as an important element of Afro-Caribbean religiosity, providing both a source of strength and solace, as well as a counter-hegemonic hidden transcript easily misunderstood by European outsiders. Yet, as this chapter has argued, it would be overly simplistic to essentialize these Black Loyalist communities and their social institutions as homogeneous expressions of a general black African Diaspora experience.[112] Indeed, in spite of these common secular and sacred threads that bound Black Loyalists together, there were intra- and interracial tensions that challenged the cohesiveness of the community. If gender, class, and ethnic differences did not undermine some of the common bonds of the community, then it was external factors related to pressures imposed by laws, normative customs, and white institutional practices that brought these differences into relief. Despite these formidable challenges, Black Loyalists asserted through their social institutions an undeniable right to live autonomously and independently even if on the margins of a non-plantation slaveholding society. As the next two chapters will demonstrate, the struggle for freedom was fought and defended on more than one level, emerging as much in the contests over labor, land, and liberty as in the desire to live in self-reliant communities.

4

LABOR, LAND, AND THE LAW

On Friday, February 27, 1789, details of a new act proposed by the members of the House of Assembly were published in the *Bahama Gazette*. The act stipulated that "all free negroes, mulattoes, musktees and Indians be required," as soon as possible "to render into the secretary of these islands a fair and impartial list of their names, ages, places of abode, and family distinguishing the sex and color under penalty of forfeiture of freedom." Apart from enumerating the number of free blacks that had recently arrived from America, the act demanded that these "negroes so selected be furnished with necessary tools, implements and other conveniences," and that they be obliged to work on the "publick roads, highways and paths until the same shall be or may be completed and furnished." Though the labor of these "free negroes" was involuntary, the act did set aside a "daily allowance of two shillings for every day they shall work." Such compensation was nevertheless followed by the oppressive stipulation that the refusal to work or neglect of duties could result in corporal punishment. A final significant detail of the proposed law was that it did not pertain to free blacks born free in Nassau. This had the effect of isolating recently arrived Black Loyalists from the thirteen colonies as the group obliged to work on the public roads.[1]

This 1789 Act underscores the challenges faced by Black Loyalists entering a hostile work environment in which their labor and skills were often exploited by leading white Loyalists. Enumerating the size and dimensions of the Black Loyalist population was just one aspect of the effort by white slave owners to curtail the freedom of black refugees seeking employment on their own. In fact, forcing Black Loyalists to labor on public works could be interpreted as a subtle way to make them more dependent on the state, while simultaneously reducing their ability to function as independent wage-earning laborers. Despite the aims of such legislation, it is apparent that Black Loyalists in Abaco and Nassau, New Providence, exerted considerable effort to carve out a space where they could labor independently of white control.

Of central importance to Black Loyalists in the Bahamas was their ability to acquire land. Yet similar to their counterparts in Nova Scotia, Black Loyalists in the Bahamas were often denied access to land, which invariably complicated their efforts to earn a living free of dependent relations with whites. Acquiring land was not the only obstacle facing Black Loyalists. They were often forced into coercive and exploitative labor relations with more affluent white Loyalists in order to pay off debt owed, or simply as a means to escape starvation and poverty. Despite the innumerable challenges facing Black Loyalists, there is convincing evidence that they succeeded in carving out important niches in the urban work environment of Nassau. Black Loyalists' labor in Nassau reflected the diversity of their skills, training, and vocational occupations as well as the considerable efforts they undertook in their pursuit of economic freedom. There was also an important gender dimension to Black Loyalist labor. In Nassau, Black Loyalist men labored as stevedores, carpenters, masons, blacksmiths, and other urban-based trades whereas Black Loyalist women were employed as cooks, domestic maids, nurses, and washers.[2] The nonplantation nature of Bahamian society also lent itself to maritime activities, so that many Black Loyalists found employment as ship's carpenters, sailors, fishermen, and wreckers. In rural Abaco, Black Loyalists likewise faced significant obstacles as a result of the effort of white Loyalists to re-enslave them. Significantly, these Black Loyalists proved extremely resourceful and creative in both avoiding entangling dependency with whites, while eking out a livelihood in a hostile frontier environment. Many lived and worked in tiny scattered communities on the mainland, where they worked small provisional grounds. Others turned to the sea and engaged in subsistence fishing to provide for their families.[3]

Where land was not available, or their status as freepersons was questioned, many Black Loyalists resorted to squatting on land or temporarily maintaining areas of land deemed fallow in order to earn a living. In some

Figure 6. Town of Nassau silk tree. The presence of the silk cotton tree in the fore-
ground along with the public library in the background suggests the transformative
impact of the arrival of the Loyalists on the Bahamas. From Craton and Saunders,
Islanders in the Stream, 235. By permission of University of Georgia Press, Athens.

instances, Black Loyalists held untitled land in commonage. Commonage, by definition, was the practice whereby land was held in common
by a kin or lineage group. Accordingly, "all land and almost all property,
was for the use of the household, but properly belonged to the extended
family, the lineage, the tribe; that is, to the people." Though not specific to
West African societies, commonage was practiced "throughout most of
precolonial West Africa, including the entire catchment area" where the
majority of enslaved persons carried to New World colonies originated.[4]

It is not surprising, then, that the practice would be replicated in Caribbean societies, although its name and particular aspects undoubtedly
were altered by local conditions. Indeed, the practice of commonage
or "family land" was widely found in Caribbean peasant communities
in the postemancipation period. This tradition grew out of the period
of formal slavery, where enslaved persons established customary rights
of use, tenure, and transmission on property designated as provisional
land or village yards. In the immediate postemancipation period these
practices mushroomed in Jamaica and other sugar islands, particularly in

traditionally uncultivated areas where small peasant farmers held small plots in common and validated this possession through oral rather than written traditions.[5]

Unlike Jamaica and other slave societies in the Caribbean, the practice of commonage in the Bahamas dates back to a much earlier pre-Loyalist period (1648–1783) when land in North Eleuthera was held in common by farmers living on the offshore cays of Harbour Island and Spanish Wells. If commonage had its roots in the pre-Loyalist era, it most certainly expanded and became more commonplace by the early part of the nineteenth century, particularly on decayed plantations and where clear land titles did not exist.[6] Black Loyalists undoubtedly took advantage of opportunities to acquire land either through commonage, squatting, or generational land distribution.

Undoubtedly in their efforts to acquire land and live free of entangling relations, Black Loyalists came into contact with other persons seeking similar aspirations. In the urban center of Nassau, particularly, the encounters with existing populations of free blacks and enslaved persons ultimately led to an accelerated acculturation process in ways that blurred the lines between Black Loyalist and the existing free black population. Additionally, the influx of new arrivals either from West Africa as Liberated Africans or from the circum-Caribbean region as West Indian regiment soldiers likely diminished the utility and usefulness of those who had previously self-identified as Black Loyalists. Once diverse and heterogeneous, by the 1820s Nassau free blacks represented a blended and creolized population forged under the fulcrum of a common lived experience with racial inequality and slavery.

This chapter examines the labor and work of Black Loyalist men and women within the urban milieu of Nassau and the rural environment of Abaco. It argues that despite being denied the opportunity to own land and other legal hereditaments, Black Loyalists continued advancing their claims to freedom by squatting on or holding land in common, by willfully participating in the market economy, and even in their adaptive means of earning a living. Through these means, Black Loyalists asserted their sense of being free subjects within the British Imperial system.

One of the central problems Black Loyalists encountered upon arrival in the Bahamas was that their legitimate claim to land was often disregarded by whites. This experience paralleled that of Black Loyalists in Nova Scotia to whom promises of land were made in return for service rendered to the British during the Revolutionary War, but upon settlement in the Maritime Provinces, they received no such land. Thomas Brownspriggs lamented this unfulfilled promise, noting that he and other "black Men Inhabitants of this Province . . . have never received any Lands." Though Governor Thomas Carleton of New Brunswick claimed that Black Loyalists received allotments in the same proportion and on the same conditions as other royal refugees, the actual experience of Black Loyalists was quite the contrary.[7] Similarly, for Black Loyalists entering rural Abaco, access to land was initially denied for a variety of reasons. First, according to instructions issued to Lieutenant Governor Powell, dated September 10, 1784, he was to grant unoccupied lands in the Bahamas as follows: "To every head of family, forty acres, and to every white or black man, woman or child in a family, twenty acres at an annual quit rent of 2s. per hundred acres."[8] For each additional dependent or enslaved person a further twenty acres was to be given. Additionally, the instructions exempted Loyalists from quit rent charges for ten years.[9]

On the surface such instructions appear to treat black and white Loyalists alike. However, by including the clause granting an additional twenty acres for each dependent or enslaved person, the land grant system tended to favor whites at the expense of blacks. Where whites arrived in Abaco in possession of blacks or even owning enslaved persons outright, they could more readily qualify for additional allotments of land. In contrast, blacks arriving from New York did not own or possess additional dependents beyond their natural kin. Thus, by listing Black Loyalists as dependents or as enslaved—even where blacks possessed certificates of freedom— white Loyalists could gain an additional twenty acres per dependent.[10] In the end, much like their contemporaries in Nova Scotia who represented contractual servants as enslaved laborers, white Abaconians manipulated household registers in order to gain a decisive advantage over Black Loyalist settlers.[11]

When land grants were finally made for the island of Abaco, white Loyalists held the majority. By the late 1780s only seven land grants had been made at Spencer's Bight, the location of the settlement of Loyalist refugees arriving from Saint Augustine. Though the combined total population was estimated at 350 persons, it appears that Lt. Col. Brown of the King's Rangers had moved 170 enslaved people to the Bahamas and was allotted 2,980 acres in 23 parcels of land. More telling for the rest of Abaco, it was reported that by 1785, 44 percent of the population of Abaco lived in

Marsh Harbour, with an additional 21 percent in Maxwell Town, 25 percent in Carleton, and about 10 percent at Spencer's Bight. Most significant, however, was the fact that Philip Dumaresq, former captain of a Loyalist privateer and son of a prominent Boston Loyalist, owned almost all the land on the north and east sides of Marsh Harbour.[12] Absent from the land grants are the names of any of the 95 passengers onboard *The William* and *The Nautilus*. This suggests that Black Loyalists arriving in Abaco did not factor into the system of land grants.

Despite the initial fervor over land grants in Abaco, it is evident that by 1790 most of the aspiring planters had removed themselves from the island. Indeed, William Wylly observed that while eighteen hundred acres had been cleared for cultivation by 1788, he also reported that the last of the true planters were moving.[13] Where did these white Loyalists move to and why? Apparently, the inability to extract and coerce the labor of blacks, as well as the infertile nature of the soil, forced many white Loyalists to move either to Nassau or to more cultivable islands in the Central Bahamas and the British Caribbean. The whites who remained removed themselves to the offshore cays, where they adopted a lifestyle of fishing and boat building similar to that of other traditional island communities throughout the archipelago. Where whites tended to move from the mainland to the cays, blacks preferred to remain on the mainland, resorting to small-scale subsistence farming and fishing. This demographic shift highlighted the existence of racial divisions within the island settlements of Abaco, initially brought to light during the early period of settlement but ultimately having a profound impact on Bahamian society.

Where Black Loyalists in Abaco struggled to survive off the land by engaging in subsistence farming, those in Nassau fared only slightly better. In one particular area—the granting of land titles—Black Loyalists in Nassau may have done better than their counterparts in Abaco. Both Johann David Schoepf and William Wylly observed that free blacks—many of them Black Loyalists—often owned land, some even becoming "opulent planters."[14] A 1788 survey of New Providence suggests that thirteen lots in the city of Nassau, thirteen in the western part of the island, and eight in the eastern part were owned by free blacks.[15] Among those who achieved land ownership was Hannah Marshall, a free woman of color who owned two lots, one in Nassau, perhaps in the western suburb of Delancey Town, and another in the eastern part of the island. Hannah's case reflects an important gendered dimension to black land ownership in the Bahamas. Black women in Nassau, like those in other British Caribbean islands, were, in a few cases, able to own land, often by working for wages in the expanding urban market that had emerged by the beginning of the nineteenth century.[16] Apart from Hannah Marshall, "Jeremiah Tinker, James Knowles, Timothy Cox, and Thomas Marshall" were listed as free black men who owned multiple properties in New Providence. Of these men, Cox apparently owned the most, possessing three lots.[17] Between 1789 and 1791, six new nonwhites became landowners when Lord Dunmore granted tracts of land to George Watkins, Edward Cox, Eve Cooba, William Cain, John Simms, and the stonemason John Williams.[18] Although these cases demonstrate that free coloreds and blacks owned property in Nassau, less certain is whether these individuals were in fact Black Loyalists.

A more direct link between property ownership in New Providence and Black Loyalists can be ascertained through an analysis of a number of wills drawn up by leading Black Loyalists.[19] Frank Spence owned six pieces of property, including two lots behind Society Hill and three tracts of land located in the vicinity of "Baillou Hills."[20] Joseph Paul likewise owned at least two pieces of property, one including his chapel which was bequeathed to his wife Susannah and two sons, the other located next to the lot of his rival Anthony Wallace, which was passed on to his daughter Mary.[21] It is important to note that in the case of Frank Spence and Joseph Paul, they both owned multiple lots of land. In addition, both had made improvements to their land, building chapels or other edifices that remained in their ownership and were bequeathed to family members upon their death.[22] The case of Anthony Wallace is also significant. Wallace provided a parcel of real property to William Means, described as "his friend and son," who had been born to a female slave named Sarah.[23] Though the location of the property is not identified in this document, according to Joseph Paul's will, Anthony Wallace's parcel of land adjoined his lot in Delancey Town. The aforementioned Prince Williams also bequeathed in his last will and testament two pieces of property located "southward of the said town of Nassau," to his two daughters Judy Williams and Lucy Williams and his granddaughter Olivia Armbrister "as joint tenants and not as servants" to be shared "in common" among them.[24] It is worth noting that in many instances, Black Loyalist men bequeathed their property to female family members. Was this simply the result of the absence of a male heir, or a reflection of a particular gendered pattern in property transference? While there were no legal encumbrances to females acquiring property through wills, from these cases it appears that male heirs were normally listed first and most likely received the largest portion of the estate. Joseph Paul, for example, provided for both his sons, but also included a clause giving his wife title to his land.[25] In the case of Prince Williams, the absence of a male heir led to transfer of the property to his surviving female children and grandchildren. Significantly, because of their marital discord and lengthy separation, Williams' wife was left out of the will.[26]

Overall, despite the fact that a few blacks in New Providence clearly owned property, an analysis of the 1789 census figures provided by Wylly suggests that the overwhelming majority of Black Loyalists in Nassau, as in Abaco, remained without clear title to real estate. According to Wylly, of a total population of 9,296, there were 3,100 whites, 5,696 enslaved, and another 500 listed as free persons of color. Added to these numbers were the 350 Black Loyalists described by Wylly as "runaways who had arrived in the Bahamas from America."[27] By tabulating property ownership among free blacks from 1788 to 1791 it can be determined that only 40 achieved the status of landowner in New Providence out of a free black population calculated at 850 persons (350 defined as "runaways from the American states" in addition to the 500 free coloreds on the enumeration list). Though it is uncertain whether the 40 individuals owning property could all be categorized as Black Loyalists, it is nevertheless telling that this group represented only 11.4 percent of the entire group of 350 fitting the nomenclature of "runaways from America." In the end, it is clear that those Black Loyalists who owned property in New Providence constituted an extremely small group within the larger free black population.

Despite the fact that only a few leading Black Loyalists ever achieved clear title to land, many Black Loyalists appropriated uncultivated land on which to eke out a living. In a notice posted in the January 25, 1799, *Bahama Gazette*, R. Cunningham noted that it had "long been the practice" of blacks on this island "to cut wood on lands not their property, which they sell to raise money to pay their wages; and the subscriber having suffered injury from such practice." Cunningham's concern for such a time-tested practice also came with a warning. He declared his intention to "apprehend and commit to gaol, any negro in future found cutting wood on his lands, and will seek for such further satisfaction as the laws will award him."[28] The general concern expressed by Cunningham reveals the practice by enslaved and free blacks of appropriating lumber for their own economic advantage. In this case, it appears these blacks were opportunistically using Cunningham's land as a source of wood they could sell in the town. Such creative engagement with the market economy in Nassau was sure to upset slave owners bent on restricting and regulating the movement of such persons. Despite Cunningham's warning, additional archival sources suggest that Black Loyalists continued to find creative ways to use uncultivated land and its resources to ply their trade as woodcutters. A November 1784 advertisement in the *Bahama Gazette* gave notice that "no person or persons, white or black, are to cut wood or burn lime above the new road, on the piece of land situated between Mr. Perpaul's and Mr. Lairy's after this." The notice further states that any person apprehended "may expect to be dealt with according to the utmost severity of the law."[29] At first glance this statement appears inconsistent with common practices and legal precedents governing woodcutting at the time. Evidently, "everyone had the right to cut wood wherever he might find it and by 1784 New Providence and the adjacent islands had been fairly well cut over."[30] The prized wood sold at the market was mahogany, valued in shipbuilding for planking the part of the vessel below the waterline; lignum vitae, a hard and oily wood used for pulleys and rigging blocks; and braziletto wood, exported for dyes.[31] However, a closer reading of the advertisement suggests that leading whites such as Richard Cunningham were determined to restrict and regulate the activities of persons, either black or white, who encroached on land claimed as private property. Such comments both reflect the growing tension over land use as well as point to the various ways in which blacks earned a living in the rural areas surrounding the town of Nassau.

Woodcutting was not the only occupation in which Black Loyalists plied their trades and skills in ways increasingly seen as a threat to slave owners. In truth, Black Loyalists continued to seek out uncultivated land on which to squat or deployed the land tenure practice of commonage in order to acquire uncultivated land. The volunteers recruited by Andrew Deveaux from Harbour Island to fight the Spanish in April 1783 had actually farmed the area of northern Eleuthera based on the practice of commonage. These volunteers included white militia officers Robert Rumer, Samuel Higgs, and Joseph Curry, along with free coloreds and enslaved persons. When Governor Powell established a system of land grants with a 1785 proclamation, all Harbour islanders who had assisted Deveaux in

reclaiming Nassau as a British colony received firmer title to the six thousand acres of farming land they had previously farmed in commonage.
Despite this individual case whereby a shift to clear title and deed occurred, commonage continued as an important land practice with the arrival of the Loyalists from North America.[32] Accordingly, Black Loyalists
settled in scattered communities on the mainland of Abaco, and those
in Nassau living in uncultivated areas to the south and west of the town
continued to hold land in commonage. "Over the Hill" areas, where free
blacks settled, did not become Europeanized until the twentieth century.
Black suburbs including Delancey Town and Grants Town often reflected
the characteristics of commonage, with movable wooden houses often
on rented or leased lots. Moreover, beyond exotic descriptions given by
white visitors, there were black community structures that continued to
owe more to West African–derived notions of family, kinship, property
ownership, and inheritance than to the official legal system of freehold
tenure advocated by leading whites.[33]

The practice of squatting on or occupying land without clear title and
deed is evident from a proclamation dated August 17, 1793: "whereas divers persons have in violation of His Majesty's right and contrary to the
warnings" have repeatedly "erected stores, shops, and other tenements,
and also fenced in several spots on the North side of the road leading from
the ordinance yard, westwardly."[34] Why were such practices viewed as
offensive? Part of the problem lay with the unwillingness of the squatters
to remove themselves despite repeated warnings. Beyond this, the community was located in close proximity to Nassau, the commercial hub and
colonial capital of the colony. Certainly in areas not so far removed from
the gaze of white slaveholders, free blacks, among whom Black Loyalists
were numbered, tilled and worked the land as independent farmers seeking a life of their own. A June 13, 1789 advertisement in the *Bahama Gazette* noted that "two new negro men" had escaped from their owner. The
advertisement alleged that these two men were likely harbored "on the
North side of the island, where negro huts have been discovered" and in
the "back of these settlements where negro fields are."[35] The advertisement
gives two important details relating to squatting and general systems of
landholding in New Providence: first, it suggests that free blacks had established huts in areas some distance removed from those inhabited by
whites. In this instance, the area was located on the north side of the
island until "discovered" by whites. Second, the advertisement indicates

that blacks tilled and worked tracts of land behind their homes. Both practices—occupying untitled land and tilling or farming it—were seen as inimical to the interests of slave owners. Indeed, whether clandestinely or openly configured, such communities of squatters not only represented a countercultural movement of self-employed persons seeking relief from the rigors of coercive labor systems, but if left unchecked could also eventually morph into full-blown marronage.

In fact, such apparent threats inevitably led to greater efforts at social control. In the December 24, 1799, edition of the *Bahama Gazette*, an act was proposed for regulating those persons "not having wherewith to maintain themselves," and as a result "live idle without employment and refuse to work for the usual and customary wages given to other laborers in the island or place where they then are shall be deemed idle and disorderly persons." Such individuals, according to the act, were upon witness before a Justice of the Peace and two credible witnesses consigned to the workhouse or jail, to do hard labor for any time not exceeding one month.[36] This particular act appears to have targeted free blacks (including Black Loyalists) who lacked the means to acquire property, but remained unattached to white employers. A number of ancillary documents point to free blacks as the target of this legislation. A few months before the passing of the act, members of the Grand Jury had expressed their concern over the presence of public houses whereby, they believed, "negroes are distracted from their duties" and "contract habits of idleness and tipping."[37] A 1794 Grand Jury also noted the want of public stocks at "proper places for the confinement of riotous Negroes and other disorderly persons on the Lord's Day." The jurors further recommended the "erection of such a jail at some convenient place in the eastern and western Suburbs."[38] Though it is difficult to ascertain the extent to which Black Loyalists as an entire group were specifically targeted as vagabonds and idlers, there are nevertheless a few cases that suggest they were victims of these legal sanctions. Take Flora Gavin, a "negro claiming to be free" in New Providence who had been jailed for a felony in 1806. While the exact nature of the offense is not given, it is noteworthy that Flora (possibly freed by Governor's Certificate in 1793) is described as a stowaway, fleeing her original owner, Mrs. Johnson of South Carolina, and eventually settling in Nassau where she birthed three children—Hester, Kinsgston, and Ramkin—by 1787. It appears that Flora remained in jail with neither family members able to pay the bond for her release, nor a slave owner willing to claim her as property. That Flora remained imprisoned reveals the precarious life of a black woman who existed on the margins of Bahamian society.[39] Black Loyalist men also appear to have been stigmatized as vagabonds. Such is the case with Mike Deveaux, alias Armstrong, who surfaces in a *Bahama Gazette* advertisement as an "idle vagabond endeavoring to get to the continent, where he alleges he was born free."[40] Apart from the obvious agency displayed in his efforts to achieve freedom, Mike Deveaux's surname hints at a possible connection to the more famous iconic white Loyalist, Andrew Deveaux, who reconquered the Bahamas for the British in April 1783.[41] Most significant, though, is the way he is inscribed into the official records as someone known about town as an idler and vagrant. In general, it appears that Black Loyalists, whether through the practices of commonage, squatting on lands in tenements, or living "idly" without proper employment, were considered subversives, potential threats to the established social order.

Outside of land issues, equally troubling for leading whites were the myriad of ways in which Black Loyalists attempted to earn a living beyond their controlling influence. While such practices appear to have been commonplace in the emerging local market economy in the Bahamas, they also reflect general practices throughout the Caribbean. As in the sugar islands in the Caribbean, free and enslaved blacks in the Bahamas tended to dominate the urban marketplace, functioning as small peddlers, traders, and hucksters. Recent scholarship underscores the central role played by enslaved persons, particularly women, in the development of an internal market economy. Of particular importance are studies focused on the urban environments of Bridgetown, Barbados; San Juan, Puerto Rico; and Kingston, Jamaica. In the urban center of Bridgetown, "hucksters" played an important role as enslaved persons met boats that docked in the bay and offshore in order to sell locally grown foodstuffs and other goods.[42] Black women in particular played an important role in the huckstering trade. Even where Barbados slave owners did not allocate provisional grounds for cultivation, enslaved women, like their counterparts in Jamaica (where such grounds were provided), demonstrated a remarkable resourcefulness in operating as independent cultivators within an expanding domestic trading market. Interestingly, Irish poor whites entered into trade and bartering relations with enslaved women, often copying their methods of selling and distributing items. Commonly sold items included drinks, poultry, and stock. Despite successive restrictions beginning in 1711 and elaborated in 1774, 1779, and 1784, these women circumvented laws in order to create an autonomous space free from the plantation and the gaze of the overseer.[43] Similarly, urban enslavement in San Juan, Puerto Rico, highlights the domestic and trading roles held by enslaved women even while facing greater social control by a modernizing and liberalizing state. Of particular relevance to this study is the fact that the shops and stores of blacks in San Juan were often targeted as unsanitary and a threat to public safety and order.[44]

Similar to Barbados and Puerto Rico, Jamaica at the end of the eighteenth century had emerged as a slave society where persons of color experienced profound inequality, regardless of legal status. Enslaved persons in Jamaica were a coerced labor force, expected to work upward of eighteen hours a day with only one day a week to rest. During cane harvest time they seldom had a rest day and could work even longer hours. Nevertheless, there a small free colored population could be found, largely in the urban area of Kingston, and often eking out a living as traders, skilled craftsmen, or petty shop owners. As in Bridgetown and San Juan, the internal market was largely controlled by black women, many of whom sold their garden crops to white slaveholders for cash. Despite their free status, as a group they were denied civil rights such as sitting on juries, holding political office, or voting unless they possessed property.[45]

Although urban space in late-eighteenth- and early nineteenth-century Nassau appears to reflect some of the general trends suggested in this scholarship, there were a number of significant differences. Similar to the pattern seen in the sugar-dominated islands of the Caribbean, free and enslaved black women in Nassau tended to control the urban marketplace, functioning as peddlers, traders, and hucksters. Yet the decline of cotton by the early 1790s changed the nature of labor organization in both the rural and urban environments of the Bahamas in ways that marked it as different from the sugar plantation complex on neighboring islands.[46] The decline of cotton as an export crop had a dramatic impact on the lifestyle and work relations of the enslaved population. As a result, enslaved Bahamians were afforded greater opportunities through a task system than in gang labor. The task system provided enslaved persons with time to work their provisional grounds and take advantage of self-hiring in the urban environment of Nassau, and it ultimately "shaped a coercive labor system into a contractual one."[47] The self-hire system that evolved with the decline of cotton eased the transition from slavery to freedom because "it not only allowed enslaved persons to purchase their freedom but also gave those who continued to work on it substantial control over their lives while they remained chattels."[48] Away from the direct control of their owner, enslaved persons "bargained with employers for wages; managed their money, and arranged for their own food, clothing, and accommodation."[49] While enslaved persons remained bound to their owner and were in fact required to return a portion of their earnings to them, the evolution of the self-hire and task system remained a permanent fixture in urban Nassau until abolition in 1834. These findings are particularly important for understanding the ways in which Black Loyalists entering the Bahamas after 1783 were integrated into a complex urban environment where enslaved and free blacks leveraged their labor potential in order to demand wages and fairer treatment from whites. In essence, though not enslaved, Black Loyalists, like many of the urban poor, attempted to negotiate and navigate unequal relations of power with landholding whites in ways that would be beneficial to them.

Efforts on the part of Black Loyalists to leverage more equitable work conditions were undoubtedly accelerated by the broader socioeconomic conditions they faced by the last decade of the eigtheenth century. Nassau in particular had become a busier, more cosmopolitan center. New stone buildings were erected, including a public library, a jail, and an assembly house. Churches were also constructed out of stone, including St. Matthew's, built in 1802 as an Anglican church servicing mostly white Loyalists in the eastern district, and St. Andrew's Presbyterian Church, built in 1810 closer to the original city limits. Apart from these buildings, "new roads were built and old ones improved, as wheeled vehicles became [a] more common sight and the town became an increasingly important market center and entrepot."[50] As a sign of the increased trade in the city, Vendue House was rebuilt in 1787 as a handsome small structure with colonnades in order to facilitate the growing trade in enslaved persons.[51] Additionally, despite the decline of cotton by the first decade of the nineteenth century, Nassau continued to flourish as a city to those remaining Loyalists, both black and white, because it was the most advanced center of commerce and trade in the colony. It was in Nassau that most whites resided as absentee plantation owners, merchants, or lawyers, either living in the secluded streets outside the commercial area, or erecting large homes on the crest of the ridge running east to west, parallel to the harbor.[52] Blacks were also drawn to the city as small trading and local markets remained a steady means of employment for many free blacks and persons of color.

It is also worth noting that while the settlement of Black Loyalists was generally concentrated in the western suburbs of Nassau in the area of Delancey Town, other free black communities had existed in the pre-Loyalist period such as Fox Hill in the east and a smaller enclave of free blacks living behind Fort Fincastle, where Frank Spence's chapel was erected. In all three locales it was likely that by the 1790s Black Loyalists had successfully assimilated into these enlarged communities, marked less by allegiance to Great Britain and more by commonage landholding practices and a collective effort to carve out an autonomous workspace of their own. Indeed, these self-contained villages thrived because of their proximity to Bay Street and the marketplace, where hucksters, peddlers, and other cultivators from within these communities could sell their wares on market day.

The marketplace in particular represented an important site where Black Loyalists and other free blacks could negotiate and leverage their economic activity in ways that were advantageous to them. Arguably, many of the "trading spaces" within Nassau's urban environment were dominated by enterprising free blacks who operated their businesses mostly independent of direct white influence.[53] In a February 24, 1789, presentment of the Grand Jury, it was noted along with the troubling concern related to Dunmore's Court whereby negro property is put on trial without a jury, that there was no law against "negroes and others, hawking goods in baskets, trays, and otherwise about the streets." While blacks appeared to be targeted as a group, the inclusion of "others" hints at the possibility that poor whites were also considered a public nuisance. A final point can be drawn from this list of grievances. Apparently, the grand jurors also suggested the need for a marketplace to be built, along with a police force and public buildings.[54] Implicit in these remarks is the general preoccupation of the elites with the unregulated and disorderly presence of free blacks selling and trading in the streets of Nassau. Their solution was to create a public space and police force that could achieve order and structure where trade could be more effectively controlled.

Though the class and racial attitudes of the ruling elite color these grievances, they also demonstrate that such practices were commonplace. The prevalence of trading and selling by Black Loyalists and other free persons of color invariably led to greater efforts at social control on the part of leading whites. In the May 8, 1795, *Bahama Gazette*, legislators attempted to create order out of the chaos they perceived was a result of a local market dominated by blacks and other marginalized racial groups. As such, the legislators determined that "no negro, mulatto, mustee or Indian, shall on any pretence, sell, barter, or carry about for sale or barter, any spirituous liquor, dry goods, wares or merchandise of any kind whatsoever." Additionally, the act also made it lawful "for any white person to take and seize all such spirituous liquor, dry goods, wares or merchandise that shall be found exposed to sale or barter in the possession of the above mentioned parties."[55] Offenders were deemed liable to receive twenty lashes on the bare back by order of the magistrate. These draconian measures were further reinforced by a provision whereby negroes, mulattoes, mustees, and Indians were forbidden to peddle "any kind of butcher's meat, fish, plantains, eggs, fruits, vegetables or other plantation provisions . . . for sale at second hand." Such actions could result in the offending parties also receiving twenty lashes on their bare backs.[56]

Despite these regulatory measures, there is evidence to suggest that free blacks, among whom Black Loyalists would have been counted, continued to participate in, and perhaps even dominate the local market. The list of grievances reported by the Grand Jury in October 4, 1799, noted that "they were particularly aggrieved at the present practice by negroes of monopolizing all fruits of roots and vegetables on board vessels from America, and the plantation boats from Eleuthera."[57] Additional sources reveal the prevalence of free blacks in the local market economy. A list accompanying a petition for closing the House of Assembly in January 1788 included free blacks such as Edward Lane, a husker who kept a gaming house; Shill Barton, a husker and "keeper of a negro gaming house"; as well as David Costable, a mulatto fisherman.[58] Such descriptions not only demonstrate the diverse occupations of urban blacks but also suggest the kind of multiracial urban culture beginning to emerge in Nassau.

Beyond participating in the marketplace, Black Loyalists, like their laboring counterparts throughout the Caribbean, found creative ways to soften coercive labor relations into more tolerable structures. Of significance, the demand for highly skilled labor in Nassau afforded Black Loyalists an opportunity to negotiate conditions of work and earn wages. Within the city limits, many Black Loyalists in fact earned substantial wages as blacksmiths, masons, and carpenters. William Paul, the son of noted Black Loyalist Joseph Paul, earned a living as a boat builder before taking over the responsibilities of Dr. Bray's School from his brother Joseph Jr. in 1811.[59] In his will Frank Spence was listed as a stonemason. Capitalizing on the demands for his trade in Nassau, by the time of his death Spence was a multiple property owner and one of the wealthier members of the free black community.[60] Likewise, Timothy Cox was described as a ship's carpenter; he apparently had earned enough wages to eventually rise to planter status, owning substantial land and even enslaved persons.[61]

Similarly, a number of advertisements in the *Bahama Gazette* indicated both the kind of work to be performed as well as the pecuniary rewards that such labor provided for Black Loyalists. In a March 18, 1796, advertisement, a young mulatto man identified as James Jones was characterized as one who could "shave and dress hair, wait in the house, drive a carriage, and take care of horses."[62] Jones can be identified as a Black Loyalist based on the corroborating account offered by the white Methodist missionary William Dowson, who wrote that Jones had arrived in the Bahamas from America with the Loyalists or refugees.[63] Likewise, an advertisement in the February 12, 1790, edition of the *Bahama Gazette* stated that a black or white mason was wanted to go to Cat Island. Suggestive of the wage-earning potential of masons was the subscriber's comment that "a good encouragement will be given."[64] Such evidence indicates the relative equality that the demand for skilled labor could create. Indeed, the fact that the advertisement noted that either a black or white man would serve indicates that what was important was the skill of the employee, not racial identity. Particularly telling is the case of Chatham Darvel, who had apparently hired himself out as a carpenter to earn wages, much to the annoyance of Elisha Swain, to whom he was apprenticed.[65] Overall, the arrival of Loyalists in the Bahamas and the subsequent economic development created opportunities for skilled black artisans.

Additionally, the expansion of public works as a consequence of the arrival of Loyalists in the capital afforded many blacks government employment. In particular, the expanding town required roads to be laid out and lands to be cleared and surveyed. The work on such construction projects was done by free blacks, many of whom had arrived with skills they had attained while laboring in colonial America. A 1784 act reflected the labor opportunities that such public works provided Black Loyalists. According to the preamble, the act was established to allow for "cutting open three new roads from the north to the south side of the island of New Providence and for appointing commissioners" in order to "superintend the same males all free mulattoes, free Indians, free negroes and slaves from the age of fifteen to sixty" which "shall be liable to work on the said roads."[66] Apart from revealing the extent to which such labor was central to the development of a more modern and cosmopolitan city and its environs, the source also indicates a mixed enslaved and free workforce. Likewise, the fact that the workers were identified as male suggests that construction work and other public projects were relegated specifically to men. Arguably, the work of clearing roads and other labor-intensive public works were sites of intraracial intermingling where enslaved and free black males worked alongside each other. Missing from the act, however, are the wages paid for such labor and a more specific description of the legal status of blacks engaged in the work. Other documentary evidence suggests that free blacks and perhaps even enslaved persons hired out by their urban slave owners did receive a wage for their work on such road projects. In a December 13, 1793, advertisement, it was announced that "laborers were wanted, twenty able-bodied people of color, to work on the new road to the south side—generous wages and good provisions will be given."[67]

In addition to clearing roads and other labor-intensive work, it appears that Black Loyalists also earned wages by working on the various forts and magazines built by Lord Dunmore during his tenure as governor. Z. Allen, writing from Exuma, posted a notice in the *Bahama Gazette* regarding an escapee named Andrew, described as a stout well made fellow; has a rather dull look, and is known in Nassau, "having for a considerable time worked at Fort Charlotte as a free man."[68] The exact way in which Andrew came to be considered the property of Allen is unknown. Still, it appears that Allen, a slave owner, identified Andrew as nominally free, at least for the time that he labored at Fort Charlotte in Nassau. The fact that Andrew surfaced as an escapee in this particular advertisement speaks to the kind of coercive work environment he most likely experienced in Exuma. Nevertheless, Andrew's case should not be taken as a general trend among laboring blacks willing to ply their trades on Family Islands. Additional advertisements in the *Bahama Gazette* suggest the extent to which Black Loyalists and free blacks negotiated favorable work relations, with provision for timely wages to be paid. A November 8, 1793, advertisement identified as "wanted for hire, from five to twelve field negroes, to be employed on Exuma." The notice added, "good wages, punctually paid and kind treatment will be given."[69]

A final employment opportunity specifically geared toward Black Loyalist men was service in the military forces. Drawing on their wartime experience during the Revolutionary War, Black Loyalists may well have been singled out for their labor expertise.

Foreshadowing the establishment of a black West Indian Regiment in the British Caribbean by 1795, Dunmore initially recruited free blacks in 1791 to defend the property of whites against local insurgents as well as the foreign threat posed by revolutionary activities emerging in nearby Saint Domingue. Drawing no doubt on free blacks' experiences as soldiers during the American Revolution, Dunmore and his executive council encouraged "all able bodied free negro men to serve as black pioneers [laborers] in His Majesty's forty-seventh or Lancashire Regiment."[70] Interestingly, the same notice also includes a pecuniary reward for enlisting, noting that "where, on being approved of, they will receive His Majesty's Bounty, with every other suitable encouragement." Another significant clause in the recruitment notice specifies that "they are hereby assured that they will not be removed from the Bahama Islands, contrary to their own inclinations."[71] It can be inferred from this particular clause that Black Loyalists apparently remonstrated against being removed to another island. Such self-conscious assertiveness reflects the way in which Black Loyalist men were able to leverage their position as wage earners in order to access better working conditions and more equitable treatment. In this respect Black Loyalists operating in the urban environment of Nassau displayed the cultural dexterity and resourcefulness of other refugees throughout the diaspora.

Take for instance the Jamaican Black Loyalist George Liele who appears to have undertaken a variety of roles in the Governor's employ to pay off his debt as an indentured laborer, including "being a trumpeter to the troop of horse . . . and . . . carrying all cannon that could be found lying about this part of the country." Epitomizing the flexibility of many in his Revolutionary generation, Liele deployed his full arsenal of talents and skills—as a soldier, trumpeter, and cart man to pay off his debt and gain a more permanent free status.[72] Having secured unequivocal freedom, Liele, like many Black Loyalists in the Bahamas, turned to institution-building, establishing the first Afro-Jamaican Baptist church on the island in 1784, with a devoted cadre of followers, many of them arriving as refugees from America.[73] Overall, it appears that the urban environment of Nassau, with its expanding roads and buildings, provided male artisans with many opportunities to leverage their skills in ways that enabled them an opportunity to earn a living by independent means.

Where Black Loyalist men and other free persons of color were able to take advantage of expanded employment opportunities in Nassau, prevailing gender norms clearly limited both the kind and nature of work for Black Loyalist women. In essence, while Black Loyalist women were able to find opportunities as wage earners in the emerging urban environment of Nassau, traditional gender assumptions often circumscribed the kind of work they were deemed fit to do. In the post-Revolutionary period in the United States there was a general retreat from the universal claims of citizenship for women; instead, founding fathers argued that wives and daughters were covered by their husbands' or fathers' civic identity. This notion of coverture not only placed sharp restraints on married women's bodies, but also essentially consigned them to supporting domestic roles and work deemed appropriate for women.[74] Did such attitudes exist in the Bahamas? It appears from a cursory glance at advertisements of the period that much of women's work fell within the limits of the domestic sphere. Thus, notices placed in the *Bahama Gazette* frequently advertised wage-earning opportunities for women as washers, maids, cooks, or seamstresses, occupational categories typically considered "acceptable" for women by Loyalist men.[75]

Though consigned to traditional female roles, some Black Loyalist women were nevertheless able to overcome these gender constraints to become successful independent landowners and wage earners. Take for example Betty Watkins, "a free woman of color who lived in the Eastern district of New Providence Island, owned a lot, a house and a female slave." Though her specific occupation is unknown, she may have been a "seamstress, a washer-woman, or a cook, the traditional occupations opened to women of that day." Interestingly, in her will she signed with an X, suggesting that despite her sizable assets she was nonetheless illiterate.[76] The gender-specific nature of the aforementioned occupations was illustrated by an advertisement in the June 22, 1792, edition of the *Bahama Gazette,* which announced an interest in hiring "a negro woman who can wash and [do] plain cooking."[77]

Such advertisements speak to the ways black women often worked on the self-hire system, performing tasks for white men to whom they may have been indentured or enslaved while also earning an additional income after such duties had been completed. Suggestive of her Black Loyalist identity, Nancy was pejoratively described as "a negro wench, well known among the free crew that came from the Carolinas by some of whom she is supposed to be harbored." Though classified as a runaway by the subscriber, Nancy had supported herself as a washer and ironer.[78] Nancy's vocational trade suggests that gender roles were reinforced through specific occupations classified as "women's work." This point is borne out by the advertisement in the August 22, 1797 edition of the *Bahama Gazette*, in which the Commissary's Office announced it "wanted immediately ten or twelve sensible Negro men and women to attend the hospitals of 33rd regiments as laborers and nurses; to whom very liberal wages and rations will be allowed."[79] Though at initial glance such an ad suggests a cross-gendered work environment, the opposite may be true. Indeed, it was most likely that the men were to be employed as laborers and the women were expected to work as nurses. Notwithstanding these gendered roles, it is significant that the advertisement attempted to entice free blacks as workers, by offering "very liberal wages and rations." In the end, even as the urban milieu of Nassau reflected the broader gendered patterns of work found throughout the eighteenth-century Atlantic world, it did provide some unusual opportunities for Black Loyalists, both men and women, to negotiate and advance more equitable work environments.

Where land-based activities did not provide Black Loyalists with any degree of freedom, many adopted the traditional means of earning a living from the sea. Given the nonplantation nature of Bahamian society, particularly before the arrival of the Loyalists, many black refugees gravitated toward sea-based activities. Black Loyalists employed their diverse maritime skills in a range of occupations as sailors, fishermen, pilots of small vessels, and possibly even as captains of larger oceangoing vessels. Johann David Schoepf's account indicates that fishing was in fact a "common employment of the poorer white inhabitants as well as of many negroes." Further suggesting the extent to which Black Loyalists participated in the existing maritime economy is Schoepf's observation that many free blacks were even in "command of small vessels."[80] This fact eventually became a source of concern among leading whites. A January 1787 Act prevented "negroes and other slaves from being masters of any turtling, wrecking or other decked vessel or boats destined to go out of the limits of this government."[81] Dunmore's executive council's concerns were not entirely unfounded. Black pilots and sailors often aided indentured servants, some of whom were likely Black Loyalists, in search of freedom.[82] If Black Loyalist pilots and sea captains deployed their maritime skills in assisting escapees, others were in the process of attaining freedom for themselves. Take for instance a shipwright by the name of Prince, who was owned by John Imrie but had recently worked for wages for Mr. Mickie before he absconded.[83] Other free blacks identified as seamen sought freedom by either fleeing to another island or finding safety in the sizable community of free blacks in the western suburbs. A July 25, 1789 escapee advertisement described both Curacao Tom and John Scott as free men and indentured servants. While Scott was listed as a seaman, Tom was identified as a carpenter by trade.[84] Arguably, while formal slavery continued to operate in the Bahamas after 1783, other coercive labor relations existed, ranging from indenture contracts to informal methods of servitude. This was in fact parallel to the situation in both Jamaica and Nova Scotia during the Loyalist settlement period as well as in nineteenth-century Cuba, where enslavement was but one form of coercive labor existing alongside indentured servitude, free wage work, and various forms of debt peonage.[85] In the case of the Bahamas, regardless of the exact nature of the labor arrangement, Bahamian sailors did not always acquiesce to white demands for their labor. It is worth noting that sailors represented the second largest occupational category listed as runaways in Nassau's newspapers.[86] In the case of the indentured servants mentioned above, their desire to live absolutely free and ply their trade outside any contractual obligations to a white person likely factored into their decision to abscond.

Beyond work relations, the city of Nassau itself also provided Black Loyalists with public spaces where they could commingle with other free persons outside the influence of slaveholding whites. The growth and expansion of Nassau as a city led to the development of a polyglot interracial artisan culture that stood in direct counterpoint to the kind of slave society imagined by leading whites. Far from being a typical plantation society, the urban environment was relatively mixed and balanced by 1801 with 1,599 whites, 752 free people of color, and 3,861 enslaved.[87] Added to this mix was the introduction of two new groups of blacks legally defined as free; West Indian troops as early as 1801, and Liberated Africans after 1810. Both groups of newcomers held an ambiguous legal space in the Bahamas as recent arrivals, freed from enslavement as a result of imperial political policies, but nevertheless often categorized as part of the un-free population by the local whites because of their perceived racial identity. For Liberated Africans, their legal status derived from the events that unfolded in London following the abolition of the trans-Atlantic slave trade in 1808. In enforcing this Imperial Act, British vessels patrolled Atlantic world waters for illegal slave traders. Upon securing illegal vessels, the British Navy brought the recaptives to the nearest Vice Admiralty Court, where, upon adjudication, the Africans were "liberated." Over a six-decade period the Royal Navy would detain more than five hundred ships found in violation of laws prohibiting trading in slaves. From such vessels, more than forty thousand rescued Africans ended up settled in British Caribbean territories, mostly under diverse labor arrangements of apprenticeship or indenture.[88] Though "liberated" or "rescued" from a life of servitude by patrolling British naval vessels, these African-born men and women were settled in the British Caribbean where it was paternalistically assumed they would be inculcated with the virtues of British civility, taught how to read and write, and converted from paganism to Christianity.[89] Between 1811 and 1828, the collector of customs in Nassau admitted 1,102 Liberated Africans, a small figure compared with those in the other resettlement territories of Guyana, Trinidad, and Jamaica. However, taking into account the small size of the Bahamian population, with only 3,190 enslaved, 1,720 whites, and 1,074 free blacks and persons of color counted in 1810, the insertion of these newcomers made an indelible impression.[90] Though technically operating as free persons in the Bahamas, many of these recaptives faced coercive labor experiences similar to those faced by Black Loyalists two decades earlier. Instead of encouraging the development of trades and useful skills, many employers exploited the Liberated African apprentices for their own personal gain by assigning them work as unskilled agricultural laborers.[91] Despite the efforts of the colonial office to keep the Africans separated from the creole populations, there was considerable mixing, particularly on market days when Liberated Africans from remote communities such as Gambier, Adelaide, and Carmichael brought their goods to Nassau to sell at the market. Perhaps because of the great distances they had to travel by foot, or the continued interactions with local creoles, including both poor whites and blacks, many Liberated Africans eventually moved closer to town, establishing the new settlements of Bain and Grants Town by the second decade of the nineteenth century.[92]

Similarly, West Indian soldiers, originating from the older sugar colonies of Barbados and Antigua, were recruited and stationed in the Bahamas by the early nineteenth century. Beginning in 1801, 272 black troops from the Fifth and Sixth West Indian regiments were brought into the Bahamas to defend the capital and outlying islands from attacks by the Spanish and French, the chief rivals of Great Britain at a time of intensifying imperial conflict. Consisting of both Caribbean-born and African-born enslaved persons, these skilled men proved invaluable during military campaigns in the region. Yet for local white elites, the garrisoning of such troops of color in the Bahamas was a continual source of friction in the first decades of the nineteenth century. For this reason, colonial authorities regularly rotated the troops in and out of the Bahamas in the hope they could keep them separate from the local enslaved and free black populations.[93] In practical terms, this did not work as the Colonial Office planned. Indeed, despite being assigned to work and live in barracks attached to Fort Charlotte, many of these West Indian soldiers interacted with the local free black and white populations in Nassau, particularly in public spaces such as the marketplace, churches, and recreational grounds. Often troops were officially stationed to guard public buildings, leading to greater interaction with both white and black persons. While these kinds of informal interactions were normally cordial, there were moments when racial tension surfaced into acts of violence. One such incident occurred in 1806 when a civilian struck a soldier stationed at a public building at 11 p.m. Though the civilian's racial identity was not revealed, the time and nature of the event suggest the assailant was a white male.[94] Such racial discord might explain the preference of black West Indian troops for marrying persons of the same color and racial identity. An analysis of the Christchurch Cathedral marriage register reveals that a large number of soldiers married free blacks. Indeed, from 1810 to 1820, more than twenty-five marriages were recorded between West Indian troops and local free blacks. In every instance the groom was a low-ranking black officer and the bride was described as either a free black or free colored.[95] Though marriage patterns suggest that the overwhelming majority of free blacks and coloreds married persons of the same color (260 to 13), in work and other social arenas it appears that a great deal of interaction occurred between working-class people of different colors.[96]

Such informal interactions were evident in frequent advertisements alleging that poor whites had escaped with blacks or even committed crimes together. An April 29, 1800, advertisement in the *Bahama Gazette* noted that a soldier named John Maddock "had broken out of the dungeon and escaped along with a negro boy named Dick, who was lodged in the same place."[97] Additionally, an April 12, 1799, advertisement in the *Bahama Gazette* described three male sailors who had absconded together from the ship *Admiral Duncan*. All three were described in ways that suggest different racial or ethnic affinities: Prince, as a stout yellow man; Ben, as a black man with a broad face; and John Crawn, possibly white, as simply a 16-year-old apprentice. It is also noteworthy that Ben and Prince were identified as "slaves" whereas John Crawn was not.[98] Apparently, daytime interactions between whites and free blacks were barely tolerated. Indeed, even as cotton profits declined, white slaveholders maintained social distinctions and continued to enact "proper laws and regulations for governing free negroes" in order to protect their property and business interests.[99] These attitudes are evident from Grand Jury reports in which the work and leisure activities of urban dwellers in Nassau are frequently characterized as "grievances" and "nuisances" with whites demanding more regulations and policing.[100]

Yet if working together in wooded lands, on vessels, or even as traders and peddlers on Nassau's streets was not troubling enough for Nassau's elites, the nighttime activities of such a motley crew of blacks, whites, mulattoes, and other less identifiable ethnic groups were certainly cause for serious concern. Of particular relevance was the emergence of taverns and public houses where free blacks and enslaved persons would congregate along with poor whites to sing, dance, and drink spirituous liquors. References to dances held at night within the Western suburbs of Nassau appear frequently in the *Bahama Gazette*. The February 6, 1795, edition of the *Bahama Gazette* reported that "all black persons who shall hereafter have dances at their houses, will be taken up and punished for promoting theft, gaming, idleness, and drunkenness among the negroes." Interesting for highlighting the interracial and cross-class encounters that such houses created is the advertisement that further warns, "all slaves who shall be detected at those dances, will be also severely punished."[101] Apart from underscoring the potentially dangerous threat presented by such nocturnal assemblies of blacks, the notice also indicates that the agrocommercial oligarchy was bent on establishing greater social control over a working class deemed idle, drunk, and engaged in unwholesome activities. The prevalence of such activities among free blacks is evident from an escapee advertisement dated July 21, 1797, indicating that "two negro boys" each about 18 years of age, and known by the names of Hamlet and Kendal, had run away from the subscriber at the beginning of the month. It was further noted that Hamlet "is well known about town and has lately been discovered to frequent the Negro Dances, to furnish himself for which entertainments he has committed several robberies."[102]

Such activities suggest the presence of a dynamic black culture that emerged in the Bahamas, largely as a result of the influx of large numbers of Black Loyalists from the garrisoned cities of New York, Charleston, Saint Augustine, and Savannah. During the British occupation of New York in particular, Black Loyalists engaged in a variety of social activities, including attending balls and formal events; they also spent leisure time in less formal and more mundane activities in the numerous tipping houses, taverns, and grog shops located throughout the city. Many of these activities reflected the extent to which crosscutting identities were forged by whites and blacks in revolutionary New York. For instance, there is evidence of the growth of "Ethiopian Balls" in which African Americans and British officers and soldiers freely mingled to the music of black fiddlers and banjo players. Even though New York remained a slave-trading center and Black Loyalists lived in segregated barracks, there is ample evidence to suggest that, employed as musicians and entertainers, they engaged and interacted with whites of different classes.[103] Taverns and tipping houses in particular were centers where a diverse multilinguistic Black Loyalist population interacted with poor white New Yorkers who shared a common work environment and similar socioeconomic position.[104] The number of advertisements in the *Royal Gazette* and *Weekly Mercury* noting the abilities of Black Loyalists as fiddlers, violinists, and banjo players suggests a reciprocal process whereby black musicians used their skills to create new spaces in New York City even as they were sought after as entertainers by white British officers.[105]

In the Bahamas, Black Loyalists invariably deployed their diverse skills as entertainers and musicians, though it appears their interactions with leading whites were far more restricted than in New York City. Perhaps owing to the marginalized nature of the Bahamas, or the efforts of white planters to establish viable cotton plantations, racial boundaries in this truncated society became increasingly marked by spatial and physical distances that made interaction between the ruling elites and their social inferiors less likely. Reflective of this cultural divide, elite whites listed grievances associated with black expressive culture, including the public playing of music, dancing, or even congregating in large numbers in public spaces. Among the October 4, 1799, list of grievances presented by the Grand Jury was the particularly offensive "meeting of negroes on the Parade and Places adjacent for their purpose of gambling particularly on the Lord's Day and we recommend that the Peace Officers may be ordered to attend to this part of their duty."[106] The fact that the peace officers were encouraged to "attend to their duty" demonstrates the way such activities were considered subversive to the established social order as envisioned by the agrocommercial oligarchy. Interestingly, within the same list of grievances were other complaints associated with the conduct of free blacks in public spaces. For instance, the Grand Jury listed as a grievance "the mode of keeping private rendezvous at Public Houses by drumming, fiddling," whereby "Negros are enticed to absent themselves from their duty, and contract habits of idleness and tipping."[107] Apart from the general concern with such indecent behavior, this remonstrance provides a glimpse into the popular culture of the urban poor, a public space inhabited by free and enslaved blacks as much as by poor whites. In such public spaces black fiddlers, drummers, and entertainers intermingled with poor whites, many with the same occupations as their laboring black counterparts.[108]

Arguably, both the work and leisure worlds of poor whites and blacks, enslaved and free, intersected in a number of interesting places: on ships, along the newly carved-out streets, in the marketplace, in churches, and most likely in taverns and grog shops. One of the more interesting accounts of cross-racial interactions was published as an editorial in the June 16, 1795, edition of the *Bahama Gazette*. The editor, John Wells, observed that white Methodist preachers in the Bahamas were so prone to "keeping Mulatto mistresses" that the Methodist church might well be called the "spotted church." In a final dismissive remark, the editor lamented that "the practice of Nassau is nearly the reverse of that of Charleston; for instead of men being Pillars of the Meeting here, black and yellow concubines are."[109] Besides revealing the presence of interracial exchanges within early Methodism (a practice that would be discontinued after 1804), the account reflects the dismissive attitude of leading whites toward black, brown, and yellow women who took on leading roles in the church. Such intraracial relations within both religious and secular spaces would be increasingly targeted by white elites who viewed such practices as a public nuisance. The May 6, 1794, edition of the *Bahama Gazette* contains a notice originating from the attorney general's office that speaks to the development of such an artisanal or laboring class culture. According to the notice, "it appears that many of the said nuisances are still continued, particularly the permitting to run at large in and about the public streets, horses," as well as "the continuing of slaughter houses in the town," and the "many unlicensed gambling houses, tipping houses and houses of resort for Negroes and disorderly persons to dance and disturb the public peace at late hours of the night." Though the notice appears to target blacks as a racial group specifically, it does include other disorderly persons, suggesting that poor whites might have been included in the group of unruly city dwellers.[110] More importantly, such evidence suggests that not only did blacks represent entrepreneurs, owning slaughterhouses, taverns, and resorts, but that disorderly persons, including the lowest ranks of white society, met in such establishments.

Suggestive of the crosscutting identities emerging among Nassau's urban poor, elite whites viewed the selling of spirituous liquors to blacks by white shop owners and tavern keepers as offensive to the establishment of good government and a stable social order. Thus, within the same list of grievances, the grand jury presented as "a nuisance, tending greatly to injure the inhabitants of this island, and to the corruption of the Negroes," the conduct of "several retailers of spirituous liquors keeping their shops open on the Lord's Day," resulting in "numbers of Negroes," being "seduced into a state of intoxication and riotous behavior particularly in the Western Suburbs." Significantly, this specific grievance not only reflected white elites' growing concern about the countless number of blacks, free and enslaved, who chose to celebrate and congregate in liquor shops and other public places, but also tied such practices to the profaning of the religious order since such "riotous behavior" occurred on the Lord's Day. Equally important was the fact that the center of this subversive and indecent behavior was the western suburbs—the very community in which Black Loyalists had settled and established churches, schools, and, apparently, liquor shops.

Given the real or imagined threat represented by a cross-racial artisan class against leading whites in Nassau, it seems inevitable that a backlash of regulatory laws bent on curtailing such activities would be promulgated. A 1795 notice in the *Bahama Gazette* hints at the kind of measures that would later be more systematically applied to Nassau's unruly underclass. According to the notice, "all black persons who shall hereafter have dances at their houses, will be taken up and punished for promoting theft, gaming idleness and drunkenness among the negroes." While this portion of the act clearly targeted Black Loyalists and other members of the free black population, the latter portion was intended for the enslaved population. As such, "all slaves who shall be detected at those dances will be severely punished."[111] Clearly these dances were subversive on two counts: they provided spaces for cultural expression that were pejoratively blackened as promoting idleness and theft; second, they allowed enslaved and free, white and black, to mingle in increasingly visible spaces.

Following this notice was the more comprehensive act of 1799 that itemized a bevy of concerns that grew out of the presence of public spaces where cross-racial artisans congregated for meetings of both sacred and secular nature. Published in the *Bahama Gazette* on December 24, the act included the observation that "the number of rogues, vagabonds, beggars and other disorderly persons daily increase . . . to the great scandal, loss and annoyance of the same," with such individuals frequently going "uncorrected and unpunished."[112] The legislators thus concluded that "such idle and disorderly persons should be convicted before a Justice of Peace, based on their confession or that of two witnesses" and "committed to the common gaol for hard labor not exceeding one month."[113]

If that were not enough, the act further stipulated that "all persons not in Holy Orders, but going about as preachers of the gospel under the denomination of Methodists, Anabaptists, Seeders, and others, without being duly licensed or authorized by law will be deemed rogues and vagabonds within the true intent and meaning of this Act." Further attempting to regulate and control the ungovernable in Bahamian society, the act also chose to define all those who "shall for hire gain, or reward, act represent, or perform, or cause to be acted . . . any interlude, tragedy, comedy, opera, farce, play or other entertainment of the stage without license by the Governor as rogues and vagabond, with the same penalty as above applying." Finally, the act stipulated that "all persons playing or betting at unlawful games or plays, and all petty chapmen or peddlers wandering abroad and not being duly licensed or authorized by law," shall likewise "be deemed rogues and vagabonds within the true intent and meaning of this Act."[114] While the portion related to plays and opera attempted, by prohibition, to stamp out the expressive elements of a secular culture that took shape at night in meetinghouses, taverns, and open spaces throughout the city, the latter portion more clearly targeted daytime activities. It was the selling and trading, the peddling and hawking, the marketplace itself that had more visibly come to represent an artisan culture—a way of living independent of white authority. Such institutions and economic activity, from the white agrocommercial oligarchy's perspective, needed to be regulated, if not expunged entirely.

Thus, by the beginning of the nineteenth century it appears that the white agrocommercial oligarchy had firmly established the legal mechanism for creating a more rigidly stratified race and caste system in the Bahamas. Despite these efforts, free blacks, including many Black Loyalists, continued to sell, barter, trade, and work in ways that put them in direct conflict with white elites. In both Nassau and Abaco, the vast majority of blacks demonstrated their preference for living autonomously, outside of relations of dependency on whites. In Nassau in particular, where blacks were forced to work for or among whites, they used a favorable labor environment to negotiate better conditions and decent wages. Such ideas highlight the cultural plasticity of the Black Loyalist experience—one in which labor relations were mutable, often needing to be renegotiated in new colonial spaces where the means of production could oscillate toward more coercive rather than contractual obligations. Emblematic of the adaptability of Black Loyalists to a potentially coercive labor environment was Caesar Brown, who refused to remain quiescent when his employer failed to pay him for his work. Brown was not alone in this respect. Indeed, the collective effort on the part of Black Loyalists to own land, ply their trade, sell their goods, and open shops and stores speaks to the tenacious ways in which they clung to the idea of freedom. As the next chapter will demonstrate, the question of civil liberties and citizenship would be yet another contested issue that would surface as a result of Black Loyalists' quest for freedom in the Bahamas.

5

CODIFYING POWER, CHALLENGING THE LAW

On December 31, 1816, the Bahamian House of Assembly passed an act that attempted to curtail the activities of black itinerant preachers, both Methodist and Baptist. Though the legislators did not admit it, the impetus behind the passing of this act was the news of a slave insurrection in Barbados. White elites, like their counterparts in Jamaica, grew concerned about controlling the free and enslaved blacks who congregated at nocturnal meetings to hear black preachers "profane" the gospel. In light of these disturbing events, Bahamian legislators stated in the preamble the need to prevent

> profanation of Religious Rites and false worshipping of God, under the pretense of preaching and teaching, by illiterate, ignorant, and ill disposed persons; and also for the better regulation of Methodist missionaries and other dissenting preachers, within these islands.[1]

If the preamble did not specifically target black itinerant preachers, the remaining portion clearly was aimed at them. The act further stipulated that no person would be allowed "to preach or teach or offer up public prayers, or sing psalms in any meeting or assembly of Negroes or persons of colour" without an annual license from the governor, "specifying the particular district and place, chapel or chapels, meeting house or meeting houses expressly appropriated for divine worship."[2] In addition to these restrictions, preachers were required to take an oath and enter into a bond of four hundred pounds with two other freeholders in order that "no doctrine or opinion shall be inculcated, preached or circulated by him unfriendly to the system of government established in this Colony, or inconsistent with the duty which slaves owe to their masters."[3] At first glance it might be tempting to read the 1816 Act simply as targeting those considered purveyors of a strange Christian doctrine. However, a closer reading of the intent of the act suggests an effort at greater social control by discouraging unregulated nocturnal assemblies where large numbers of free and enslaved persons gathered for worship. The legislators likely reasoned that these night meetings would contaminate the minds of the oppressed, and perhaps even inspire a revolt of the kind that had enveloped the colony of Saint Domingue two decades earlier.

Trepidation about a Haitian-inspired insurrection was likely more acutely felt by Bahamian legislators in 1816 because of the close proximity of the archipelago. The southern islands of the Bahamian archipelago, particularly the island of Inagua, "though sparsely inhabited at the time, [were] little more than sixty miles distant [from Hispaniola] while the Caicos Islands (then a part of The Bahamas) were not much farther away."[4] Despite its proximity to Saint Domingue and the fear of a contagion of revolutionary ideas spreading to the Bahamas, enslavers in the Bahamas continued to pass punitive legislation bent on curtailing the activities of both free blacks and enslaved persons in the colony. Legislators in the Bahamas could support their actions by pointing to recent upheavals in the pan-Caribbean world that had been inspired by the Haitian Revolution. In nearby Cuba, the 1812 Aponte Rebellion had drawn inspiration from the revolutionary leaders in Haiti, evident in the discovery there of paintings of Toussaint, Henri Christophe and other notable heroes of the Revolution. Despite the haunting images of the Haitian Revolution invoked by Cubans during the Aponte Rebellion, the ruling class resorted to brutal repression in punishing the rebels. In essence, although images of the Revolution served to confirm for Cuban slave owners their deepest apprehensions, these images did not lead them to consider ameliorating working conditions or even abolishing slavery.[5] Likewise, in Richmond, Virginia, slaveholders were convinced that Gabriel Prosser and the other ringleaders of the 1800 plot had conspired with French émigrés arriving from the island of Hispaniola. Here again, slaveholders resisted the opportunity to reform or abolish the institution of slavery, choosing instead wide-scale suppression and execution of the ringleaders. More directly bearing on the minds of Bahamian legislators was the massive, island-wide revolt that erupted in Barbados in 1816. By the time British soldiers had crushed the insurrection, a quarter of the island's sugarcane crop had been destroyed. In the course of the revolt, nearly 1,000 rebels were killed, with an additional 214 executed and 123 transported from the island after the rebellion. These examples suggest a paradoxical process in which distant northern locales in the Atlantic world were more apt to abolish slavery (New England) whereas in places located within the epicenter of revolutionary activity, slaveholders chose to continue to import slaves and pass draconian legislation.[6]

Thus it was no coincidence that Black Loyalist men—educated, politically conscious, and connected with other black religious leaders throughout the black Atlantic—were perceived as unfriendly to the system of established government in the Bahamas. Indeed, by forcing itinerant preachers to apply for a license to preach, the legislators not only curtailed the freedom and activity of the black preachers but also created a legal mechanism to monitor the doctrines expressed at the meetings where enslaved and free blacks undoubtedly met. Moreover, by requiring sectarian preachers to post a substantial bond, the legislators tacitly reduced the number of blacks who could legitimately apply for such licenses.[7] The act further obstructed the activities of black itinerant preachers by stipulating that the preaching license was good only for one year, and subject to renewal on application to the governor. The fact that the renewal was left to the discretionary power of the governor to either accept or reject, speaks to the precarious position of black preachers as a result of this act.[8]

Such legislation reflects the tensions between an enlarged free black population advocating greater inclusion into the body politic, and the small, politically empowered white minority bent on regulating and controlling the black majority. For elite whites, the 1816 Act attempted to address the vexing problem of whether free blacks—among whom a considerable number were holders of certificates of freedom from Lord Dunmore—ought to be considered full members of the body politic. Exacerbating the issue was the work of many white missionaries, some of whom appeared to view free blacks as spiritual equals, and likely social and political equals as well. More troubling to white merchants was the fact that Black Loyalists themselves—despite laws that curtailed their liberties and tended to exclude them as active members of the body politic—continued to engage in activities that suggested they were in fact fully free. Among these activities were bearing witness in civil suits and congregating in public spaces alongside the poorer class of whites. Blacks also deftly and creatively responded to the challenge to white agrocommercial hegemony by establishing self-help organizations and even appealing to the governor for legal redress. Where their political rights were trampled upon, Black Loyalists also sought safety and refuge in the strength of their community institutions, particularly their churches and schools. Thus, like their counterparts throughout the Atlantic world, leading Black Loyalists in the Bahamas often combined the dual role of political and religious leaders. As protopolitical leaders, Black Loyalist evangelicals provided tangible support for their congregants, often witnessing land transactions, funding manumission efforts, and administering wills and testaments in order to safeguard the property of their members.[9] Such leadership reflects not only the politicization of Black Loyalist communities but also the increasingly oppressive and restrictive conditions they faced in the early nineteenth century. Indeed, as a reflection of the growing racial discord, blacks increasingly withdrew from the fellowship of white missionaries, preferring to pastor congregations that were entirely black, and with the kind of autonomy that allowed for an expansion of Afro-Caribbean religious experiences. This shift toward autonomous self-governed religious institutions in the Bahamas paralleled similar processes at work in the larger black Atlantic world, from South Carolina and Georgia to Philadelphia, and as far North as Nova Scotia.[10] Thus black evangelicals in the Bahamas joined a chorus of religious leaders across the black Atlantic in forging religious institutions that heralded a distinctive brand of evangelical religion that was by its very nature politically charged.

This chapter focuses on the ongoing political battles that emerged in the late eighteenth and early nineteenth centuries between Black Loyalists and the white agrocommercial oligarchy. The central argument advanced is that despite gaining freedom from bondage, Black Loyalists faced challenges from a series of legislative acts passed between 1795 and 1817 that ultimately undermined their efforts to enjoy the civil liberties they had anticipated receiving as loyal subjects of the British Empire. It argues that despite the efforts of elite whites to codify power and hierarchical socioeconomic relations, Black Loyalists refused to remain quiescent and submissive. On the contrary, efforts by these elites to deny civil liberties remained a constant source of friction, contested and challenged by Black Loyalist leaders in various public spaces.

By the time the act for controlling sectarian preachers was passed in 1816, the social and political environment of the Bahamas had changed. Particularly important was the emergence of a sizable free black population inclusive of Black Loyalists. Demographically, the population of free blacks had essentially doubled in size within the span of a decade from 1,074 in 1810 to 2,034 by 1822.[11] Concomitant with the rise of a large free black population was the development of a politically astute group of white businessmen and landowners who coalesced to form a singularly powerful, self-serving group of mercantile elite. Thus, the initial tensions between existing inhabitants and newly arrived Loyalists that prevailed in the 1780s was supplanted by the growth of an agrocommercial oligarchy that increasingly dominated the meager export sector of the economy and commercial trade. Elite whites were also engaged politically, holding important offices in the colonial government, as well as seats in the House of Assembly and appointments to the judiciary. Members of both the executive and legislative branches cooperated to protect the fragile agricultural sector, preserve slavery, and place free blacks and persons of color in a subordinate position.[12] Indeed, despite the collapse of the cotton industry by 1810, the mercantile elite remained committed to creating a fixed social and racial hierarchy.[13] As a result, they placed greater emphasis on policing and regulating those interlopers who attempted to make a profit from the meager commercial market in the colony. Indeed, the dominance of the small-scale internal market economy by free blacks, among whom Black Loyalists were counted, invariably put them in direct competition with the enterprising efforts of white elites. Consequently, white elites from the 1790s onward passed a series of laws in an attempt to curtail the movement and activities of a segment of the population they viewed as a threat to the established social order, if not to their entire way of life.

In order to appreciate the ways in which Black Loyalists attempted to gain greater civil liberties, it is necessary to first examine the legal edifice erected to deny them these rights. The first attempt was an act for governing "Negroes, Mulattoes, Muskees and Indians," passed in May 1795. The act curtailed free blacks' trading activities, particularly selling of butchered meat, eggs, spirituous liquor, and dry goods.[14] Six months later, on

December 14, 1795, another act was passed to establish a patrol or night guard under the authority of the vestry or three or more justices of the peace. The rationale for this set of laws was to "prevent all mischief happening by fire, and all murders, burglaries robberies," as well as "breaches of the King's peace, riots, and other outrages and disorders, and tumultuous meetings of negroes and People of Color or other persons."[15] Like the earlier act in May, this legislation specifically targeted free blacks and enslaved persons who apparently were in the habit of holding "tumultuous meetings at night." The act further stipulated that the guards were authorized to "arrest and apprehend in the guard house of the town, any persons found wandering about or misbehaving themselves in the town or suburbs after nine o'clock at night." Assuming the worst of the black population who were given to attending nocturnal meetings, the act pejoratively added that "every person or persons whomsoever committing or aiding or abetting any such murders, burglaries, robberies, breaches of the peace, riots and disorder" shall be "arrested and placed in the common jail or guard house." Such language all but stigmatized and criminalized blacks even if the specific reference to race went unmentioned. If this section did not explicitly link blacks to criminal behavior, it is apparent from the remaining portion of the act that free and enslaved blacks were indeed the targets of this law. The law went on to direct that "all negroes, mulattoes and other people of color who shall be found in the streets, lanes and other places of town after the aforesaid time," without satisfactory "proof or account of themselves, or slaves and other Negroes otherwise without a ticket from their owner or employer may be carried to a magistrate the following morning, to be dealt with according to the law." Thus, authorities could apprehend and detain people for as many as five days in the town guardhouse or jail. More importantly, the far-reaching discretionary power built into this legislation suggests that the government was preoccupied with controlling disorderly subjects deemed incapable of fully participating in the body politic as active citizens. A final section is noteworthy because it allowed persons of color to be armed and to join the night patrol provided they not exceed "two non-commissioned and twelve privates of any company or corps," under the command of a "white constable of good repute."[16] Such provisions reflect an attempt by the legislators to divide the free black community, providing status, rank, and even badges of respectability for those blacks willing to aid in patrolling their own neighborhoods.

Another set of laws was passed on January 22, 1796. The preamble to the law made its intentions clear. It was "an Act for regulating the police of the town of Nassau and the suburbs thereof." However, the specific issue addressed within the act had to do with liquor sales in Nassau. The act proclaimed that all licenses "for selling spirituous liquors shall be granted by a certificate from under the hands of the Church Wardens and a majority of the Vestry of the parish of Christ Church for the time being."[17] The act placed the power to grant liquor licenses in the hands of the established church, making it difficult, if not impossible, for anyone deemed disreputable or disorderly to receive a license. Additional legislation aimed at the growing free black and enslaved population was reflected in the Consolidated Slave Act of 1797. The laws focused mainly on enslaved persons, providing them with the legal framework to cultivate provisional and garden lots around their quarters, as well as some degree of protection from masters by outlawing the use of iron collars and chains. Despite these efforts at reform, the act still maintained that owners could impose corporal punishment on their enslaved.[18] More telling, the largest number of clauses dealt with the problems of controlling the movement of enslaved persons, and the increasing issue of escapees and petit marronage. Yet most significant for this study were clauses meant to divide and rule the black community. For example, enslaved persons who returned escapees were rewarded in the same fashion as free blacks. Additionally, those who served against enslaved rebels were not only paid five pounds for each insurgent killed and ten pounds for each captive, but were also awarded "a blue cloth coat with a red cross on the right shoulder." Such regulations were also applied to free blacks who aligned themselves with enslaved persons. Any free black, mulatto, or Indian who concealed an escapee or forged a ticket of leave was liable to lose his freedom and be transported, in addition to punishments "short of life or limb."[19] In the end, the Consolidation Slave Code of 1797 attempted to demarcate and divide enslaved from free, and those loyal to upholding a slave order from those subversive to that order. Equally important was the policy that gave enslaved and free persons incentives to reinforce the agrocommercial oligarchy's control.

Further efforts at social control were evident in legislation passed at the turn of the century. The 1799 Act mentioned in the previous chapter established a series of laws to prevent the congregating of "rogues, vagabonds," and those deemed "idlers" in the streets of Nassau. The act also lumped together as rogues and vagabonds, dissenting preachers, those prone to performing plays, operas, and comedies, as well as peddlers and sellers. Another law was passed on December 23, 1800, with the vague purpose of preventing "slave assertion." Though the preamble appears ambiguous, the intent of the act was to more effectively police the free black population through a systematic process of registration and identification. Accordingly, "every negro, mulatto, mustee and Indian" was required "to repair to the Office of Police, and enroll their names, ages, and places of abode."[20] The law also specified that inspection by a magistrate would determine whether the individual "was born free or otherwise, of which a certificate, specifying the same," would be issued "to every such free person of color, without any fee charge whatever." However, if such a person were to neglect or refuse to enroll with name, age, place of abode, and birth, he or she would be held in custody until able to pay all legal fees incurred upon arrest. In an effort to provide more accurate statistics and documentation of a group that was increasingly a threat to the established social order, the 1800 Act also mandated that a fit book be kept in the Office of Police in which to record the number of certificates of freedom granted. Though intended to function as a regulatory mechanism, it is significant that the law also stipulated that the fit book be open to the inspection of any person, upon the payment of legal fees to the magistrate of police, and that such a book be considered "good evidence in any court of law in these islands, against any negro, mulatto, mustee or Indian, whose name shall not be enrolled therein in all question where his, or her, or their freedom shall come in contest."[21] The legislation appeared to favor whites for a number of reasons. First, by requiring a payment of legal fees to the magistrate, the legislators reduced the number of blacks that could legitimately afford such a pecuniary investment. Second, in contests where the status of a person of color was questioned by a white, the fit book could be used against the person of color in ways that would jeopardize his or her efforts to achieve freedom. Despite the negative implications of this clause, it is conceivable that the fit book could be utilized by Black Loyalists who were officially registered as a legal mechanism against the encroachment of opportunistic slave-owning whites. As such, blacks could point to registration in the book as proof that they qualified or were "fit" for freedom. Additionally, where the certificate of freedom was lost, the fit book could be used to verify the claim to freedom of a black person. In the end, the dual functions of the fit book clause reflect

the ways in which Black Loyalists operated within an extremely contentious and ambiguous legal space at the turn of the nineteenth century.

Added to the regulatory and legal mechanisms embodied in the 1800
Act, an additional section addressed the vexing issue of escapees and pe-
tite marronage. The act empowered magistrates to respond to reports of
five or more runaways on the island of New Providence by ordering a
"sufficient number of the male free people of color between the ages of
sixteen and sixty years to turn out in search of the said runaway slaves."[22]
This section of the act was intended to function as a way to divide blacks,
separating loyal and duty-bound free blacks who enlisted in a search party
from those who would more readily align themselves with escapees in
deliberately subverting the colonial order. The divisive nature of the remaining portion of the act is borne out by the fact that these recruits were
to be registered on "a correct roll or list of all the said free persons liable
to be employed and alternately summoning them," under the command
of a "fit and proper white person." For further encouragement and induce-
ment to betray black neighbors harboring escapees, the 1800 Act mandated that free blacks be paid out of the treasury "such sums of money as
his Excellency the Governor by and with advice of His majesty's council
shall deem adequate and proper."[23] Further inducements included arms
and the authority to fire upon any runaway if attacked. Significantly, in
the event that these armed black recruits were to injure or cause death to
an escapee, they could invoke this particular clause in their defense, as
justifiable evidence. Such legal machinations speak to the ways white legislators set dangerous rebels apart, while simultaneously deploying loyal
blacks as part of the policing mechanism of the state. It is ironic and char-
acteristic of the internal contradictions of a slaveholding legal system that
if black recruits refused "the summons to search for runaways they would
be imprisoned at the discretion of the magistrate to the gaol for any time
not exceeding twenty days and liable to pay all legal fees."[24]

A final segment of the 1800 Act made it mandatory for those free blacks
with certificates issued by the Office of Police to wear "a silver medal of the
size of a dollar, on which shall be engraved in legible character the initial
letters of the name of such free person of color, with the number of his or
her certificate," and with the word "free" inscribed on it.[25] Additionally,
such medals were required to be exposed for public view and worn at all
times in order to distinguish these persons from the enslaved population.
In the event that free persons of color were found in public without such

a medallion, any white person could apprehend the violators and secure them in the jail until "they shall provide such medal, and pay all legal fees upon such commitment."[26] Clearly, the burden of proof in this instance fell on family members and kin who undoubtedly were forced to produce the required medal as well as pay the necessary legal fees in order to secure the release of their relative from jail. Interestingly, in a separate piece of legislation, enslaved persons working or hiring out their labor in the urban streets of Nassau were now required to wear a bronze medal, in recognition of their servile status in the colony.[27]

The regulatory mechanisms behind the 1800 Act may have been influenced by events occurring directly to the south of the archipelago where the Haitian Revolution had the impact of spreading fear throughout slaveholding societies in the Atlantic world. This fear, verging on paranoia, was only exacerbated by reports from Saint Domingue of the slaughter of thousands of whites at La Cap, the most populated city in the French colony.[28] Just as traumatic, though, was the report of thousands of émigrés forced onto ships and exiled from Saint Domingue as a consequence of the destruction at La Cap. Conservative estimates suggest that upward of 10,000 émigrés fled La Cap, many destined for the United States, although a sizable number migrated to Cuba, Louisiana, and other locations throughout the Atlantic World.[29] Elites in the Bahamas surmised that because of the archipelago's close proximity to La Cap and the obvious sea routes that would take U.S.-bound ships through Bahamian waters, a flood of refugees was poised to engulf the struggling colony. Against this backdrop, Bahamian legislators ostensibly passed the 1800 Act as a way to ensure the continuation of slavery while also attempting to buffer the Bahamas against unregulated refugees who were likely to spread the contagion of revolutionary activities among the existing enslaved and free populations. Overall, the 1800 Act served two purposes: first, it provided a comprehensive method by which white legislators attempted to regulate and make conspicuous the previously invisible social networks that already existed among free blacks. Second, it implemented a more rigorous form of social control through the time-tested method of dividing and conquering the group in question.

Subsequent legislation passed in the early nineteenth century echoed a familiar refrain whereby local legislators were preoccupied with both regulating and demarcating free persons from those deemed enslaved. Additionally, with the increasing size and complexity of the black population

within the Bahamas, the agrocommercial oligarchy was fearful of the potentially subversive activity that might occur in places where Liberated
Africans, West Indian troops, Black Loyalists, and other free and enslaved
blacks might congregate. These fears appear to have been behind the 1816
Act that authorized the governor to order out patrols of the colored militia
in Nassau on Sundays, because it had "of late been a common practice for
white persons as well as free people of colour, free blacks and slaves, to
meet and assemble together upon the public grounds and other places in
and about the town and suburbs." The purpose of these meetings according to the report was "for playing at ball and other sports and pastimes,
thereby profaning the Sabbath or Lord's Day."[30] Where such activities no
doubt represented elements of a polyglot African-derived culture, among
white elites, such practices were viewed as disorderly, profane, and subversive to the order of a slaveholding society. Ultimately, it was these kinds
of activities that led to the 1816 Act for controlling and regulating sectarian
preachers as well as the ancillary Police Act of 1817. Indeed, the Police Act
passed on January 1, 1817, specifically forbade any religious meetings between 6 p.m. and 6 a.m. In effect, this act made it impossible for enslaved
or free blacks to meet for religious services except on Sunday—the one
day they were given relief from their work.[31] This act remained in force
until March 5, 1821. In more general terms, these legislative acts, passed
between 1795 and 1817, reflect a comprehensive effort of white Bahamian
elites to systematically deny blacks—of various social statuses—the rights
for which they had fought during the American Revolution. Such legal
mechanisms would reverberate among black communities in Nassau and
Abaco in ways that would have lasting repercussions on the future of their
quest for freedom in the Bahamas.

The foreclosure of religious tolerance in the Bahamas was echoed
across the Atlantic world. Indeed, by the last decade of the eighteenth
century there had emerged in the Atlantic world a shift from interracial
church alliances to segregated institutions. Such shifts in religious and racial sentiments required leading black churchmen to adopt new strategies
to deal with the changing world that confronted them.[32] In the Bahamas,
Black Loyalist preachers, like their counterparts throughout the Atlantic
world, shifted their political strategies, developing more self-reliant and
autonomous religious structures while also continuing to fight the government and white officials bent on restricting their activities. The black
church, as an autonomous institution led by self-assertive and politically

empowered black men, became a politicized venue in which congregants found not only faith, hope, and love, but also refuge from a racially hostile world. Put another way, the churches founded by Prince Williams, Joseph Paul, and Frank Spence in the Bahamas became a political space in which a collective consciousness was forged in response to violent persecution.

In order to effectively understand the extent to which the black church served as an agent of political mobilization for Black Loyalists in the Bahamas, it is first necessary to expand our understanding of politics itself. This is necessary given the fact that Black Loyalists in the Bahamas and elsewhere throughout the Atlantic world rarely, if ever, cast a ballot, sat in the House of Assembly, or held an appointment on the executive council.[33] Nevertheless, in the case of Bahamian Black Loyalists, much of the political activity that an outsider would have considered simply an expression of a peculiar form of religious revivalism was in fact a powerful symbol of resistance. Parallel to the experiences of Black Loyalists in Jamaica and Nova Scotia, Black Loyalists in the Bahamas found in their churches a place of communion where the spiritual and the secular converged. Put another way, black churches offered "post-slavery communities unique opportunities for self-governance, mutual assistance, leadership development and education."[34] Equally important, black churches in the Bahamas, as elsewhere in the Atlantic basin, generated competing understandings of black displacement, enslavement, racism, and emancipation, shaped by their differing theological, class, and gender perspectives.[35] In essence, black churches, founded by Black Loyalists in the Bahamas, emerged in the late eighteenth and early nineteenth centuries as a primary venue for black political organization, cultural expression, and race consciousness.[36]

One form of Black Loyalist activism was their effort to defend and represent church members on issues related to civil liberties. Given that many congregants were illiterate or nominally educated, Black Loyalist church leaders, as the most educated members of their communities, often represented their members in litigations related to property transfer or administration of wills. The extent to which leading male Black Loyalists functioned as administrators of the wills of their fellow congregants is shown by a number of cases. On October 4, 1799, Prince Williams placed a notice in the *Bahama Gazette* for "all persons having demands against the estate of Amos Williams, a free man of color, late of this island, deceased." The notice also requested that all persons with such demands were to deliver them to the subscriber, in this case Prince Williams, who requested immediate payment of any debts due the same.[37] The fact that Prince Williams functioned as the administrator of Amos Williams' will underscores an important connection: both men had played leading roles in the establishment of a Baptist congregation in New Providence, with Amos most likely the initial founder, but with Prince Williams and Sambo Scriven taking more prominent roles after 1800. It may have been because of Amos' failing health and ultimate death in October 1799 that Sambo Scriven was appointed as preacher and Prince as his assistant. Notwithstanding these changes in the leadership of Bethel Baptist Church, Amos and Prince clearly had forged a close relationship as leading figures in the local Baptist movement. By signing on as the administrator of this will, Prince ensured that any earthly possessions his friend had held, and all outstanding debts owed to him, would be managed and secured for Amos' relatives in the future.

For Prince and other Black Loyalists, ensuring that land, estates, and property remained in the hands of members of their community was a tremendously important political act, particularly in a slaveholding society in which racial prejudice remained deeply entrenched. Such concerns were likely the reason Samuel Lambert, a free black man, appointed Joseph L. Paul, the son of Joseph Paul Sr. as administrator of his 1809 last will and estate notice.[38] In the case of Samuel Minors, it appears that his wife Judy Minors posted a notice stating, "all persons having demands against the estate of Samuel Minors, late of the island of New Providence, free black man, deceased, are desired to render in the same property attested." Like the notice posted by Prince Williams for Amos, Judy Minors as the administrator encouraged "those anywise indebted to the said estate, to make payments" directly to her.[39] Though interesting parallels exist between the ways in which Prince Williams, Joseph Paul Jr., and Judy Minors functioned as administrators for deceased free blacks who owned property, the latter case highlights a gendered element of Black Loyalist actions. Evidently Judy Minors operated in a space most often dominated by black or white men. Yet, as a free black and educated woman, Judy Minors moved outside the usual domestic sphere in order to become the administrator of her late husband's estate, even asserting that financial transactions and debt payments were to be handled by her.

It is tempting to see the actions of Prince Williams, Judy Minors, and Joseph Paul Jr. as simple, mundane, and uncalculated transactions related to property rights common throughout the late-eighteenth-century Anglo-American world. However, the right of these Black Loyalists and former convicts to pass on inheritance including property and privilege like that of any freeborn English person reinforced a sense of pride and significant achievement.[40] For Black Loyalists dispersed around the globe, owning property and bequeathing it to relatives provided a tangible expression of their legal status as free English subjects; thus, the mundane legal transfer of property in the Bahamian context takes on greater significance. Black Loyalists in the Bahamas reinforced their sense of being free imperial subjects when they defended their right to bequeath property with clear title to their descendants.

Apart from administering wills, Black Loyalists in the Bahamas petitioned the government, ecclesiastical authorities, and even white elites in ways that reflected their political activism. Notwithstanding the restrictive measures embodied in the 1816 anti-sectarian act, and the subsequent Police Act of 1817, Anthony Wallace and the Black Loyalist James Jones, along with thirteen other petitioners, organized politically in order to challenge the offensive legislation.[41] Such political maneuvers speak to the ways in which Black Loyalists, as leading members of the free black community, continued to offer a dissenting voice to those attempting to circumscribe their full participation in civil society. In fact, the petition expressed both their disappointment in recent legislation as well as the relevance of an African-derived evangelical experience imparted by black preachers:

we may say Both Body and soul Deprived of such means that is our Night Meeting[,] wich stiks us to the very quick. for this reason we trust when this coms to your deare hands and [is] look[ed] into . . . [you] May be able[,] and I trust will[,] make a way for us. We are stoped for no cause whatever. We are thankfull to our preachers[.] they take Evry measure to bring souls to God. No comp[laint] is among us for this reason[.] we can't see how this cause should be put upon by men of the world. once we were in Greate darkness[.] thanks be to God[,] deare Fathers in London[,] for this light and Liberty of the Gospel[.] We wish to worship God in spirit and in truth[.] this is our Aim[,] and by so doing[,] deare Fathers who stand for the cause we beg your a sistence in the name of our Lord God Almighty . . . dear fathers don't forget us in N. Providence[.]

this from the hands of our brothers and sister leaders of Coular in this place[.] Many of them in years [past] pray[ed] for Methodists to be Established hear[.] We know the Lord he[ars] prayer that [we] can say. from one to seven we put our hands to our hearts to this [to ask you] to relieve us our distress [which we] lay under . . . [and] to keep us or our ways from bad men.[42]

A close analysis of the petition reveals that the petitioners felt the injustice of an act that obstructed their meetings for "no cause whatever." The petition also demonstrates the ways in which the appropriation of Christian theology provided this "light and liberty of the Gospel." Equally telling is the fact that as politically informed members of a church body, these petitioners marshaled the Crown to intervene on their behalf. Such appeals were in fact tailored to a humanitarian and ameliorationist audience in England in ways that would elicit a favorable opinion from metropolitan politicians.

The petition is also remarkable for underscoring gendered elements in Black Loyalist thinking in the Bahamas. Notably, all fifteen of the petitioners were men. Nevertheless, in spite of the absence of a single female petitioner, subtle references are made to the kinds of roles women played in the Methodist congregations in the Bahamas. Accordingly, the petitioners reminded their listening audience not to "forget us in N. Providence," from the hands of "our brothers and sister leaders of coular in this place."[43] The inclusion of women of color as leaders suggests that within the supposedly invisible institution of the black church, women played a central role. Arguably, an ambiguous duality emerged: black women could sing, dance, chant, and teach within an "invisible" informal church, but in the public arena where a virulent battle between leading whites and blacks was being fought, women were consigned to a private, supportive, yet ultimately silent role.[44]

The petition offered by these fifteen men also reflects the global dimension of the struggle for freedom in which Black Loyalists throughout the Atlantic world were engaged. Apart from the fact that the petition was clearly intended for a white audience of abolitionist or humanitarian inclination, it was also apparently circulated among both white and black sectarian evangelicals within the colony and beyond. In a journal entry dated January 17, 1817, William Dowson noted in relation to the passing of the recent acts that Brother Rutledge, a white missionary stationed in

Nassau, along with a Mr. Wilson, "wrote a joint letter to the committee (most likely in England)." Other letters from white members of the
Methodist society were also written to England, including one "by Mr.
Butterworth and another to Thomas Thompson, Esq. M.P. for Hull." Remarkably, attached to this remonstrance is the notation that the "black
leaders have written one to Mr. James Wood, London."[45] Though an exact connection between this reference and the petition cannot be made,
there is compelling evidence to suggest they are one and the same. First,
Dowson mentioned the correspondence immediately following his journal entry regarding the offensive acts. Second, the date of Dowson's entry
occurred within three weeks of the passage of the act. Finally, as a white
Methodist missionary in the Bahamas, Dowson was referring to black
leaders in Nassau who wrote to London. This fact considerably narrows
the potential authorship of the correspondence. Thus, it appears likely
that this petition was circulated as part of a larger group of documents
destined for London.

Arguably, reading this petition in concert with others authored by
Black Loyalists throughout the Atlantic world underscores the view that
the movement of these ideas unequivocally shaped the emergence of an
outer-national black consciousness.[46] This was particularly evident in
the work of John Marrant and George Liele, two Black Loyalist writers
who circulated their ideas for attracting a larger black Atlantic audience.
Writing from Kingston, Liele had his 1796 covenant document printed
and circulated by John Rippon, a prominent Baptist stationed in London,
England. Despite its conciliatory tone, the document had a pragmatic and
subversive element, affording enslaved persons in Jamaica access to evangelical religion provided they had written proof of their master's permission to attend. Through Rippon's *Baptist Annual Register*, the covenant
became widely circulated and was adopted as an article of faith by black
evangelicals throughout the Atlantic.[47] Liele also had his letters printed
and distributed in ways that spoke to a political awakening within the
black Atlantic.[48] Simply put, black thinkers and writers, including Loyalists, not only maintained important social networks that spanned the
Atlantic littoral, but also, in their documents, articulated political ideas
that moved beyond colonial boundaries.

In the Bahamas, apart from the 1816 petition, other Black Loyalists defended their civil liberties whenever white authorities challenged
them. Particularly germane is the petition written on behalf of the Baptist

congregation by Prince Williams, dated January 1826 and addressed to the governor of the colony, William Munnings. The circumstance surrounding the petition was the governor's recent revocation of Williams' license to preach. Indeed, according to correspondence preceding the petition, Governor Munnings had learned from the elders of the congregation that "the conduct of the said Prince Williams has been of a highly immoral and improper nature reflecting disgrace upon his character and calling." As a consequence of Prince Williams' conduct, Munnings "thought it fit to revoke, ban and conceal" his license.[49]

Williams' response offers a fascinating glimpse into the rhetorical strategies deployed by Black Loyalists in order to defend their right to preach, work, and live freely. The first part of the petition establishes the fact that Williams had long been a leading member of the Baptist society. He in fact alludes to the role he played in securing the property in the southern part of Delancey Town in 1801, on which to erect a church building. Moreover, Williams notes that he remained a faithful member, appointed by the congregation to assist Sambo Scriven as preacher until 1812, when he married Peggy Wilson.[50] According to Williams' narrative, it was the "ungovernable temper" of his wife that forced him to remove himself from the society to Harbour Island for a "temporary ease of mind." Williams remained in Harbour Island until 1819, when "he received a letter from his aforesaid wife." Though the details of the letter were apparently "annexed," they were not included in the Colonial Office Records.

While Williams' explanation for his separation from his wife is important for understanding domestic conflicts within Black Loyalist families, it also informed his broader defense against allegations of moral misconduct brought by the governor and some dissenting church members. According to Williams, after 1819 he received many pressing invitations to return to Nassau in order that he might prevent "the flock from going astray."[51] One of his additional reasons for returning to Nassau was that Sambo Scriven was gravely ill and near death. Such factors certainly motivated Williams to return to Nassau. Yet Williams observed that those among "the flock that would later secede (amounting to between twenty and thirty persons) wrote many of the invitations for him to return to Nassau."[52] Such comments by Williams reveal that the contentious issues he would ultimately face in Nassau were initiated from within the congregation. It was in fact the death of Sambo Scriven in 1820 that brought the charges of immorality and misconduct to the forefront of a public debate.

Figure 7. Old Bethel Baptist Church. Possibly the earliest photograph of the original edifice. The building has since undergone a number of extensions. By permission of Pastor Timothy Stewart, Bethel Baptist, Nassau, Bahamas.

According to Prince Williams, upon Sambo Scriven's death, the congregation sought to provide a proper burial by utilizing the funds of the society "amounting to forty dollars and 3/8."[53] However, Williams argued that "Archy Parker and certain seceders" had clandestinely taken this "sum along with many other articles belonging to the society at large." As a result of the actions of this dissenting group, Williams was forced to raise the necessary funds for Scriven's funeral by "applying to the individuals of his congregation for the means necessary for the performing of the funeral services of said deceased Scriven which they readily granted."

From this narrative, it is clear that Williams' initial conflict with his congregation centered on the appropriation of funds established by the trustees and elders of the church. Where Williams saw fit to use the funds to provide an adequate funeral service for Scriven, the dissenting group felt that such funds should not be used in that manner. These concerns brought to the forefront the thorny issue of who controlled the finances of the church and to what extent the preacher had authority to raise funds from congregants independent of the elders. Apart from the issue of appropriating funds, the elders increasingly challenged Williams in regard to the unusual arrangements he had with his wife. Williams noted that upon his return from Harbour Island, and "wishing to gratify the Society by a reunion with his wife—he authorized the elders to propose it to her—which they did several times ineffectually."[54] Not to be outdone by the efforts of the elders, Williams also sent, of his own volition, Andrew Frazier, a free man of color, to see if he could effect the same object, with similar results. At this point, with little or no hope of reconciliation, Williams' marriage appears to have become a burden—and perhaps even an embarrassing spectacle. This, of course, was played out in a racially hostile environment in which dissenting preachers and sectarians were already perceived as immoral practitioners of strange doctrines. Moreover, the elders may have felt additional external pressure, given that the licensing of itinerant preachers was still controlled and determined by the governor. It was likely under such mounting pressure and concerns that Williams caustically remarked that he was "directed by your Excellency to attend with his said wife before the Rev'd Mr. Hesworth to see if he could affect [sic] reconciliation between the two parties." Even though Williams no doubt was frustrated at having to air his private matters before an Anglican clergyman, he nevertheless noted with pride that the "Rev'd gentleman discharged the parties observing the said Peggy Williams, that the fault was entirely her own."[55] Yet despite the assertion that his wife was at fault, Williams' problems were far from over. Without a wife to perform her traditional domestic duties, Williams "applied to the elders and the society to allow him to have a housekeeper which under the above mentioned circumstances they gave their sanction to."[56]

The general argument constructed in the petition of Prince Williams thus achieved two goals. It declared Williams innocent of immoral activity based on the notion that he had, first, followed the legitimate legal avenues for redress and had acted according to, and within, the legal framework normally afforded to free subjects in the Imperial system of governance. In addition to upholding the customs and practices established by British common law, Williams argued that he had cooperated with the elders, the governor, and even Reverend Hesworth in order to resolve his embarrassing personal situation legitimately. Equally important for validating his actions was his argument that in looking for a housekeeper to fill the vacuum left by his wife's absence, he had gained the sanction of the elders. In essence, his first line of reasoning against the accusations of immorality and impropriety was to frame his petition as an argument of legitimation—sanctioned by common law, custom, government, and religious officials. It is significant that Williams' appeal to legitimacy was not unusual for a black writer working within the black Atlantic world. Indeed, Thomas Peters, David George, and other Black Loyalists dispersed throughout the Atlantic often crafted their petitions by appealing to white humanitarians who sympathized with their sense of being legitimate subjects of the Empire—governed by the same laws, constitutions, and Crown that all freeborn Englishmen enjoyed.[57]

Williams' second line of reasoning was to cast blame on the conduct of the elders and those dissenting members who apparently took issue with his actions. In this respect, Williams argued that the only reason the elders took issue with him was that they no longer had the "same influence over the funds of the society as they had" under Sambo Scriven.[58] Williams, in fact, charged that these men, acting in their own interest, had usurped control of the church's finances under his predecessor and appropriated funds in ways they saw fit. It was thus his opinion that the only reason this dissenting group had seceded from the Baptist congregation was that Williams had managed to wrest control of the church's finances from them, putting management of the funds and collections back into the hands of the majority of the congregants. In addition to casting blame on the elders and dissenting members for misappropriating funds, Williams clearly saw his wife as solely to blame for his predicament. In this vein, Williams noted that he had attached a copy of a letter written by his wife that represented "a fair specimen" of the "ungovernable temper" that had driven him to separate from her.[59]

Though casting blame and legitimating his actions formed the two pillars of his argument, Williams also provided more tangible proof that his work with the church had met with approbation by the majority of the congregation. He noted that ever since he had taken charge of the society in 1822, his congregation had grown steadily to three hundred and fifty souls, all of whom were entirely satisfied with his performance. In defending his role as the leader of the congregation, Williams alluded to the fact that he had not broken any colonial law that he was aware of. More importantly, he highlighted the potential impact that the revocation of his license would have on his congregation. As Williams argued, the vast majority of the congregants who supported his leadership "did not have the means of going to law to compel the parties to deliver up the possession of the meeting house and lots" that had apparently been taken possession of by the elders and dissenting members in collaboration with the governor.[60] By emphasizing the impact that such a decision would have on the majority of his congregants, Williams rhetorically positioned himself as the defender of the rights of those dispossessed, enslaved, or otherwise un-free church members who undoubtedly could not make claims to property or estates contested by the dissenting eldership. Moreover, such a discursive strategy effectively aligned Williams with the majority of the congregation who supported his position, thus casting the elders as the disruptive minority. Wary of the power and position the governor wielded in a slaveholding society, Williams' posturing reflects a sense of deference toward the intended reader, particularly in his expression that "your Excellency taking his case into consideration as well as that of those of 350 individuals alluded to."[61]

Despite the language of deference, Williams' petition nevertheless represents a powerful and collective expression of resistance. This is substantiated by the remaining portion of the petition in which Williams explicitly indicted the governor for being "instrumental in dispossessing them of the same by delivering up the key to those who had the right to it." Williams further argued the complicity of the governor in trampling the rights of his congregation when he noted that "your honor still retains possession of the key of the aforesaid meeting house," and he therefore requested "that your honor will be pleased to direct the same to be delivered up to your petitioners for and on account of so great a majority of the members of the Baptist Society."[62] In essence, Williams argued that the land, building, and keys were not only unjustly taken away, but that it was the natural right of the congregation to have such possessions returned to them. In the end, Williams' petition reflects a careful blend of ideas: a concern for duty, honor, and deference as a loyal subject to the crown; but also a more radical sense of the idea that liberty and property rights are inalienable privileges accorded to both black and white Englishmen. Equally important was the collective nature of the claim. Indeed, Williams' petition was in fact signed and marked by 424 individuals, most likely free and enslaved blacks, living in the polyglot community of Delancey Town.[63] In boldly signing the petition, the vast majority of congregants and free citizens of Delancey Town not only showed their support for their maligned leader, but also demonstrated their claim to land, a building, and ultimately liberty.

What was the long-term impact of Williams' petition? Evidently, the impasse between the preacher, the trustees, and the governor lasted long enough and with sufficient ill will that Williams decided to move his members to a new location where he could establish himself as the unquestioned leader of the church. As a powerful act of defiance and resistance, Williams chose as his new location a piece of property on Meeting Street, located across from Bethel Baptist, and most importantly, servicing the same community of Delancey Town. Williams and his followers named their new congregation St. John's Native Baptist church. At the same time, the remaining congregation at Bethel appointed Sharper Morris as pastor.[64]

Apart from the petition of Prince Williams, other documents suggest that Black Loyalists were at the forefront of a struggle for freedom from bondage and for greater civil liberties. Arguably, Black Loyalist thinking in the Bahamas combined Afro-Christian principles with the radical abolitionism that was gaining currency throughout the Atlantic world. Emblematic of this emancipatory message was a notice in the *Bahama Gazette* dated March 29, 1792, in which the writer, identified as John Baptist, argued that the "nine new negroes, found by him starving on Romano Cay, and supposed to have been landed from a French Guinea man," had since been "seized along with the boat in which they arrived by Harry Webb, Esq. and His Majesty's Attorney, Advocate, and Solicitor General." The rationale for such seizure, according to the writer, was simply that these persons were considered "goods, wares and merchandise, imported contrary to the Free Port Act and other British statutes."[65]

Like Prince Williams and Anthony Wallace, "John Baptist" articulated the legal issues surrounding the "cargo" in question. Moreover, it is most likely that the writer used the nomenclature "John the Baptist" as a way of hiding his true identity in order to avoid facing reprisals for openly expressing such progressive views in a politically hostile environment. If not explicit in his earlier comments, Baptist made it clear in the latter portion of his notice that he opposed the seizure of these persons based on abolitionist principles. Accordingly, he noted with outrage that "the absurdity of considering Human Creatures snatched from the jaws of death, as contraband goods, is so apparent, that he need not caution the public against purchasing any of the said Negroes."[66] While it is difficult to determine the actual identity of "John Baptist," the nomenclature itself suggests that it may have been one of the leading black Baptists. In this light, Frank Spence, the leader of Saint John the Baptist Church, or even Amos Williams or Prince Williams might have been the author of the letter. In any event, the defense of these enslaved blacks as "Human Creatures," rather than merely as chattel, speaks to a progressive, if not humanitarian sentiment.

Black Loyalists in the Bahamas also provided invaluable support of self-liberation on the part of enslaved individuals seeking freedom from bondage. One of the most singular and unique cases of self-liberation is the letter of Caesar Brown.[67] One of the few surviving documents written by an enslaved person, Brown's letter, in fact, was addressed to the daughter of his former owner in order to request he be granted freedom, or otherwise be allowed to purchase it through a reduced manumission rate. Reflective of the agency and volition of enslaved persons seeking freedom, Caesar argued that "I beg you so far to indulge me as to lower the price at which I am valued and I will try to purchase my own freedom, with the assistance of some friends in this place."[68] Although Caesar Brown never mentions the friends willing to assist him, we can speculate that Caesar gained support for his efforts at manumission from members of the Black Loyalist community.

In fact, a number of documents show that Black Loyalists helped to manumit enslaved persons. In particular, Anthony Wallace's last will and testament is remarkable for the list of enslaved persons he wished to have manumitted through his estate and real property. In his will, Anthony Wallace declared that "after payment of all my debt and financial expenses . . . the remaining 'purchase money' [should] go towards the manumissions of the said Alexander and Alick." Apart from Alexander and Alick, Anthony Wallace allocated funds for the manumission of a "negro girl slave named Sarah formerly the property of a certain Mary Neglam." Wallace also provided "the funds for the purchase" or to "obtain manumission of Elizabeth Blatch from attorneys or owners."[69] In total, by his will alone dated December 9, 1830, Anthony Wallace managed to manumit four enslaved persons. This intentional act appears significant in light of the fact that by 1830, slavery in the British Caribbean had come under attack by a number of forces both within and outside the region. Indeed, in addition to British abolitionists based in the metropole who railed against slavery, in the colonies enslaved and free blacks had earnestly sought freedom from the shackles of slavery. Anthony Wallace's effort to manumit enslaved persons came almost exactly a year before the Christmas Day revolt in Jamaica, led by Sam Sharpe, a deacon in the black Baptist congregation on that island; and within the same period of time (1829–1830) when Pompey, an enslaved person working on Lord Rolle's plantation in Exuma, spearheaded the most famous insurrection in the Bahamas.[70] Arguably, the activities of Anthony Wallace, along with the enslaved insurgents mentioned above, reflect the way black abolitionism played a central, but often ignored role, in pushing the issue of slavery from simply a concern for amelioration or reform to its most radical end—the complete and immediate abolition of slavery throughout the empire.

In addition to arguing for manumission and writing petitions, Black Loyalist communities at the beginning of the nineteenth century continued to provide protection and refuge for escapees seeking freedom in the urban environment of Nassau. Most notable in the escapee advertisements listed in the *Bahama Gazette* were references to Negro Town as well as to the role that the Baptist church appeared to play in harboring runaways. It was to Negro Town in 1800 that the black man Cesar, formerly the property of Lord Dunmore (and therefore likely regarding himself as free), was thought to have fled from his new master, Edward Shearman, no doubt to be harbored by free blacks living in the community.[71] Much later, and more directly implicating black sectarians in harboring escapees, was the advertisement in 1821 for the enslaved Boatswain and his family (owned by William Wylly), who sought sanctuary with the black Baptist preachers who dominated the area. Similar to Boatswain, a short elderly man well known about the town by the name of James, along with his wife, Venus, and their daughters Hannah and Eve, absconded from Nathaniel M'Queen in March 1818. Three months later they were still at large, although it was convincingly reported that "James is connected with Black Preachers and is supposed to be harbored by them."[72] Most significant in these cases is the fact that many of the escapees included entire families who sought protection within an established community of free blacks. Equally revealing is the fact that the subscribers of the advertisements, and most likely the escapees themselves, saw in the Baptist church and the actions of their preachers a locus of slave resistance, a place to symbolically, and perhaps literally, loosen their chains.[73]

If blacks increasingly viewed the Baptist church as a site of resistance, whites became increasingly more critical of the practice of black preachers.

Indeed, despite the fact that by 1822, the colonial government had repealed the offensive 1816 legislation related to licensing requirements for sectarian preachers, the government and leading whites continued to view black preachers and their followers with contempt. Put another way, the decision to repeal the 1816 Act was not elite liberalism. Instead, the government opted to support the expansion of missionary activity by white missionaries aligned either with the established church or with Methodism. This unofficial policy allowed for de facto racial discrimination to exist in the Bahamas, while disabling Black Loyalist preachers from challenging the system. This new political order was evident from the correspondence between Governor Lewis Grant and Lord Goderich. According to Governor Grant, there were, apart from the white Methodist missionaries, three licensed "Anabaptists and Baptist" preachers in New Providence. Grant added, "they are black men, and their Hearers comport themselves in a very creditable manner when attending worship"; however, Grant further argued that

> It nevertheless, if it can be temperately effected, would be desirable that the last description of persons were brought on a different footing and embodied into either the Established Church or the Wesleyan Mission. But though this may be kept in view, it is too soon, perhaps, at present to take any immediate steps regarding it. I mean any steps savouring of compulsion because I think it possible to bring it about otherwise by degrees.[74]

From Grant's account it appears that not only was the established church preferred as the agency to Christianize the enslaved and free blacks, but that increasingly the Methodist church was also gaining respectability with the ruling class. Conversely, only a few of the black Baptists were tolerated, and they were always kept under tight scrutiny. Attempts to extend the influence of the Anglican church and to establish it as an official agent for the Christianization of enslaved and free blacks were evident when in 1827 the rector of Christ Church, William Strachan, was appointed to the Executive Council of the Anglican Church in the Bahamas. In that same year, St. Paul's, which had been started by Joseph Paul, was made an official chapel of the Church of England, and its black preacher granted an annual allowance.[75] Such concessions invariably reflected on the one hand a political strategy whereby leading whites and colonial officials attempted to divide the black community by offering respectable blacks positions of power. Yet these concessions came at a price. Respectable and striving blacks would be forced to assimilate, acculturate, and mimic the behavior and practices of whites in order to receive such benefits. On the other hand, black preachers and their fellow congregants who followed the path of resistance and nonconformity would continue to be ostracized and discursively stigmatized as strange and profane. In all likelihood the choice was not easy. Still, the majority of blacks cast their lot with the invisible institution: the expressive and popular forms of religious experience grounded in religious revivalism and West African worldviews.

The conflicted world of visible and invisible, between those deemed respectable and those of ill repute, was pointedly expressed by members of the House of Assembly. In a letter printed in the *Bahama Argus,* the legislators not only lamented the dangerous consequence that would result if more Baptist preachers were given official sanction in the colony, but also revealed a predictable lack of sensitivity to black worship and ritual. The Assemblymen revealed their overwhelming hostility toward Bahamian black Baptists when they remarked,

> A quick and apt sense of the ludicrous, and of its concomitant combinations, are the leading features of the mind in a state of ignorance . . . more particularly so of that of the Bahamas Negro; and although temporary fear of censure may induce a degree of demure decorum among them, yet there would be a proportionate want of real reverence for what they will deem a "John Canoe" exhibition. That there will be an abundance of followers we admit; but their worshipping would be more in conformity with the noisy rites of Bacchus, than with the sober doctrines of the Christian faith.[76]

Evidently, the writers of the article drew upon a longstanding tradition of demarcating the practices of African descended people as simply barbaric, profane, or "ludicrous" expressions of individuals whose minds were still in a state of ignorance. In contrast to the noisy rites of Bacchus that were prevalent in these "disorderly" meetings, the writers presented the rituals of the established church as reflecting the sober and staid doctrines of the Christian faith. Despite the clear racial and class assumptions explicit in these remarks, the authors, perhaps unwittingly, highlighted a number of ways in which African-derived customs were central to black community identity and religious practices. Most interesting is the mention of "John Canoe," a cultural practice that emerged during this period in which enslaved and free blacks collectively celebrated their release from work requirements at Christmas time by beating drums, dancing, and masquerading around town. More broadly, the authors hint at an ecstatic, emotive religious and cultural experience that was far removed from the formulaic, orderly, and sober church services in which the Anglican and white congregations participated. Arguably, and until more sources become available, it would seem that the former practices were adopted and appropriated by Black Loyalists, Liberated Africans, and other free black populations in ways that expressed a commitment to another kind of political order, one squarely rooted in Afro-Caribbean cultural practices away from the unequal relations of power with whites.

Indeed, by the 1820s and just before the abolition of slavery in the Bahamas, free blacks constituted themselves into segregated communities. In 1825, Liberated Africans and other members of the free black population in New Providence established Grants Town as a black community just south of the town of Nassau, an action most likely driven by blacks seeking more lucrative employment in domestic work or trade in Nassau. Invariably, personal connections between Liberated Africans, Black Loyalists, and other existing black populations occurred in this nascent black suburb. As an African suburb, Grants Town was essentially a squatter community until formal arrangements were made in May 1825, when Charles Poiter, the collector of customs, purchased four hundred acres of land at that site. Liberated Africans could then purchase quarter-acre lots at a rate of ten shillings per lot, or two pounds per acre. Liberated Africans dominated Grants Town, and substantial evidence indicates a great deal of intermingling across various African ethnic lines.[77] Grants Town was hardly the only cross-racial African community that emerged in these years. Besides the older Delancey Town, settled largely by Black Loyalists, Bain Town on the south side of Meeting Street and to the west of Blue Hill Street also emerged as a locus of black intraracial activity by the late 1830s.[78]

The efforts of Black Loyalists to advance claims to greater political inclusion in the body politic met with challenging, even formidable obstacles. This is evident in the efforts of the agrocommercial oligarchy to pass a series of laws geared toward circumscribing the liberties of Black Loyalists at the turn of the nineteenth century. When faced with restrictive legislation, Black Loyalists were in the forefront of a movement by free blacks to have such offensive laws repealed. In addition to writing petitions, Black

Loyalists also advanced the cause of freedom and greater political liberties by supporting self-liberation efforts through the process of manumission. Additionally, acting as administrators, leading Black Loyalists provided much needed assistance for illiterate blacks seeking a degree of freedom through landownership and estate transfers. Of equal significance is the fact that the churches established by Black Loyalist preachers became important centers for black political consciousness. Church leaders not only established autonomous religious institutions but also composed the vanguard in the fight for civil liberties, including access to property and other privileges normally available to free subjects of the British Empire. Refusing to give up their right to preach and teach, Black Loyalist preachers continued to uphold the invisible institution, even in the face of virulent attacks and pejorative ridicule. Such political actions underscore the fact that Black Loyalists not only thought and acted politically, but they did so even while living in a society increasingly hostile to their goals.

CONCLUSION

In 1833, one year before slavery was officially abolished in the Bahamas, Prince Williams once again found himself entangled in a battle over control of his church. Unlike the 1826 contest, this time external forces initiated the controversy: the Baptist Missionary Society (BMS), located in London, sent white Baptist missionaries to the Bahamas. Upon arrival in 1833, these white missionaries attempted to influence and control both Bethel Baptist and its sister congregation, Saint John's Native Baptist. Bethel, under the leadership of the Black Loyalist Sharper Morris, accepted the British white missionaries as leaders and actually proposed that BMS ministers take over the administrative and pastoral duties of the church. On December 13th, 1834, the Committee of the Baptist Missionary Society of London became associated trustees of Bethel. Prince Williams chose a different path. Offended by their demands to take over as trustees of his church, Williams in a bold move broke away from the BMS, forming the St. John's Particular Church of Native Baptists Society.[1]

Williams' decision to reject the controlling influence of the British Baptists had important implications. As in his earlier petition to the governor, Williams showed a determined effort to maintain his church as an autonomous and independent institution. In taking such a stance, Williams also advanced a momentous political position in which black institutions, particularly churches, would be led by black preachers, constituted of black congregants, and based on a form of worship squarely rooted in revivalist religious experience. By rejecting the trusteeship of

Figure 8. New Bethel Baptist Church. The oldest Baptist church in the Bahamas proudly displays the date of its foundation, circa 1791. Photo by the University of The Bahamas student Clethra Dean.

the BMS, Williams and his congregation entered the era of formal freedom proudly committed to resisting the controlling influences of white missionary supervision.[2]

Equally salient, though less self-evident, is the way in which Williams' actions echoed the black politics emerging throughout the Atlantic world during this period. In Nova Scotia, John Marrant combined an evangelical Calvinism, made popular by George Whitefield, with a republican ideology that perceived Black Loyalists as a covenanted people.[3] Yet for Marrant and other free blacks, this Zionist impulse was born out of the gradual disenchantment with liberty—a realization that such ideals could not protect blacks from scorn, poverty, and degradation. Recognizing that liberty itself was, at best, a civil status requiring continual defense, black evangelicals such as Marrant increasingly urged their followers to secure freedom and liberty through spiritual transformation and regeneration along with a commitment to ritual, if not physical, return to Africa.[4]

Likewise, the Baptist preacher and Black Loyalist David George would also echo Marrant's sentiments in Nova Scotia. Tired of the continual harassment by white settlers who felt threatened by his popularity with both blacks and whites, George took on an increasingly political role, eventually moving toward the kind of African Zionist impulse that informed Marrant's decision to reject relations with the Anglo-American world. Eventually, George would be numbered among the 1,190 Black Loyalists who would resettle in Sierra Leone by 1792.[5] Though not driven so much by a Zionist impulse, similar efforts to mold unique African churches and institutions occurred in Rhode Island, Boston, and Philadelphia. Most telling is the fact that in each instance, these black founders—men such as Prince Hall, Richard Allen, and Absalom Jones—established churches based on notions of Africanness and African identities.[6]

Where do Prince Williams and other Black Loyalist institution builders in the Bahamas fit within this black founding tradition? Williams, for one, clearly understood the tactical and strategic importance of creating a separate black church. In this regard, appellation became significant. In breaking away and forming his own society of Baptists, Williams established a new name and identity: St. John's Particular Church of Native Baptists Society. Though lacking a specific referent to "Africa" as was the case with Allen, Hall, and Marrant, Williams nevertheless invoked a "native" and "particular" society that delineated a group that would be different from white religious institutions. Equally telling was the fact that Frank Spence, another leading black Baptist and Loyalist, crafted a similar nomenclature for his society, calling it "John the Baptist Christ Church."[7] Were such expressions and the invocation of John the Baptist simply a case of coincidence? Perhaps we can speculate that such naming reflected the centrality of baptism for a religious movement that continued to reflect the primacy of ecstatic experiences, emotive forms of worship, and a corporate sense of religiosity rooted in communal celebrations. Such social practices suggest that while white elites attempted to compel conformity to what they considered acceptable and respectable religious practices, the majority of blacks in the Bahamas continued to engage in alternative religious expressions.[8]

Yet even as Black Loyalists such as Frank Spence and Prince Williams demonstrated an oppositional stance in leading their congregations to secede, others such as Joseph Paul and Sharper Morris chose an accommodationist stance. How do we explain these differences? The actions of Morris and Paul serve to remind us how important it is for scholars of the African Diaspora to avoid essentializing their subjects as a singular or monolithic community of Africans or African Americans. Likewise, notions of identity and racial consciousness need to move beyond nationalist narratives that present blacks as objects fixed in time and without a sense of the dynamism and complexity of their lived experiences.[9] In the case of Black Loyalists in the Bahamas it is important to conceptualize these communities not as static and immutable settlements, but rather as dynamic, multilayered societies in which members often adopted varying strategies for dealing with inequality. For Paul and Sharper Morris, accommodation provided a vehicle for achieving greater respectability and acceptance by the white community. Leading whites proved equal to the task in their willingness to grant concessions and privileges to the few "loyal" and "trustworthy" blacks and free persons of color. Such concessions nevertheless came at a price for these Black Loyalists, providing them social advancement, but also requiring them to adopt and mimic Euro-American religious expressions, and in the case of Sharper Morris, actually yielding administrative control of his church to whites. Paul's accommodationist stance was demonstrated not only in his shift to Anglicanism, but also in the rewards that came with his association with Dr. Bray's Associates School.[10] In time, Paul was elevated to the lofty status of principal and teacher, and his building would eventually become a separate parish church where respectable striving blacks could worship.[11]

The political strategies of Paul and Morris, juxtaposed against those of Frank Spence and Prince Williams, express the polycultural features of Bahamian society that had emerged by the 1830s. Blacks—free and enslaved—maintained two related yet distinguishable lifestyles: one based on interactions with whites, often negotiated unequally through coercion or co-optation, and reflecting accommodationist tactics. The other, displayed beyond the gaze of the host society, expressed a rich clustering of African-descended people whose various identities were refracted through the emergence of a creolized revivalist Christianity. In Nassau and its outlying suburbs settled by Black Loyalists, Liberated Africans, and existing free black populations, two streams of African-based Christianity developed. One stream moved toward accommodation and acceptance by white society, while the other—the invisible institution—remained more African and community-based.

The development of a distinctly Afro-Caribbean religious experience was due in part to the efforts of Black Loyalist itinerant preachers. Not only did Black Loyalists establish the first lasting footholds for sectarians in the Bahamas, but also, by the third decade of the nineteenth century they had begun to advance independent missions to the Family Islands.

Such activities had serious political implications as they often undermined the government and the efforts of the official established church
to create a more orderly and "churched" society through the missionary
efforts of whites. Often the work of black itinerants was ridiculed and
mocked by white missionaries. For example, when Prince Williams sent
one of his own Native Baptists to the mission field in the Out Islands, Mr.
Winder, a white missionary, wrote to the governor:

> James Burns was sent by Prince Williams to rebaptize into the Bap-
> tist society, followers of John the Baptist, whom they believe were
> equal to if not greater than Jesus Christ, persons who have already
> been baptized by the established church. Burns was paid three shil-
> lings and six pence for this.[12]

Winder also argued that the BMS missionaries had frequently complained
about these men and asked the governor to use his authority to suppress
their meetings and their "sitting up all night."[13] Such views underscore
the ways itinerant black preachers continued to be discursively projected
by their contemporaries as profaners of the gospel, ignorant men, held
in suspicion by those who were far more educated and therefore legitimate purveyors of the gospel. Despite these pejorative narratives, the fact
remains that Black Loyalists continued to spread sectarian Christianity
throughout the Bahamas.

Even as Black Loyalists were identified as important institution builders, by the 1830s there had been sufficient intermixing among existing free
blacks, Liberated Africans, and members of the West Indian regiment that
the very notion of being a loyal black had likely been supplanted by new
ethnic or racial affinities. Arguably, the black urban landscape of Nassau reflected a polyglot community comprising Liberated Africans, the
majority of whom were ethnically identified as Yorubas or Congos; West
Indian soldiers, mostly creoles arriving from Barbados or Antigua; and
an existing free black population that was, as a result of unusually high
natural birth rates in the Bahamas, essentially a creolized population by
the time slavery was abolished in 1834. Significantly, in comparing Liberated Africans in Trinidad and the Bahamas, it has been determined that
in the former case, as in Cuba, the absence of extensive Christian missionary work, and the relative remoteness of many of the communities,
inevitably led to the proliferation of West African–derived religious sects,
particularly Santeria and Orisha cults associated with the Yorubas. Yet,

in the Bahamas, despite a heavy Yoruba and Congo influx between 1810 and 1860, a syncretistic revivalist Christianity became the more dominant expression of religiosity for the majority of blacks.[14] While recently it has been suggested that the development of Afro-Christian practices in the Bahamas was due to the more deliberate and systematic efforts of sectarian missionaries to convert enslaved and free blacks to their various denominations, a more explicit connection to the work of Black Loyalists is missing.[15] But the evidence elaborated in this study demonstrates that Black Loyalists were instrumental in the establishment of vigorous self-reliant social structures and sacred institutions as well as the development of a distinctly African-based form of religious expression. Over time, such religious expressions were transmitted to large numbers of enslaved and free blacks in ways that would indelibly impact the internal dynamics and development of a unique Afro-Bahamian society.

Beyond the religious realm, Black Loyalists in both Abaco and New Providence made significant contributions to the development of Bahamian society. Their desire to defend freedom in Dunmore's Negro Courts reflects a kind of political consciousness in which Black Loyalists were increasingly aware of their rights as subject-citizens of the British Empire. Though imbued with a sense of their legitimate rights as British subjects, Black Loyalists nevertheless did not espouse a coherent black republican ideology. Their struggle for freedom was deeply personal and individualized. This motivation, however, should not be interpreted as a lack of political acumen or awareness. Indeed, in many respects the hostility toward black claimants reflects the ways Dunmore's Negro Courts functioned as a highly politicized theatre in which the hidden transcript became public and personal liberty was contested, challenged, and sometimes constrained by black and white Loyalists alike.

Black Loyalists acted politically in other ways, particularly when the courts failed to provide a favorable ruling, or where their claims were either ignored or the arm of the law failed to extend to their jurisdiction. Escaping from slaveholders, squatting on unclaimed land, participating in the local market economy, and deploying various strategies for survival suggest that Black Loyalists were keen to create a life of their own outside relations of dependency with whites. When all else failed, Black Loyalists resorted to outright rebellion. This was certainly the case in Abaco where, in late 1787, Black Loyalists took up arms and defended their right to freedom. Though small in scale, the incident is still worthy of the attention of scholars given the cause for which the insurgents fought and the long-term repercussions of this event on race relations in the Bahamas. Lord Dunmore certainly recognized the severity of the revolt, acting quickly to establish a special tribunal of his Negro Court in Abaco by May of 1788. The fact that only one out of thirty claimants received a favorable ruling reflects the ways in which justice was ultimately denied for Black Loyalists pursuing freedom in Abaco. The combined force of Dunmore's ruling and the continued economic imperatives of their white Loyalist counterparts undermined their claims to freedom. In reality, despite Dunmore's claim that his actions in Abaco had made the island permanently peaceful, not only were plantations never successfully established on the island, but the conflict initiated during this period would also establish a permanent racial divide.

In fact, well into the twentieth century the racial divide continued to exist, with many of the offshore cays—including Elbow Cay, Guana Cay, Man-O-War Cay, and Cherokee—constituted as all-white settlements. In these communities where the labor of blacks was still needed, Afro-Bahamians were forced to leave the island before sunset, in order to comply with the rigid racial policies of these all-white communities.[16] Other cays were established as biracially bifurcated communities where the descendants of white Loyalists tended to occupy the best land, and a strict adherence to racial divisions was manifested in both social distancing and the spatial separation of black and white homes. Examples of such communities include Green Turtle Cay, located almost directly across from the original settlement of Carleton, and the mainland settlement of Marsh Harbour.[17] Recent studies conducted by sociologists and anthropologists have found that such racial divisions are still imprinted in these small settlements in Abaco.[18] In a study of the biracial community on Green Turtle Cay in 1972, it was found that a number of forces—including the relative physical isolation, residential segregation, segregated work schedules, recreational segregation, and social distance—have kept the two ethnic groups apart. Within the social distance framework, the preference for socializing within one's own ethnic group was noted. As a result, on Green Turtle Cay, differences in culture are maintained or even created by and derived from differences in resources, personal association, and shared ideas.[19] Even the Loyalist Memorial Garden erected by the whites in 1983 (as part of the bicentennial celebration of the Loyalists' arrival), symbolizes the community's racial segregation with its central icon a heroic white

Loyalist woman waving the union flag and a loyal female enslaved person a "suitable" step or two behind.[20] The image is a powerful reminder of the erasure of the Black Loyalist presence in Abaco and the racial divisions that remain largely in place throughout the Abacos.

More broadly, such iconographic representations demonstrate the ways in which Black Loyalists remain hidden in Bahamian historiography in spite of the crucial role they played in the development of self-reliant communities and political ideas related to abolition during an era of enslavement. Though Bahamian scholars have rightly addressed the significant contributions made by white Loyalists to the development of the Bahamas, such master narratives overlook two important elements of the Black Loyalist story. First, Black Loyalists experienced tremendous violence, both personally and collectively, at the hands of whites. Black Loyalists in fact were the victims of coercive and exploitative labor arrangements, particularly where whites in possession of blacks attempted to exert a form of apprenticeship or absolute bondage over individuals who were rightfully and legitimately free. Such stories bring into relief the profound inequalities and racial antagonism that existed in a non-plantation society that was, nevertheless, built on the Western and Anglo-American legal edifice of racial slavery.

Second, apart from blurring the real inequalities that existed between blacks and whites in the Bahamas, the master narrative also conceals the manifold ways in which Black Loyalists acted as subjects, making contributions to Bahamian society even while challenging the claims of those bent on re-enslaving them. If Black Loyalists were subjects in their own right, we ought to be careful not to fall into the same trap as the hagiographers of white Loyalist history. Black Loyalist communities were dynamic and fluid, composed of real men and women who often quarreled with each other over land, space, religious views, and political strategies. Highlighting intraracial contests and conflict as much as alliances speaks to an effort to recover the voices of Black Loyalists, their interiority and subjectivity, rather than projecting a flat and fixed representation. Yet understanding the differences within Black Loyalist communities does not deny the existence of a collective consciousness, a consciousness based on the desire for freedom from bondage forged in the fulcrum of the American Revolution. Later these ideas were transferred to the Bahamas where Black Loyalists continued their struggle for freedom: fighting for personal liberty, demanding access to land, and establishing important social institutions. As agents of change, Black Loyalists in the Bahamas also found creative and novel ways to practice their politics: in courts, in pubs, in the marketplace, and even in their churches. In the end, Black Loyalists were thought of as objects ready for exploitation by whites, but in myriad political acts, blacks proved they were subjects who could think, act, and react to the changing contours of the spaces they inhabited. Their story is worth telling as it is situated within the larger panorama of the Age of Revolutions and Humanitarianism. Their contribution lay in their herculean efforts to secure freedom through a variety of actions— in courts, in sacred spaces they founded, and in wooded areas in Abaco where they took up arms in order to extend the liberty denied to them.

NOTES

Introduction

1. Bahamas Register Office, N, 219–221 quoted in Peters, "American Loyalists," 121–122.

2. Jasanoff, "The Other Side," 208.

3. Herbert Aptheker was the first to argue that the American Revolution represented a powerful epoch of slave revolt; *American Negro Slave Revolt.*

4. Quarles, *The Negro,* vii.

5. Pulis, *Black Loyalists,* xiv.

6. Carole Troxler discusses the debate between Walker and Cahill, noting that it has been a useful exchange for clarifying the term "Black Loyalist." She also notes that most Black Loyalists, particularly in the Southern theater of war, would have initially been enslaved fugitives drawn to the promises of freedom declared in various proclamations issued by British officials. Other scholars such as Sharma and Pybus refer to their protagonists as "escaped slaves," "runaway slaves," and "black refugees." However, as Walker and others have pointed out, once behind British lines, black fugitives qualified for the distinctive appellation by their direct military service rendered to the British military during the war (as was the case for white Loyalists), or through compliance with the terms of the various proclamations; Troxler, "Re-enslavement," 72–73.

7. Cahill, "Black Loyalist Myth," 79.

8. See Cahill, "Black Loyalist Myth," 77; Walker, "History and Revisionism," 88.

9. Walker, "History and Revisionism," 89.

10. Walker, "History and Revisionism," 89. Carole Troxler makes a similar distinction, noting that "throughout the Southern Campaign, there had been efforts—both by British officials and by white Loyalists—to distinguish between Black Loyalists and 'sequestered Negroes.'" According to Troxler, "the latter were enslaved persons who had been confiscated as the property of prominent revolutionaries. 'Sequestered Negroes' could be

purchased and sold or taken away. Black Loyalists, by contrast, were free, under the provisions of proclamations of freedom for all black persons who went into the British lines of occupation and provided their services as laborers or soldiers;" "Re-enslavement," 73.

11. Wylly, *A Short Account*, 7. Prince Williams is a classic example of a Black Loyalist who was redefined by enslavers in the Bahamas as a "runaway" in an advertisement posted in the *Bahama Gazette*, July 23, 1785.

12. Governor Thomas Shirley reported in 1772 that Nassau, New Providence, had 1,024 whites and 1,800 "reputed blacks," Harbour Island had 410 whites and 90 blacks; Eleuthera had 509 whites and 237 blacks. Exuma, a scarcely settled island, had 6 whites and 24 blacks. Whittington Johnson thus concludes that in the immediate pre-Loyalist era, blacks constituted a small majority on New Providence and were significantly outnumbered on the two other major islands, Eleuthera and Harbour Island. Thomas Shirley, COP 23/22/59, cited by Whittington Johnson, *Race Relations*, xvii. For a broad overview of the emergence of free black communities in the British Caribbean, see Sio, "Marginality," 166–182. Some of the exclusionary measures passed by the House of Assembly in The Bahamas included an act in 1799 that classified "Methodist, Anabaptist and Seceder [probably referring to sectarians in general] ministers as Rogues and Vagabonds" and required them to have a license to preach. Though the language did not target a specific ethnic group, most unlicensed Baptist and Methodist itinerant preachers were in fact free blacks. This was reinforced in 1804 when a Negro man "Simon Whitehead" was "taken up as a preacher" according to an advertisement in the *Royal Gazette* of October 29th, 1805. See Canzoneri, "Early History," 14.

13. One of the prize-winning monographs that explores the transnational repercussions of the American Revolution is Christopher Brown's *Moral Capital*. Of particular importance is chapter 5, where he argues that Black Loyalists in distant locales throughout the Atlantic world deployed an abolitionist argument in ways that reflected their collective and personal self-identification as free subject-citizens; *Moral Capital*, 284, 294.

14. The surrender of Nassau, New Providence by the Spanish is noted in a letter by Elizabeth Brown-Maunsell, dated April 29, 1783. Brown Family Correspondence and Miscellaneous Items, 1 box, New York Historical Society. For attacks by Spanish and Patriot forces see Peters, "The Plantation Period," 18–19.

15. Report of John Wilson, Saint Augustine Historical Society.

16. Pulis notes that the Revolution represents not simply a military campaign, but a war of words. As such, the term "loyalist" was used in a discursive arena—a war of proclamations, declarations, and oaths—and it was not uncommon for families to be divided over the issue of identity and affiliation; *Black Loyalists*, xiii.

17. R. Scott, *Degrees of Freedom*, 6.

18. Berlin, *Many Thousands Gone*, 17. It is worth noting that Berlin's usage of the term refers to what he calls the charter generation of Africans who operated in the netherworld between the African and European continents. I have adopted the term for Black Loyalists operating in the late-eighteenth-century Atlantic world.

19. Gilroy, *The Black Atlantic*, 4, 17.

20. Maya Jasanoff in her footnotes indicates a total of 30,000 Loyalists settled in the Maritime provinces in Canada, including 3,000 blacks; 6,000 in Quebec; 5,000 in East

Florida; 3,000 in Jamaica; 1,000 in the Bahamas; 7,000 in Great Britain; to these numbers must be added 5,000 to 7,000 Black Loyalists not included in these tallies. John Pulis has estimated that the number of Black Loyalists entering Jamaica amounted to 200 in addition to some 5,000 slaves and 65,000 blacks seized as contraband. Mary Beth Norton estimates roughly 1,200 free blacks were in London by 1786, though these figures include those freed based on the Somerset case of 1772. See Pulis, *Black Loyalists*, xx; Jasanoff, "The Other Side," 208; Norton, "Fate of Some Black Loyalists," 406.

21. Though the British had established their presence in the Caribbean in St. Kitts in 1624, Nevis in 1628, and Montserrat and Antigua in the 1630s, it was in Barbados, settled in 1627, and Jamaica, in 1655, that sugar plantations were most successful. See Gomez, *Reversing Sail*, 84–85.

22. Gomez, *Reversing Sail*, 85.

23. Engerman and Higman, "Demographic Structure," 48.

24. Michael Craton and Gail Saunders note that in the mid to late seventeenth century in particular, there was a blurring of class, and even racial lines, through familiarity and interdependence; *Islanders in the Stream*, I: 90–91.

25. Craton and Saunders, *Islanders in the Stream*, I: 136.

26. Despite efforts to establish cotton plantations, by 1810 the Bahamas represented a decayed plantation system. Brown's comments may well have reflected the initial optimism that the Bahamas could be transformed into a thriving plantation. Bahamas Register Office, N, 219–221 quoted in Peters, "Plantation Period," 121–122.

27. Governor Dunmore to Lord Sydney, Nassau, New Providence, November 28, 1787, COP 23/27.

28. Wylly included a petition written by white Abaconians in which they claimed Captain Mackay had misled their slaves by telling them to leave their plantations and travel to Nassau where they would be declared free. See Wylly, *Short Account,* 40; Richard Pearis to William Coleman, May 8, 1788, COP 23/29.

29. John Tattnall was the Surveyor-General. See Lord Dunmore to Lord Sydney, December 20, 1787, COP 23/27.

30. Dodge, *Abaco*, 7–9.

31. Copy of Letter written to Lieutenant Wilson, acting Engineer at Saint Augustine, ordering him to the Bahamas, from Guy Carleton, New York, July 14, 1783. BHP, Box 34, #8431. A similar report by a German traveler in 1788 described Abaco as "fertile," with the potential for its residents to do well "once they have gone through with the hardships exacted in clearing and preparing wild land." Schoepf, *Travels,* II: 259

32. Craton and Saunders, *Islanders in the Stream*, I: 101.

33. Schoepf, *Travels,* II: 263.

34. Craton and Saunders, *Islanders in the Stream*, I: 172.

35. Pascoe, *Two Hundred Years*, I: 221; Craton, "Loyalists Mainly to Themselves," 44.

36. Graham Russell Hodges notes that the "war experience taught them powers of self reliance, inculcated survival skills and imbued them with a deep desire for republican liberty;" *Black Loyalist Directory*, xv. Also Pulis, *Black Loyalists*, xx–xxi.

37. E. Williams, *Capitalism and Slavery*, ix; Mintz, *Caribbean Transformations*, 9; Shepherd, *Slavery without Sugar*, 1.

38. Tannenbaum, *Slave and Citizen*, 91.

39. Critics of Tannenbaum are numerous. Early scholars such as Eugene Genovese focused on material conditions rather than the law as a major factor in shaping the relative severity of a slave system. Others such as anthropologist Marvin Harris asserted that demographic factors and local conditions were more important, noting the gender imbalance in Iberian colonies leading to population increase mainly through miscegenation with enslaved and indigenous populations; *Patterns of Race in the Americas*. Other scholars have pointed to harsh conditions that existed across much of the Americas and how legal authority emanating from a remote imperial or metropolitan center rarely actually impacted the daily lives of enslaved persons in the colonies. See for example Degler, *Neither White Nor Black*, 41–47. Recent work by Jane Landers, Herman Bennett, Michelle McKinnley, and Alejandro de la Fuente have underscored the importance of revisiting Tannenbaum's work but without accepting his flawed judgments regarding the relatively benign form of slavery in Latin America that produced a postemancipation racial democracy. These scholars attempt to look at how enslaved and free persons of color utilized courts of law and the church to forge personal lives, advance individual liberties, and create crosscutting community identities. Bennett, *Colonial Blackness*; Landers, *Black Society*; McKinley, "Fractional Freedoms"; Fuente, "Slave Law and Claims-Making."

40. Christopher Schmidt-Nowara has recently used Berlin's original formulation of Atlantic Creoles to suggest that the concept of an overlapping, interconnected, and fluid Atlantic world in motion is a more fruitful way of analyzing the relative severity of slavery across the Americas; "Still Continents," 378.

41. Landers, *Black Society in Spanish Florida*, 2.

42. Whittington Johnson mentions Betty Watkins and Timothy Cox as two free blacks who were also slave owners; *Race Relations*, 30–31.

43. Saillant, "Antiguan Methodism," 96.

44. Prince Williams' advertisement posted in the *Bahama Gazette*, July 23, 1785. Wallace may have been the owner of up to six enslaved persons. Will of Anthony Wallace, dated December 9, 1830; Supreme Court Wills, W–Y, Department of Archives, Nassau, Bahamas.

45. It is important to note that while Black Loyalists in the Bahamas left far fewer written testimonies or memoirs compared with their counterparts in other locales in the Atlantic world, their political mobilization can still be excavated from the historical record through a reading of other kinds of documentary evidence, especially wills and testaments, ship registers, and newspaper advertisements. Beyond utilizing different kinds of evidence, I have made an effort to reread traditional sources against the grain of conventional scholarship. Scholars have sometimes been hesitant to use documents written by white writers as a way to access the voice of the subaltern blacks. However, as recent literary scholarship has demonstrated, there is much value in decoding and deconstructing the language and discursive context of documents written by whites in which blacks are the featured subject. Lois Brown argues that despite the absented subject (blacks), memorializing narratives in obituaries often provide haunting glimpses of individuals who survived the Middle Passage, pined for their African homes and

families, established themselves in new and foreign communities, and in their final hours negotiated the symbolic, religious, and social demands of Anglo-American culture. John Saillant and Joanna Brooks have argued for readers to be alert to the rich intertextuality of the Black Loyalist writings in their collection. As they further note, none of them, not even an apparently straightforward autobiographical narrative, stands independent of its historical context or the beliefs and denominational loyalties of its author. Similarly, Rosalie Murphy Baum suggests that black voices have traditionally been ignored in the canon of Early American literature, despite the existence of numbers of sermons, lecturers and novels. Baum further argues we should broaden our concept of what constitutes canon in order to include a number of different genres of literature produced by blacks. See Lois Brown, "Memorial Narratives," 38; Baum, "Early American Literature," Brooks and Saillant, *Face Zion Forward*, 31.

46. The notion of lived experience is drawn from Herman Bennett's work on Africans in colonial Mexico City; *Africans in Colonial Mexico*, 3.

47. Pybus, *Epic Journeys of Freedom*, xvii.

48. Pybus, *Epic Journeys of Freedom*, 168.

49. Kelley, *Race Rebels,* 4, 7. James Scott discusses how behind the scenes, serfs and slaves will create and defend a social space in which offstage dissent occurs as a hidden transcript. Robin Kelley applies Scott's idea to black resistance, providing a more narrow definition based on racial resistance in the United States; James Scott, *Domination*, xi.

50. William Wylly observed the tendency of Black Loyalists to hide in the huts near the hospital. See Wylly, *Short Account,* 22.

51. Hilary Beckles has argued that slave resistance had long been conceived of as a lower species of political behavior, lacking in ideological cohesion, intellectual quality, and philosophical direction. He contends that current work by Caribbean scholars is now assessing the extent to which the rebellious actions of enslaved persons were informed by ideological choices in the context of maturing political consciousness; "Caribbean Anti-slavery," 869–878. It is argued that as free persons possessing greater cultural plasticity, linguistic dexterity, and adaptability, Black Loyalists would undoubtedly have possessed the mature political consciousness necessary to engage in collective resistance.

52. Shirley, "Migration, Freedom and Enslavement," 10–11.

53. Police Magistrate's Report on trial of Lord Rolle's slaves, May 10, 1830, cited in Cash, Gordon, and Saunders, *Sources of Bahamian History,* 209. Craton contends that the enslaved led by Pompey had an intrinsic ideology grounded in the belief that they deserved the freedom to make a life of their own, to develop their own Afro-Caribbean culture and religion, and, above all, to live as peasant farmers as independently as possible from the plantation system; "We Shall Not Be Moved," 19–35.

54. Governor to Colonial Office, October 1, 1833, cited in Cash, Gordon, and Saunders, *Sources of Bahamian History,* 209.

55. Viewing Black Loyalists within an outer-national framework reflects my engagement with recent historiography in Latin America and the Caribbean, particularly Truett and Young, *Continental Crossroads.*

Chapter 1. Roots and Routes

1. See Prince Williams' claim in the Loyalist Claims Commission, Sept 1, 1783, Great Britain Public Record Office, Audit Office, Class 12, Volume 99, folios 353–354.

2. Prince Williams' claim in the Loyalist Claims Commission, Sept 1, 1783, Great Britain Public Record Office, Audit Office, Class 12, Volume 99, folios 353–354.

3. Symonette and Canzoneri, *Baptists in the Bahamas*, 3.

4. The advertisement further described Prince Williams as "a little bow legged and turns on his great toes, has his Country marks down his face; went away four days ago." The Notice also described Sambo Scriven as "a Negro Man with a long lip and chin and well known as a Baptist Preacher." *Bahama Gazette*, July 23, 1785. The Negro Freedoms Register along with other manumission records have been tabled and conveniently transcribed by Paul Shirley. See Shirley, "Migration, Freedom and Enslavement," 301.

5. Amos Williams was possibly married to Judy Williams. Both noted in Register of Freed Slaves, Department of Archives, Nassau, Bahamas. Cited in Shirley, "Migration, Freedom and Enslavement," 296.

6. Pugh, "Great Awakening," 371.

7. January 2, 1788, under hand by George Barry, Receiver General and Treasurer, John O'Halleran and Thomas Smith, Justices of the Peace, COP 23/29, folio 279.

8. Gilroy, *Black Atlantic*, 16–17.

9. Kramnick, *Republicanism and Bourgeois Radicalism*, 4.

10. Sidbury, *Becoming African in America*, 69–70.

11. Pugh, "Great Awakening," 367.

12. Brooks, "Silver Bluff Church," 173.

13. In his narrative of his conversion, David George noted the influence of a powerful sermon preached by Liele on his decision to be baptized; "Account of the Life," 180.

14. Brooks, "Silver Bluff Church," 173.

15. Interestingly, Henry Sharpe's family attempted to rescind Liele's manumission. Fearful of being returned to bondage, Liele indentured himself to a British army officer who befriended him. Liele would later accompany this officer to Jamaica, where he would eventually free himself from this indenture. See W. Johnson, *Race Relations*, 57.

16. Pugh, "Great Awakening," 371.

17. Pugh, "Great Awakening," 372.

18. James Sidbury notes that preachers from Savannah maintained their connections with one another as they moved out across the Atlantic world. Liele particularly played a pivotal role in fostering these ties, maintaining contact with David George in Canada and Sierra Leone as well as with Andrew Bryan, who remained in Savannah to found the First African Baptist Church of Savannah. Sidbury appears to have been unaware of the significance of the Bahamian Baptist connection through the work of Amos Williams; *Becoming African in America*, 71.

19. The Negro Freedoms Register cited in Shirley, "Migration, Freedom and Enslavement," 295.

20. Craton, "Loyalists Mainly to Themselves," 62.

21. *Book of Negroes*. See also Hodges, *Black Loyalist Directory*, 124; Hodges, *Slavery, Freedom and Culture*, 75.

22. Boston King was recorded as being evacuated onboard *L'Abondance* bound for Port Roseway; Moses Wilkinson onboard *L'Abondance* bound for Port Roseway; Paul onboard *The Nautilus* bound for Abaco on August 21, 1783; and Murphy Steele onboard the *Joseph* bound for Annapolis Royal. *Book of Negroes*.

23. Riley, *Homeward Bound*, 140.

24. W. Johnson, *Race Relations*, 51; see also Craton, "Loyalists Mainly to Themselves," 62.

25. Catron, "Evangelical Networks," 106.

26. Negro Freedoms Register, cited in Shirley, "Migration, Freedom and Enslavement," 306.

27. Catron, "Evangelical Networks," 107–108.

28. Catron, "Evangelical Networks," 80.

29. King, "Memoirs," cited in Brooks and Saillant, *Face Zion Forward*, 105–110; 157–158.

30. For spiritual narratives and their uniform pattern see Brereton, *From Sin to Salvation*.

31. Pybus, *Epic Journeys to Freedom*, 219.

32. May, "John Marrant," 554.

33. May, "John Marrant," 553.

34. May, "John Marrant," 554.

35. Hodges, *Black Itinerants of the Gospel*, 1.

36. Pugh, "Great Awakening," 358.

37. Sobel, *World They Made*, 188.

38. Wigger, "Taking Heaven by Storm," 173.

39. W. Johnson, *Race Relations*, 56.

40. W. Johnson, *Race Relations*, 56.

41. Wigger, "Taking Heaven by Storm," 170.

42. Brooks and Saillant, *Face Zion Forward*, 10.

43. Sobel, *World They Made*, 18.

44. Expressions of West African religiosity that were manifested in Christian beliefs included the ring shout; wakes and funerary practices that celebrated the parting of a loved one for the afterlife; water baptism as it related to general rites of adult initiation; and the shared beliefs in spirit power, its nature, and its possible control. For a discussion of African religious practices see Stuckey, *Slave Culture*; M. Mullin, *Africa in America*; Sobel, *Trabelin' On*; Joyner, *Down by the Riverside*; and Genovese, *Roll Jordon Roll*.

45. George, "Account of the Life," 180.

46. George, "Account of the Life," 180.

47. Marrant, "Narrative," 51.

48. Marrant, "Narrative," 52.

49. Hodges, *Black Loyalist Directory*, xv. For an additional account of Stiel's vision see Hodges, "Liberty and Constraint," 93.

50. Diviners among the Kalabari would often meditate in a trancelike state to provide valuable messages for the living from the dead. See Sobel, *Trabelin' On*, 20, 47.

51. James Piecuch notes that the British were unreliable liberators, often wavering and indecisive regarding the status of blacks and other persons of color who had found their way to British camps during the war; "Three people, one king," 20–21. See also Frey, *Water from the Rock*, 63.

52. Morgan and O'Shaughnessy, "Arming Slaves," 187.

53. Frey, *Water from the Rock*, 63.

54. Lord Dunmore's proclamation, November 7, 1775, cited by Quarles, *Negro in the American Revolution*, 19.

55. Morgan and O'Shaughnessy, "Arming Slaves,"189. Additionally, the authors convincingly argue that Dunmore's policy did not free enslaved persons belonging to Loyalist slave owners and in fact steps were taken to ensure their continued servitude.

56. Frey, *Water from the Rock*, 63.

57. Walker, *Black Loyalists*, 2.

58. Walker, *Black Loyalists*, 2.

59. It is important to note that women were employed in the army in various capacities, most notably as launderers and cooks. David George recalled how his wife used to wash for General Clinton; "Account of the Life," 182.

60. Douglas Egerton notes that although Black Loyalists never cast a ballot, they helped shape the politics of the era through their demands and actions; *Death or Liberty*, 14.

61. Frey, *Water from the Rocks*, 107

62. *Book of Negroes*, cited by Hodges, *Black Loyalist Directory*, xxi.

63. George, "Account of the Life," 182.

64. W. Johnson, *Race Relations*, 57.

65. *Charleston Royal Gazette*, March 9, 1782.

66. L. Harris, *In the Shadow of Slavery*, 55.

67. *Royal Gazette*, September 9, 1778.

68. *Royal Gazette*, July 25, 1778.

69. *Royal Gazette*, December 19, 1781.

70. *Royal Gazette*, February 2, 1779.

71. *Royal Georgia Gazette*, June 6, 1781.

72. Piecuch, *Three Peoples, One King*, 310.

73. Piecuch, *Three Peoples, One King*, 319.

74. Piecuch, *Three Peoples, One King*, 309–310.

75. Hodges, *Slavery, Freedom and Culture*, 68.

76. Hodges, *Roots and Branches*, 147.

77. *Royal Gazette*, October 8, 1783.

78. Pybus, *Epic Journeys to Freedom*, 219.

79. Hodges, *Slavery, Freedom and Culture*, 68.

80. Troxler, "Refuge, Resistance, and Reward," 565.

81. Under Spanish rule escapees were traditionally granted freedom in exchange for allegiance to the Crown and the Catholic faith. The best study on Spanish Florida during the Revolutionary period is Jane Landers, *Black Society in Spanish Florida*. See also Landers, "Black Community and Culture," 117–134.

82. Patrick Tonyn to Germain, St. Augustine, October 18, 1776. COP 5/557.

83. University of Florida Special Collections Library, Census Records 1784–1814, East Florida papers, microfilm reel 148, list of Negroes with Certificates of Freedom.

84. Proceedings and other records of the Board of Police, 1780–1782, July 11, 1780; July 14, 1780, South Carolina State Archives, Columbia.

85. Buskirk, *Generous Enemies*, 7.

86. Buskirk, *Generous Enemies*, 136.

87. *Royal Gazette*, August 23, 1780.

88. Petition, Dinah Archery, August 8, 1783, Henry Clinton papers, Clements Library, cited by Buskirk, *Generous Enemies*, 141.

89. Orders establishing Board of Commissioners for superintending Embarkations, April 15, 1783, *Book of Negroes*, 2.

90. Minutes of the Board of Commissioners for superintending Embarkations held on May 30, 1783, *Book of Negroes*, 2.

91. E. Wilson, *Loyal Blacks*, 68.

92. Minutes of the Board of Commissioners for superintending Embarkations held on August 2, 1783, *Book of Negroes*, 11–12.

93. Minutes of the Board of Commissioners for superintending Embarkations held on August 2, 1783, *Book of Negroes*, 10–11.

94. Marcelle Wilson argues that women and ethnic minorities used courts and other means to achieve their goals outside of their gender-assigned spheres. Yet of the 35 Black Loyalists who filed claims, not a single black woman is listed; "Loyalists," 13, 70–74.

95. Report of Lieutenant John Wilson with instructions from Robert Morse, dated July 14, 1783, Box 5, file 4, Saint Augustine Historical Society, St. Augustine, FL.

96. Craton, *History of the Bahamas*, 11.

97. Michael Craton and Gail Saunders note that Hispaniola, the largest and richest of the Greater Antilles, was far more attractive than the Bahamas to the Spanish *conquistadores; Islanders in the Stream*, I: 51.

98. Michael Craton and Gail Saunders note that Ponce de León observed on traveling through the Bahamas in 1513 that the islands were completely empty of people; *Islanders in the Stream*, I: 55.

99. For general work on the Eleutheran Adventurers and their Bermudan origins see Henry C. Wilkinson, *Adventurers of Bermuda*, 246–280. For their settlement experience in the Bahamas, see Craton, *History of the Bahamas;* Albury, *Story of the Bahamas*; Riley, *Homeward Bound*.

100. Craton and Saunders note that Sayle would eventually serve a third term as governor of Bermuda; *Islanders in the Stream*, I: 78.

101. Craton and Saunders argue that the grant establishing Proprietary Government in the Bahamas on November 1, 1670, echoed that for Carolina, particularly in its impractical combination of feudal and liberal ideas. This plan they speculate was conceived by John Locke, at the time the personal secretary to Lord Ashley, the chief Lord Proprietor; *Islanders in the Stream*, I: 92.

102. John Darrell, Calendar of State Papers, Vol. 7 (1669–1674) cited by Craton and Saunders, *Islanders in the Stream*, I: 79.

103. In *A short account of the Bahama Islands*, John Graves highlighted not only the strategic importance of the Bahamas but also the importance of protecting the salt pans in Exuma that supplied Atlantic seaports in Jamaica, the Carolinas, and Nova Scotia. John Graves, *A memorial: Or, a short account of the Bahama Islands* . . . (London, 1707), 3–4, Gale Eighteenth Century Collections Online, http://galenet.galegroup.com.ezproxy .lib.uconn.edu/servlet/ECCO (accessed January 12, 2010).

104. John Darrell, Calendar of State Papers, Vol. 7 (1669–1674), cited by Craton and Saunders, *Islanders in the Stream,* I: 79.

105. Fort Nassau was built under the governorship of Nicholas Trott (1694–1696). Apart from building the fort, he laid out plans for the town and renamed the city Nassau, after William of Orange. See Craton and Saunders, *Islanders in the Stream,* I: 101.

106. Craton and Saunders, *Islanders in the Stream* I: 80.

107. Craton and Saunders, *Islanders in the Stream,* I: 108.

108. Craton and Saunders, *Islanders in the Stream,* I: 104.

109. According to John Oldmixon's account, during Governor Trott's rule (1695), "there was established a church in Nassau." However, this church was quickly destroyed by the Spanish in 1703; *History of the Isle,* 18.

110. Dodd, "Wrecking Business," 174.

111. Craton and Saunders, *Islanders in the Stream,* I: 88–89.

112. W. Johnson, *Race Relations,* 19.

113. Saunders, "Slavery and Cotton," 22.

114. Craton, "Historiography," 666.

115. On the uniqueness of the Bahamas as a society dominated by the legacy of slavery, colonialism and European conquest, but lacking an export staple such as rice or sugar, see Howard Johnson, *The Bahamas in Slavery and Freedom,* vi.

116. Engerman and Higman, "Demographic Structure," 49.

117. Knight, *General History,* III: 5.

118. Knight, *General History,* III: 5.

119. Engerman and Higman, "Demographic Structure," 49.

120. Saunders, *Bahamian Loyalists,* 2.

121. Craton and Saunders, *Islanders in the Stream,* I: 119–120.

122. Craton and Saunders, *Islanders in the Stream,* I: 120–121.

123. Craton and Saunders, *Islanders in the Stream,* I: 122.

124. Craton and Saunders, *Islanders in the Stream,* I: 124–125.

125. Thomas Shirley, COP 23/22/59, cited by W. Johnson, *Race Relations,* xvii. For a broad overview of the emergence of free black communities in the British Caribbean, see Sio, "Marginality," 166–182.

126. Craton and Saunders, *Islanders in the Stream,* I: 149.

127. Craton and Saunders, *Islanders in the Stream,* I: 149.

128. Craton and Saunders, *Islanders in the Stream,* I: 149–150.

129. Craton and Saunders, *Islanders in the Stream,* I: 150.

130. Morgan cited by Saunders, "Slavery and Cotton," 31.

131. Saunders, *Bahamian Loyalists,* 3. See also H. Johnson, *Slavery and Freedom,* 2.

132. Saunders, "Slavery and Cotton," 33. See also H. Johnson, *Slavery and Freedom,* 16.

133. Scholars have long noted the importance of provisional grounds in the development of a proto-peasantry in the Caribbean. See particularly Sidney Mintz and Douglas Hall. Hilary Beckles has recently argued that even in Barbados, enslaved persons were able to use their garden plots to grow food that could be either consumed or sold in the local internal market system. The uniqueness of the Bahamas is that the development of the task system and the underdevelopment of the islands allowed the emergence of a proto-peasantry to take hold much earlier and on a much wider scale. Mintz and Hall, *Origins*; Beckles, "Economic Life," 33.

134. Berlin and Morgan, *The Slaves' Economy*, 6.

135. Saunders, "Slavery and Cotton," 37.

136. Craton and Saunders, *Islanders in the Stream*, I: 119.

137. Craton and Saunders note that the 1729 slave code was copied from an earlier Bermudan code, though both owed much to the Barbados laws of 1665; *Islanders in the Stream*, I: 136.

138. Regarding laws for better governing of the colony, Woodes Rogers noted that the "Act had its rise . . . upon a combination which was discovered among the Negroes to rise and destroy the white inhabitants, and is no more than what is agreeable to the laws of our neighbouring colonies in the method of trying and punishing these savages." Governor to Board of Trade, September 7, 1731, cited in Cash, Gordon, and Saunders, *Sources of Bahamian History*, 184.

139. Craton, "Loyalists Mainly to Themselves," 46.

140. Craton and Saunders, *Islanders in the Stream*, I: 183.

141. Craton and Saunders, *Islanders in the Stream*, I: 183; Brigadier General McArthur reported, "six hundred souls have been brought here from East Florida at the expense of Government, and about fifty at their own." Letter from Brigadier General McArthur to Lord Sydney, March 1, 1784. COP 23/25.

142. Craton and Saunders, *Islanders in the Stream,* I: 183.

143. Craton and Saunders, *Islanders in the Stream,* I: 188.

144. Schoepf, *Travels,* II: 263.

145. C. F. Pascoe, *Two Hundred Years*, 221.

146. Wylly, *Short Account,* 10.

147. Wylly, *Short Account,* 7.

148. Most of the Black Loyalists in Nassau, including Frank Spence, Prince Williams, Sambo Scriven, and Amos Williams, appear to have arrived from Saint Augustine. See Symonette and Canzoneri, *Baptists in the Bahamas,* 1–3.

149. Craton, "Loyalists Mainly to Themselves," 45.

150. Lieutenant John Wilson, cited in Craton and Saunders, *Islanders in the Stream*, I: 186. The more favorable report noted that Abaco abounded "with Timber, Fir, Madeira Wood, Mahogany, Fustick, Lignum Vitae, Brazeleto, Logwood, and Sundry Woods fit for dying. The Soil is Capable of Producing all the West India Produce & c." See letter addressed to His Excellency Guy Carleton from Thomas Stephens, John Davis, Henry Smith, John Pintard, Thomas Sirtor, New York, June 25, 1783. BHP, Box 34, #8227.

151. Pulis, "Bridging Troubled Waters," 190.

Chapter 2. Their Struggle with Freedom from Bondage

1. Struder was in fact the son-in-law of Ann Nelson. See John Martin Struder's affidavit, COP 23/29.

2. The story of Mary Postell mirrors Sara Moultrie's narrative. Carole Troxler notes that despite initially having a certificate of protection issued by General Leslie in Charleston, Mary Postell was forced to give up the document to John MacDougal who used the pretext of wanting to look at it. No longer possessing the document certifying her freedom, Postell was eventually persuaded by MacDougal and her husband to go to East Florida in the service of Jesse Grey who, once they arrived in Saint Augustine, claimed that she was in fact his slave. Though Grey denied any relationship to Postell prior to arriving in Saint Augustine in 1783, it is clear that his ability to acquire her as property was accelerated by the fact that Postell no longer had documents in her possession. She therefore became part of that ambiguous group of blacks who were often sold as part of business transactions conducted at the East Florida state house; Troxler, "Re-enslavement of Black Loyalists," 80.

3. Sarah Moultrie's case was heard before receiver-general George Barry and two justices, J. Martin and T. Smith, on April 14, 1788. The affidavit of Struder is dated April 22, 1788, and was witnessed by Robert Scott and Stephen Haven, both justices of the peace and notaries. COP 23/29.

4. Dayton, *Women Before the Bar*, 4–5.

5. The case of Mary Postell represents the kind of political opening emerging throughout the North Atlantic world at that time. Despite her claims to have possessed a certificate of freedom after coming within British lines in Charleston by 1780, Mary was still adjudged a slave of Jesse Grey. Yet her case was far from an isolated instance of loss of freedom rendered by a court of law in Nova Scotia or Nassau; Troxler, "Re-enslavement of Black Loyalists," 75–79.

6. Jane Landers notes how Spanish Florida remained a viable sanctuary for escapees desiring freedom. Governor Zespedes honored the petitioner's demand for protection under Spanish law, despite the objections of Patrick Tonyn, the former British governor of East Florida; *Black Society*, 2, 76–77. Notably during the revolutionary period enslaved persons in the thirteen colonies often appropriated the rhetoric of liberty to advance claims to freedom in various courts. See Emily Blanck's comparative study of Boston and Charleston where two enslaved individuals—Leander and Caesar—brought their manumission efforts before the court of law; "Manumission and the Law." For other locales across the Atlantic world where courts remained accessible to blacks, see Alejandro de la Fuente, "Slave Law," 339–369; Michelle McKinley, "Fractional Freedoms," 749–790.

7. C. Brown, *Moral Capital*, 295.

8. Siebert notes that these instructions regarding land grants and quit rents were issued fifteen days before a fleet arrived in New Providence carrying McArthur as the new military commander-in-chief for the Bahamas; Siebert, *Legacy*, 20. For a definition of quit rents see Vianna, *American Heritage Desk Dictionary*, 778.

9. In total, 941 settlers sailed from New York to Abaco between August and October

1783, augmented by some 650 persons who reached Abaco from Saint Augustine, Florida. Craton and Saunders, *Islanders in the Stream*, 1: 183.

10. Craton and Saunders, *Islanders in the Stream*, I: 185.

11. Craton and Saunders, *Islanders in the Stream*, I: 185.

12. Paley, "Mansfield," 176. Paley examines two brothers, Ephraim and Ancona John, who were like the Black Loyalists in this study, highly creolized but unfortunately the subject of white efforts to confer slave status on them. See also Randy Sparks, *Two Princes*.

13. The concept of "foreign country" did not mean literally "outside a British colony," as Paley demonstrates in the Mansfield ruling; "Mansfield," 169–170.

14. Walker, *Black Loyalists*, 41.

15. Troxler, "Re-enslavement of Black Loyalists," 77.

16. See for example Jack, who was listed as being formerly the property of John Longley, "purchased from Sarah Aymer as per Bill of Sale produced," In *Book of Negroes*.

17. Craton and Saunders, *Islanders in the Stream*, I: 185.

18. Ship Register for *The William*, August 22, 1783, *Book of Negroes*.

19. Ship Register for *The William*, August 22, 1783.

20. Ship Register for *The William* and *The Nautilus*, August 21 and 22, 1783.

21. Kathleen Brown argues that white women embodied the privileges and virtues of womanhood, while "women of African descent shouldered the burden of its inherent evil, sexual lust;" *Good Wives*, 2.

22. The exact location of Carleton was unknown until 1979 when Steve Dodge discovered it. See Dodge, *Carleton*, 1.

23. Brigadier General McArthur, Commanding in East Florida and the Bahama Islands, Nassau, New Providence, March 1, 1784, to Right Honorable Lord Sydney, Colonial Office Papers, 23/25.

24. McArthur noted that upon being ordered to appear in court to account for their nonperformance of duties, two refused to appear and three others treated the court with "insolence and contempt." Most alarming was that many of the inhabitants signed a petition in support of the actions of these five. McArthur to Lord Sydney, COP 23/25.

25. Craton and Saunders, *Islanders in the Stream*, I: 185.

26. McArthur to Lord Sydney, COP 23/25.

27. Craton and Saunders, *Islanders in the Stream*, I: 186.

28. Message from the Governor, John Maxwell, to the General Assembly September 29, 1784, COP 23/25.

29. Maxwell, October 15, 1784, to Lord Sydney, COP 23/25.

30. Maxwell, October 15, 1784, to Lord Sydney, COP 23/25.

31. G. Barry to Governor Maxwell, June 30, 1786, COP 23/26.

32. The wide circulation of the Mansfield ruling is evident from the fact that at least thirteen British newspapers and twenty-two out of twenty-four North American colonial newspapers reported the arguments of decision. Cleve, "'Somerset's Case,'" 625. Scholars have long debated the significance of Mansfield's ruling in the Somerset case. Justin Buckley Dyer has argued that the ruling reduced the status of slavery to local positive laws. Increasingly slavery would be viewed as abhorrent to natural law and British common law. Thus, Somerset's premise would be commandeered as a rallying

cry for Anglo-American abolitionists. George Cleve argues that Mansfield attempted to juggle the West Indian interests and the exegesis of late-eighteenth-century British politics, which was increasingly influenced by humanitarians. In an effort to provide a compromise, Mansfield produced a ruling that was purposefully ambiguous. Daniel J. Hulsebosch argues that Mansfield's ruling reflected a more conservative imperial tradition, whose aim was to keep slavery out of England, but within the Empire; Dyer, "After the Revolution," 1422–1434; Hulsebosch, "'Somerset's Case,'" 647–657; Cleve, "'Somerset's Case,'" 601–645. See also Ruth Paley, "After Somerset."

33. According to Cleve, Mansfield's ruling posited that only positive laws in specific jurisdictions could determine the status of slavery in that colony, thereby limiting Imperial judicial power over slaves; "'Somerset's Case,'" 643.

34. Cleve, "'Somerset's Case,'" 645.

35. Craton and Saunders, *Islanders in the Stream*, I: 186–187.

36. Blanchard to Powell, April 6, 1785, cited by Riley, *Homeward Bound*, 170.

37. September, 27, 1786. Interestingly this case was presided over by G. Barry, mentioned above, John Boyd, and Thomas Ross. COP 23/29, folio 279–280.

38. June 15, 1786. COP 23/29, folio 279.

39. For Spanish Florida, see Landers, *Black Society*. For Nova Scotia, see Troxler, "Re-enslavement of Black Loyalists," 70-85.

40. Troxler, "Re-enslavement of Black Loyalists," 83.

41. It is worth noting that Major General Alexander Leslie issued these certificates of protection leading up to the evacuation of Charleston. Troxler, "Re-enslavement of Black Loyalists,"74.

42. Rosemarie Zaggari notes that American political leaders rejected the "full implications of equality and natural rights, with a resultant hardening of boundaries between the races and the sexes. The legacy of the Revolution was redefined and circumscribed so as to limit its full benefits to white males;" *Revolutionary Backlash*, 185; K. Brown, *Good Wives,* 367.

43. Landers, *Black Society*, 78–79.

44. Troxler, "Re-enslavement of Black Loyalists," 75-76.

45. Troxler, "Re-enslavement of Black Loyalists," 75-77.

46. Willis' document of freedom and purchase of Hester from Cameron, ORG, Book B, 338, cited in Riley, *Homeward Bound,* 141. Cameron was initially assigned to "whose possession they are now," evident in the records of the *Book of Negroes* pertaining to *The William*. See *Book of Negroes* in Riley, *Homeward Bound,* 266. The date of the payment for Hester's freedom in Abaco is noted in Registry Office Book M, cited by Paul Shirley, "Migration, Freedom and Enslavement," 296.

47. An analysis of the wills, deeds, and records found at the Georgia Historical Society, Savannah, provides clues to the kind of work relations that existed in this early Loyalist period. Many of the records of indentured relations include the fee paid or the value of the indenture paid upon release from the contract. See for example a man named Sturrup, who paid £294 to the deeds and conveyance office for his release. Of course, these official transactions obscure the countless other illegal contracts that existed. Wills,

Deeds, and Records, Nassau, Bahamas, 1700–1845, Georgia Historical Society, Savannah, Georgia.

48. For the case of Liele and his indentured status, see Holmes, "George Liele," 344, and Morrison, "George Liele," 5–6. For John Singletary, see Carole Troxler, "Re-enslavement of Loyalists, 75–76.

49. The November 1775 Proclamation by Dunmore and its impact on Black Loyalists in both the Bahamas and Virginia is succinctly summarized by Paul Shirley in "Migration, Freedom and Enslavement," 179–180.

50. Governor Dunmore to Lord Sydney, Nassau New Providence, November 28, 1787, COP 23/27.

51. Governor Dunmore to Lord Sydney, COP 23/27.

52. Governor Dunmore to Lord Sydney, COP 23/27.

53. Wylly, *Short Account*, 21. Paul Shirley notes that Wylly's *Short Account* was intended to show how a despotic governor, acting out of personal hostility, venality, and misplaced sympathy for black people, established "an unconstitutional tribunal" administered by "the most improper persons"; "Migration, Freedom and Enslavement," 11.

54. Wylly, *Short Account,* 22.

55. Wylly, *Short Account*, 22

56. Douglas Egerton has as his subject black activists of the founding generation who pushed hard against the tide of mounting racism. He notes that though no black during this generation cast a ballot, former bonds people, and even the enslaved (such as Gabriel Prosser, Mum Bett, Olaudah Equiano, and Harry Washington) helped to shape the politics of the Early Republic through their demands and actions; *Death or Liberty*, 14. For work on Toussaint Louverture see James, *Black Jacobins*. David Brion Davis argues that the specter of the Haitian Revolution was symbolically significant, looming large in slave societies across the Atlantic world; "Impact," 5.

57. Lord Dunmore was often accused of using the Negro Courts to enlarge his plantation's labor force. Wylly noted in the case of Mary Brown, that her slaves were taken to Lord Dunmore's plantation where they were "set to work upon the 22nd of January 1788" without a trial pending. William Wylly, to Jonathan Michei, COP 23/29, folio 261–262. In the case of John Ross, the magistrates ruled in favor of the slave owner but stipulated that Binah, the female slave, be sold to Lord Dunmore. Affidavit of John Ross, April 23, 1788, COP 23/29.

58. Governor Dunmore to Lord Sydney, COP 23/27.

59. Dunmore's Proclamation, November 7, 1787. COP 23/27 f. 78.

60. Dunmore's Proclamation, COP 23/27 f. 78.

61. Abstract of Act of Assembly, Bahama Islands, passed November 24, 1787. COP 23/27. It is interesting to note that a number of Indian Loyalists arrived from the Mosquito Coast, off Honduras. See the memorial of Mary Brown dated November 13, 1788, in which she claims Dunmore unfairly removed her Mosquito Coast Indians from her property and put them to work on his plantation. Memorial of Mary Brown to Lord Sydney, November 13, 1788. COP 23/28. See also Craton and Saunders, *Islanders in the Stream*, I: 129.

62. Abstract of Act of Assembly, Bahama Islands passed November 24, 1787. COP 23/27.

63. Abstract of Act of Assembly, CO 23/27.

64. The magistrates presiding over this case were G. Barry, Receiver-General, John O'Halleran, J.P., and Henry Yonge, J.P. November 26, 1787, COP 23/29.

65. January 2, 1788, COP 23/29.

66. Letter written by O'Halleran to William Green, October 30, 1787, COP 23/29.

67. Trial of Mathias, a negro man, on a claim of freedom. William Green, claimant, COP 23/29.

68. *Bahama Gazette*, February 21, 1789.

69. Bennett, Colonial Blackness, 1–2.

70. Bahamas Register Office, Box O, 62, cited by Thelma Peters, "Plantation Period," 58.

71. Another certificate held by Charles Williams testifies to the personal and political nature of such documents. Williams' certificate was issued by J. Bluck, "by order of the commandant," and dated New York, October 14, 1783. The certificate states that the bearer hereof, a Negro named Charles Williams, aged sixty-eight years and formerly the property of Samuel Williams, Eastern Shore in the province of Virginia, appears to have come within British lines, under the sanction, and Claims the Privilege of the Proclamation respecting Negroes, heretofore issued for their security and protection. Bahamas Register Office, Box O, 424, cited by Peters, "Plantation Period," 58.

72. Wylly, *Short Account*, 40

73. Parish, "Some Southern Loyalists," 419–420.

74. Richard Pearis to William Coleman, May 8, 1788, COP 23/29, cited in Riley, *Homeward Bound*, 176.

75. Wylly, *Short Account*, 41.

76. Wylly, *Short Account*, 22.

77. Wylly, *Short Account*, 41.

78. Wylly, *Short Account*, 41

79. Wylly, *Short Account*, 23.

80. Governor Dunmore to Lord Sydney, Nassau, July 18, 1788, COP 23/27, folio 164.

81. Although the bill for amending previous acts was published as early as February 26, 1788, it was not officially passed by the Assembly until July. Events in Abaco likely created a greater sense of urgency for the bill to be passed as law. See COP 23/29.

82. Baylis, like Wylly, was a strong critic of the 1788 Act. See letter dated February 26, 1788, COP 23/29. Wylly noted in a letter dated September 27, 1789, that "under this Act, the Court could be held only in the Court House at Nassau. Yet contrary as well to this Act, as to a maxim of the Common Law these trials have generally been had at the Hut of the Receiver General (when he has been able to do business) and a court has lately been held by special commission and under the Governor's immediate inspection upon the island of Abaco, one hundred miles from Nassau." COP 23/29.

83. Letter of Provost Marshall William Baylis, dated February 26, 1788, COP 23/29.

84. William Wylly, September 27, 1789, COP 23/29, folio 272–279.

85. William Wylly, September 27, 1789, COP 23/29, folio 272–279.

86. For locales in the Atlantic world where enslaved persons used the courts to their advantage, see Alejandro de la Fuente, "Slave Law," 342, 360. Fuente notes that when legal disputes arose, where a judge was thought to be partial to the slaveholder, the enslaved had the right to challenge him and to ask that a new judge be appointed, 360.

87. Troxler, "Re-enslavement of Black Loyalists," 78.

88. See Shirley, "Migration, Freedom and Enslavement," 164; Berlin, *Many Thousands Gone*, 228–255; Blackburn, *Overthrow*, 117–121.

89. William Wylly, September 27, 1789, COP 23/29, folio 276; Wylly, *Short Account*, 21.

90. William Wylly, September 27, 1789, COP 23/29, folio 272–279.

91. Though Wylly may well have been referring only to Dunmore's proclamation, his experience as a Virginian, and later as a refugee in New Brunswick, Canada, would have provided him with an appreciation of the other proclamations relative to Black Loyalists.

92. Cornelia H. Dayton has argued that in seventeenth-century Connecticut, women entered courtrooms often: suing and being sued over debt and slander, petitioning for divorce, and prosecuting for sex crimes. However, by the early 1800s, women's participation in courtrooms had diminished because of the expansion of a legal fraternity, a growing group of professional men including judges, justices of the peace and professional attorneys as well as wealthy heads of households who rotated on and off duty as jurors; *Women Before the Bar*, 4–5, 8–9.

93. Zaggari, *Revolutionary Backlash*, 10.

94. William Wylly, September 27, 1789, COP 23/29.

95. William Wylly, September 27, 1789, COP 23/29.

96. *Bahama Gazette,* May 29, 1792.

97. *Bahama Gazette,* August 31, 1790.

98. Peters, "Plantation Period," 124.

99. Case of Binah found in a letter written by G. Barry to Thomas Ross requesting his presence in the court. Dated February 19, 1788, COP 23/29.

100. Affidavit of John Graham Ross, April 23, 1788, COP 23/29.

101. *Bahama Gazette,* February 7, 1789.

102. *Bahama Gazette,* November 21, 1789.

103. Shirley suggests that the Abaco community of maroons evolved from petit marronage to the more permanent grand marronage. The short length of time in which the Abaco group remained in hiding suggests otherwise. See Shirley, "Tek force wid force," 33.

104. Shirley, "Tek force wid force," 33.

105. *Bahama Gazette*, January 6, 1792. A similar proclamation was issued in the *Bahama Gazette,* June 18, 1790.

106. Negro Act of 1784, passed June 25, 1784. COP 23/29.

107. Negro Act of 1784. COP 23/29.

108. *Bahama Gazette*, February 24, 1789.

109. *Bahama Gazette,* February 24, 1789.

110. W. Johnson, *Race Relations*, 1784–1834, 42.

111. Shirley, "Migration, Freedom and Enslavement," 175–176.

112. Shirley, "Migration, Freedom and Enslavement," 177.

113. Shirley, "Migration, Freedom and Enslavement," 177–178.

114. Shirley, "Migration, Freedom and Enslavement," 185–188.

115. Shirley, "Migration, Freedom and Enslavement," 190.

116. Shirley, "Migration, Freedom and Enslavement," 182.

Chapter 3. Setting Their Feet Down

1. The account of Joseph Paul in the footnotes is actually part of a letter written by William Turton, the first white Methodist missionary sent to the Bahamas in 1800 by the Methodist Conference in Manchester, England. The letter dated from New Providence on March 22, 1817 was addressed to the Missionary Committee and hand delivered to Dowson. Peggs, *Dowson's Journal*, 48.

2. Peggs, *Dowson's Journal*, 49.

3. The location of the school is noted by Sandra Riley in *Homeward Bound,* 140. See also W. Johnson, *Race Relations*, 51.

4. See James Scott, *Domination*, xi; Kelley, *Race Rebels*, 7–8.

5. Kelley notes that such public performances occur in places of tension, including public buses, organized demonstrations, and even nightclubs and bars; *Race Rebels*, 4, 7.

6. A number of scholars refer to the ruling elites in the Bahamas as an "agro-commercial oligarchy," both implying their hegemonic grip on Bahamian society as well as suggesting an appropriate appellation for a group that never derived its power from sugar cultivation. See for example, Craton, "Bay Street," 71–94; Craton and Saunders, *Islanders in the Stream*; H. Johnson, *Slavery and Freedom*. Regarding slave codes, see for example the Consolidated Slave Act of 1797 passed by the Loyalist-dominated House of Assembly. The act placed strict restrictions on enslaved persons, including prohibiting the possession of hunting weapons, assembling in numbers exceeding twelve, and using drums and horns for that purpose. See Consolidated Slave Act of 1797, cited by W. Johnson, *Race Relations, 6.*

7. Kelley notes that there has been a tendency to essentialize African American communities as singular, rather than as diverse and heterogeneous; *Race Rebels*, 13.

8. W. Johnson, *Race Relations,* xiii.

9. *SPG Journal*, vol. 26, Minutes dated November 21, 1794, cited in C. Williams, *Methodist Contribution,* 31. The actual year the family migrated has been debated among scholars. Craton argues that Paul migrated sometime shortly after he arrived in Abaco, although he does not give a precise date when he left. Craton, "Loyalists Mainly to Themselves," 62. Sandra Riley surmises that they migrated to Nassau in 1784, citing Samuel Kelly, a visitor to Nassau in 1784, who observed a colored man preaching in the eastern districts of the town. In her footnote Riley argues that since Joseph Paul's name does not appear on the 1788 Plan of Nassau, he may not have arrived there until 1790; *Homeward Bound*, 140, 248. Finally, Colbert Williams, relying on the records of the Society for the Propagation of the Gospel, suggests Paul was in Nassau by 1790; *Methodist Contribution*, 30.

10. Riley, *Homeward Bound,* 140.

11. Nassau, May 12, 1795. Letter from John Richards to Rev'd Dr. Morrice, Secretary, SPG, Gorver Street, London. SPG Records, microfilm reel 2.

12. Scholars dispute the significance of William Hammett's influence on black preachers and the spread of evangelicalism to the Caribbean. Bundy argues that Hammett's foray into mission work in the Bahamas was largely self-serving as a way to gain political capital in his struggle against the evolving U.S. Methodist episcopacy. Further, Reily notes that Hammett had initially castigated Coke for buying slaves, but by 1795 had become a slaveholder and defender of slavery in America. On the other hand, Catron suggests that he was an important individual who spearheaded an evangelical movement across the Greater Caribbean. See Bundy, "African and Caribbean," 175; Catron, "Evangelical Networks," 104; Reily, "William Hammett," 41.

13. Coke, *History of the West Indies,* III: 200.

14. Dowson mentions all three by name: Johnson, Rushton, and Meriday, whereas Thomas Coke preferred having their names consigned "to oblivion." The size of the congregation is given by Coke as numbering about sixty. See Coke, *History of the West Indies,* III: 200–201; Peggs, *Dowson's Journal,* 48.

15. Catron, "Evangelical Networks," 105

16. Coke, *History of the West Indies,* III: 201.

17. Nassau, June 12, 1794. Letter from Richards to Morrice. SPG Records, microfilm reel 2.

18. W. Johnson, *Race Relations,* 51.

19. Coke attributes these divisions to the work of the three white missionaries sent out by William Hammett. However, it is evident that even after these three men left, both groups remained split, with one group meeting with Paul in the meetinghouse he helped erect, and the other meeting in the house of Anthony Wallace. This view is supported by Dowson's account. See Coke, *History of the West Indies,* III: 201.

20. Peggs, *Dowson's Journal,* 48.

21. W. Johnson, *Race Relations,* 51.

22. Will and testament of Joseph Paul, dated April 19, 1802, Supreme Court Wills, P, folio 241, Department of Archives, Nassau.

23. W. Johnson, *Race Relations,* 51.

24. Richard Roberts, cited in W. Johnson, *Race Relations,* 52.

25. John Stephen, cited in W. Johnson, *Race Relations,* 52.

26. Underhill, *West Indies,* 473.

27. Correspondence of D. W. Rose, Exuma, Bahamas, Sept. 2, 1803, SPG Records, microfilm reel 2.

28. Reports of Richard Roberts and John Stephen, cited in W. Johnson, *Race Relations,* 51.

29. Saillant, "Antiguan Methodism," 89–95.

30. Rooke, "Pedagogy of Conversion," 372.

31. Holmes, "George Liele," 347.

32. It is worth noting that while many black evangelicals such as John Marrant emphasized an antischolastic approach to sermonizing and teaching of the word, they did not outright reject educational instruction. Indeed, as Cedric May has argued, Marrant advocated a "proper training" based on a simple and plain understanding of the

scriptures rather than creeds and doctrines developed by men. See May, "Narrative Construction," 566–567.

33. Significantly, in the immediate postemancipation era, where the agrocommercial oligarchy tended to ignore the educational needs of the majority of Bahamians, black Baptists were at the forefront of providing schooling for the black masses. In Nassau by 1856 there were Baptist churches and schools in the communities of Adelaide, Carmichael, Grants Town, and Bain Town. A Sunday school was also started at Good Hope Hill with James Rutherford as the teacher. Curry, "Baptists' Contribution," 378.

34. Whittington Johnson notes that when the rector of the parish school of Christ Church in Nassau was asked in 1814 to give an account of the number of colored children currently attending, he responded that they were equal to the number of whites. According to Johnson, this is remarkable in light of the 1815 population figures, which show that whites greatly outnumbered free blacks and coloreds combined; *Race Relations,* 55.

35. For figures on the number of students, see W. Johnson, *Race Relations,* 51. For total population figures see Wylly, *Short Account,* 7.

36. John W. Catron provides the best corroborating evidence supporting Anthony Wallace as a Black Loyalist, noting that he evacuated from South Carolina as a free black and eventually settled in New Providence with his wife, old Mrs. Wallace. His ties to William Hammett and the primitive Methodists in Charleston and Nassau, his literacy and trans-Atlantic connections suggest that he was a leading figure in the spread of evangelical Christianity to the Greater Caribbean region. Wallace in fact wrote a letter to Thomas Coke, head of the Methodist Episcopal [American] Conference in 1796 requesting a missionary be sent to the Bahamas; "Evangelical Networks," 107; C. Williams, *Methodist Contribution,* 35.

37. The 1816 Act is mentioned in Peggs, *Dowson's Journal,* 102–104. For the 1817 Act see Craton and Saunders, *Islanders in the Stream,* I: 332.

38. Whittington Johnson speaks of three stages of Methodism in the Bahamas, the first marked by the work of Paul and the three American missionaries; the second, the small remnant left after the split from Paul controlled by Wallace; and the third stage inaugurated with the arrival of Turton in 1800; *Race Relations,* 62–63.

39. Peggs, *Dowson's Journal,* 49.

40. Peggs, *Dowson's Journal,* 49.

41. See Coke, *History of the West Indies,* 203; Peggs, *Dowson's Journal,* 49.

42. Report of Turton given in Coke, *History of the West Indies,* III: 205.

43. Coke, *History of the West Indies,* III: 205–206. Apparently, Forbes advanced the money to purchase land, and "others gave credit for such things wanting."

44. Coke, *History of the West Indies,* III: 206.

45. Coke, *History of the West Indies,* III: 206. In a less specific report dated August 1804, Turton gave the total for 1803 at 162, including 7 whites, 9 brown, and 146 blacks. This total appears to exclude the chapel in the Eastern district. Turton, "New Providence," 382.

46. It is worth noting that a similar trend was echoed in the 1805 and 1806 reports. In 1805 New Providence society equaled 11 whites, 8 colored people, and 120 blacks. In 1806 the society in New Providence under Rutledge comprised 170 people of whom 15 were

white; the others were colored and black people. In Eleuthera, now under the jurisdiction of Turton, there were 84 congregants, so that the entire Bahamas had 254 people connected to the Methodists. Coke, *History of the West Indies*, III: 208, 216.

47. C. Williams, *Methodist Contribution*, 277.

48. Peggs, *Dowson's Journal*, 66

49. Peggs, *Dowson's Journal*, 81–82.

50. Dowson noted that in Harbour Island there were about 50 new members. See W. Dowson, "Letter from Mr. Dowson," 952.

51. Peggs, *Dowson's Journal*, 81–82.

52. Joseph Ward documents a letter written by twenty-one white slave owners in Abaco requesting Turton be sent as a Methodist preacher to their community. Apparently Ward went instead of Turton, embarking from New Providence on June 17, 1815 for Green Turtle Cay, Abaco. Upon arriving, he preached to a congregation of 120 to 130 individuals. Though he noted faithful members totaling 29 whites and 10 blacks, these two groups were most likely segregated. By 1823 the Methodist District Minutes noted that Green Turtle Key "has two schools one for white children and the other for blacks." See Joseph Ward, "Letter," 71; Methodist District Meeting Minutes, March 23, 1831.

53. Underhill, *The West Indies*, 473.

54. Letter from John Richards, October 1791, SPG Records.

55. Symonette and Canzoneri, *Baptists in the Bahamas*, 1.

56. Symonette and Canzoneri, *Baptists in the Bahamas*, 1.

57. Pugh, "Great Awakening," 363.

58. Spence Street is the first street south of Mason Street, just east of East Street. Canzoneri, "Early History," 10.

59. Canzoneri, "Early History," 10.

60. Will of Frank Spence, Supreme Court Wills, S, Department of Archives, Nassau.

61. John Asplund, "The Annual Register of the Baptist Denomination in North America," quoted by Canzoneri, "Early History," 9.

62. Register of Freed Slaves, Public Archives, quoted by Canzoneri, "Early History," 10.

63. Of note, Sandra Riley attributes Kelly's reference to Joseph Paul. It would be difficult, however, to trace Paul to such early activity in New Providence, given that he had only settled in Abaco by October 1783. Amos, on the other hand, came to New Providence directly from St. Augustine; *Homeward Bound*, 140; W. Johnson, *Race Relations*, 57.

64. W. Johnson, *Race Relations*, 57. See also Liele, "Letters," 73. In his letter titled "An Account of Several Baptist Churches Consisting Chiefly of Negro Slaves," Liele recorded that "Brother Amos is at Providence, he writes me that the Gospel has taken good effect, and is spreading greatly; he has about three hundred members."

65. W. Johnson, *Race Relations*, 57.

66. W. Johnson, *Race Relations*, 58.

67. Petition of Prince Williams, COP 23/81, folio 316.

68. Jenkins noted in the same report that the Methodists have two preachers and are more numerous. He was most likely referring to Rutledge and Turton. Implicit in his report is that the Baptists were more of a threat than the Methodists, given that the latter

were organized under the tutelage of white missionaries from England. Henry Jenkins' report, Nassau, Oct, 5, 1805, SPG Records, microfilm reel 2.

69. Slave laws in the Bahamas were first enacted in 1723 and expressly prohibited the meeting of enslaved persons at night in groups of six or more. See Cash, Gordon, and Saunders, *Sources of Bahamian History*.

70. Sobel, *World They Made*, 3.

71. As Gomez has advanced, "African converts to Protestantism may have very well reinterpreted the dogma and ritual of the Christian church in ways that conformed to preexisting cosmological views," but once removed from the gaze of whites, enslaved and free blacks were at liberty to Africanize the religion; *Exchanging Our Country Marks*, 10.

72. Curry, "Christianity and Slavery," 2–7.

73. The report by D. W. Rose is found in both the SPG Records for the West Indies and C. F. Pascoe's ecclesiastical history of the West Indies. See letter from D. W. Rose, Long Island, Oct. 14, 1799, SPG Records, microfilm reel 2; C. F. Pascoe, *Two Hundred Years*, 224.

74. Letter from D. W. Rose, Oct. 14, 1799, SPG Records, microfilm reel 2.

75. Mechal Sobel among others has pointed out that healing, prophecy, and visions were a fundamental part of the enslaved person's own African heritage. As such, through visions and prophecies of the Baptist faith, enslaved and free blacks could experience God and a sense of liberation from this world; *Trabelin' On*, 97.

76. Isaac, *The Transformation of Virginia*, 172.

77. Letter from D. W. Rose, Oct 14, 1799, SPG Records, microfilm reel 2.

78. Rev. H. Groombridge, Nassau, New Providence, July 9, 1802, SPG Records.

79. Marrant, "Narrative," 51. For Murphy Stiel, see Hodges, *Black Loyalist Directory*, xv.

80. Rev. H. Groombridge, July 9, 1802, SPG Records.

81. Townsend, *Diary of a Physician*, 20–21, 36.

82. Sterling Stuckey contends that for most West African–descended people, expressive music and dance accompanied the "settin up" in order to prepare the deceased for arrival in the ancestral world. This practice reflected West African beliefs in the interconnectedness of the living and the dead, the sacred and the secular. This belief stood in stark contrast to Western culture's division of secular and sacred, and its view of lively celebrations at funeral services as profane and sinful; *Slave Culture*, 25–27.

83. Townsend, *Diary of a Physician*, 36.

84. Townsend, *Diary of a Physician*, 13, 17

85. *Bahama Gazette*, May 9, 1790.

86. *Bahama Gazette*, February 28, 1794

87. Wylly, *Short Account*, 42.

88. Pascoe, *Two Hundred Years*, 221.

89. Wylly, *Short Account*, 7.

90. Schoepf, *Travels*, 263.

91. For census data, see W. Johnson, *Race Relations*, 38–39.

92. Craton and Saunders, *Islanders in the Stream*, I: 195.

93. *Bahama Gazette*, July 18, 1789.

94. Will of Anthony Wallace, dated December 9, 1830. Supreme Court Wills, W–Y, Department of Archives, Nassau, Bahamas.

95. See Petition of Prince Williams, COP 23/81, folio 316.

96. W. Johnson, *Race Relations,* 31.

97. W. Johnson, *Race Relations,* 30.

98. W. Johnson, *Race Relations,* 32.

99. Arguably, such tactics were not too dissimilar from the conservativism of Nova Scotian Black Loyalists such as Samuel Blucke and Isaiah Limerick, who often aligned with the white Anglican officials and colonial establishment in order to gain better land and privileges at the expense of others. Whites used Limerick, in particular, to roust more controversial black Anglican and Methodist preachers from Nova Scotia communities. He later joined the Sierra Leone project both as an appointed screener of prospective black emigrants and as a migrant. See Brooks and Saillant, *Face Zion Forward,* 9.

100. Brooks and Saillant, *Face Zion Forward,* 12.

101. In chapter 3 of his study, James Sidbury shows how Pharoah and Tom, the slaves who revealed Gabriel's plans and thus undermined their success, were not mere betrayers. Their actions demonstrate that there existed no single identity for black Virginians, but rather a tangle of conflicting identities that placed slaves on opposite sides of the same issue—even when that issue was freedom versus slavery; *Ploughshares into Swords,* 95–117.

102. Beckles, *Centering Woman,* 192; Beckles, "Freedom without Liberty," 193–223.

103. Symonette and Canzoneri, *Baptists in the Bahamas,* 1.

104. Booby Hall, Registry Office Records, Box T, 4, cited by Thelma Peters, "Plantation Period," 121.

105. Beckles, "Freedom without Liberty," 193–223.

106. W. Johnson, *Race Relations,* 121.

107. Craton, "Loyalists Mainly to Themselves," 63.

108. Coke, *History of the West Indies,* 203.

109. Will and testament of Joseph Paul, dated April 19, 1802, Supreme Court Wills, P, folio 241, Department of Archives, Nassau, Bahamas.

110. Petition of Prince Williams, January 1826, COP 23/81, folio 316.

111. Roy Finkenbine and Richard Newman argue that the black founding generation built an impressive array of autonomous institutions to buttress rising free black communities: independent churches, burial societies, Masonic lodges, insurance organizations, small businesses, and educational groups; "Black Founders," 85–86.

112. Gilroy, *The Black Atlantic,* 3–4.

Chapter 4. Labor, Land, and the Law

1. Minutes of House of Assembly reports, February 27, 1789, COP 23/30.

2. Comparatively speaking, Black Loyalists laboring in the urban environment of Nassau worked at many of the same kinds of jobs as those found in the garrisoned cities they had left. Leslie Harris notes for New York City that black men "helped to build fortifications, served as cart men, woodcutters, cooks, and military servants." According to Harris, "Black women labored as cooks, washerwomen, and prostitutes. Though there

are no examples of prostitution in the Bahamas at that time, the other trades mentioned appear frequently in the *Bahama Gazette* from 1784 to 1802; *In the Shadow of Slavery*, 55.

3. Michael Craton notes that many of the Black Loyalists who stayed in Abaco after failure of the initial settlement phase chose to settle in small scattered communities throughout the mainland, rather than live with white Loyalists on the offshore cays of Abaco; "Loyalists Mainly to Themselves," 48.

4. Craton, "Evolution," 90.

5. Besson, "Religion as Resistance," 47.

6. The best example of commonage developed in Exuma on the decayed plantations formerly owned by Lord Rolle, the largest slave owner in the Bahamas. His four plantations were eventually transformed into lands held in common, with the formerly enslaved taking on the name of Rolle and working the land collectively. See Craton and Saunders, *Islanders in the Stream*, I: 390–391.

7. Walker, "Myth, History," 89–90.

8. Siebert, *Legacy*, 20.

9. Dodge, *Abaco*, 36.

10. Dodge, *Abaco*, 36, 39. It is significant that a similar process by which Black Loyalists were falsely listed as dependents also occurred in County Harbour, Nova Scotia. Troxler, "Black Loyalists," 43.

11. Troxler, "Re-enslavement of Black Loyalists," 84.

12. Dodge, *Abaco*, 42-44.

13. Wylly, *Short Account*, 7.

14. Wylly and Schoepf, cited by W. Johnson, *Race Relations*, 29–30.

15. W. Johnson, *Race Relations*, 30.

16. For the opportunities afforded to black women in urban environments, see Beckles, *Centering Woman*.

17. W. Johnson, *Race Relations*, 30.

18. John Williams was most likely a Black Loyalist, based on his relationship to Prince Williams and Bethel Baptist Church. John and Prince Williams were recorded as the purchasers of the property in 1801 on which Bethel Baptist would later be built. See chapter 4, W. Johnson, *Race Relations*, 30.

19. Whittington Johnson notes that this index becomes a valuable source for determining how much and what kind of property free blacks and persons of color owned; *Race Relations*, 31.

20. Will of Frank Spence, Supreme Court Wills, S, Department of Archives, Nassau, Bahamas.

21. Will of Joseph Paul, Supreme Court Wills, P, Department of Archives, Nassau, Bahamas.

22. Wills of Franck Spence and Joseph Paul, Supreme Court Wills, S and P, Department of Archives, Nassau, Bahamas.

23. Will of Anthony Wallace, Supreme Court Wills, W, Department of Archives, Nassau, Bahamas.

24. Will of Prince Williams, Supreme Court Wills, W, Department of Archives, Nassau, Bahamas.

25. Will of Joseph Paul, Supreme Court Wills.

26. Will of Prince Williams, Supreme Court Wills.

27. Wylly, *Short Account,* 7

28. R. Cunningham, *Bahama Gazette,* January 25, 1799.

29. J. Mackenzie, *Bahama Gazette,* January 25, 1784.

30. Peters, "Plantation Period," 50.

31. Peters, "Plantation Period," 50.

32. Michael Craton points out that although the initial land grants to Loyalists seem to suggest movement toward absolute freeholds, the practice of commonage in fact continued to be widespread. He notes that in the Family Islands, commonage developed most prominently on decayed plantations where absentee owners and the decline of cotton created conditions whereby a sense of community and attachment to a particular location were forged between actual and fictive kinship groups. Commonage was also evident in the urban environment of Nassau, particularly among free black communities that developed in the area south of the city, known as Over the Hill; "Evolution," 94–97.

33. Craton, "Evolution," 99.

34. *Bahama Gazette,* August 17, 1793.

35. *Bahama Gazette*, June 13, 1789.

36. *Bahama Gazette,* December 24, 1799.

37. Presentments of Grand Jury, *Bahama Gazette,* October 4, 1799.

38. List of grievances of Grand Jury, *Bahama Gazette,* May 1794.

39. Johnston and Hallett, *Early Colonists*, 119. If the "Flora" noted in the Register of Freed Slaves and Negro Freedoms Book is indeed Flora Givens, then her imprisonment suggests a woman who continued to live on the margins of Bahamian society, even after achieving free status. See Register of Freed Slaves, tabulated by Shirley, "Migration, Freedom and Enslavement," 301.

40. *Bahama Gazette*, September 30, 1800.

41. For an account of Andrew Deveaux's retaking of the Bahamas, see Craton and Saunders, *Islanders in the Stream*, I: 169–171.

42. Welch, "Views from Bridgetown Barbados," 183–198.

43. Beckles, *Centering Woman*, 140–155. For an interesting Atlantic world perspective, see Olwell, "Slave Women," 97–110.

44. See Rodriguez, "Abolition of Slavery," 248–272; Rodriguez, *Women and Urban Change*.

45. Beckles and Shepherd, *Liberties Lost,* 104.

46. The rise and subsequent decline of cotton production has been observed by both contemporaneous writers and recent scholars. Writing in 1789, William Wylly observed that the area of cultivated land had risen from 3,434 to 16,322 acres between 1783 and 1788, and that total would most likely double to peak around 1793. Craton and Saunders have more recently suggested that initial cotton exports amounted to 124 tons in 1785 produced on 2,476 acres, rising steadily to 219 tons of cotton in 1787 and 442 tons of cotton in 1790, grown on roughly 12,000 acres of land. After this peak in 1790, there was a slow and precipitous decline in the tonnage of cotton exported as well as in land under cultivation. Various reasons can be given for such a decline, including the appearance of

the chenille bug, a cotton-eating worm "that looks like a caterpillar," and the scattered nature of the archipelago that made transportation difficult. Most importantly, cotton declined due to the inadequacy of Bahamian soil. See Wylly, *Short Account,* 5–6; Craton and Saunders, *Islanders in the Stream,* I: 156, 192, 196. See also Saunders, *Slavery in the Bahamas,* 23–27; Craton, *History of the Bahamas,* 156.

47. Saunders, "Slavery and Cotton," 129–151. Craton refers to the conditions favoring the development of a proto-peasantry lifestyle as a decayed open plantation system, particularly prevalent in Exuma; "Two Extremes," 349.

48. H. Johnson, *Slavery to Servitude,* 42.

49. H. Johnson, *Slavery to Servitude,* 42.

50. Craton and Saunders, *Islanders in the Stream,* I: 194.

51. Craton and Saunders, *Islanders in the Stream,* I: 194. The original wooden structure appeared as early as 1769.

52. Craton and Saunders, *Islanders in the Stream,* I: 195.

53. The notion of trading spaces is taken from Jane Mangan's study of colonial Potosi, where indigenous and African-descended people carved out unique market space within the urban city streets. Mangan, *Gender, Ethnicity.*

54. Grand Jury presentations, February 24, 1789; COP 23/29; *Bahama Gazette,* February 28, 1789.

55. *Bahama Gazette*, May 8, 1795.

56. *Bahama Gazette*, May 8, 1795. Lane was also a slaveholder. See Negro Freedoms Book, cited by Shirley, "Migration, Freedom and Enslavement," 304

57. *Bahama Gazette*, October 4, 1799

58. List with remarks after petition for closing of General Assembly and petition for new general election. COP 23/27.

59. C. Williams, *Methodist Contribution,* 122.

60. Will and Testament of Frank Spence, Supreme Court Wills, S, Department of Archives, Nassau, Bahamas.

61. Case of Timothy Cox, cited by W. Johnson, *Race Relations,* 32.

62. *Bahama Gazette,* March 18, 1796.

63. Peggs, *Dowson's Journal,* 81–82.

64. *Bahama Gazette,* February 20, 1790.

65. *Bahama Gazette*, January 13, 1794.

66. *Bahama Gazette,* December 11, 1784.

67. *Bahama Gazette,* December 13, 1793.

68. *Bahama Gazette,* May 13, 1791.

69. *Bahama Gazette,* November 8, 1793.

70. *Bahama Gazette,* August 2, 1791.

71. *Bahama Gazette*, August 2, 1791.

72. Morrison, "George Liele," 6.

73. Liele, "Letters," 71.

74. Kerber, *No Constitutional Right*, xxiii.

75. See for example the May 2, 1800, *Bahama Gazette,* in which an advertisement called for an "active, hardworking and careful Negro woman, capable of plain cooking,

a good washer and complete house servant." The ad went on to describe other character traits required, including "she must be sober, honest and of good disposition."

76. W. Johnson, *Race Relations,* 31.

77. *Bahama Gazette,* June 22, 1792.

78. *Bahama Gazette,* July 14, 1796.

79. *Bahama Gazette,* August 22, 1797.

80. Schoepf, *Travels,* II: 276, 301.

81. Act proposed in Executive Council, January 15, 1787, COP 23/27.

82. The case of Thomas Flinn, who is 19 or 20 years old, is particularly germane. Flinn apparently had been apprenticed as a baker to Michael Specty and John Lewis Fraser before escaping onboard a vessel captained by William Thompson. The affidavit of his employers, Michael Specty and John Lewis Fraser, also claimed that Lord Dunmore had authorized the said Thompson to carry Flinn away without the necessary bond or security required by law. Though Thompson's racial identity is not indicated, Flinn no doubt was black. Affidavit of Michael Specty and John Lewis Fraser, COP 23/27.

83. *Bahama Gazette,* March 21, 1789.

84. *Bahama Gazette,* July 25, 1789.

85. For diverse but coercive labor arrangements in Nova Scotia, see Troxler, "Re-enslavement of Black Loyalists;" Walker, "Myth, History." See also Walker's earlier monograph, *Black Loyalists.* For Jamaica see Pulis, "Bridging Troubled Waters"; Morrison, "George Liele." Finally, for Cuba see R. Scott, *Slave Emancipation.*

86. This was because they had access to boats and the ability to sail them. See MacIntosh, "Runaway Slaves," 9.

87. W. Johnson, *Race Relations,* 38.

88. Adderley, *New Negroes from Africa,* 2.

89. Adderley, *New Negroes from Africa,* 8.

90. W. Johnson, *Race Relations,* 39.

91. W. Johnson, *Race Relations,* 93.

92. For a study of Liberated African communities see Adderley, *New Negroes from Africa,* 2006.

93. W. Johnson, *Race Relations,* 86.

94. W. Johnson, *Race Relations,* 87.

95. Examples include the marriage on April 8, 1808, between Eustache Peyer, a private of the Seventh West Indian Regiment and Marceline, a free woman of color of the island of Martinique. On that same date another West Indian soldier identified as Jean Francois Cooper of the Seventh West Indian Regiment married Sarah Millar, a free black woman of Nassau. Finally there was the marriage on May 29, 1813, between John Nixon, Sergeant of the Second West Indian Regiment, and Mary Pindar, a free black woman of this place. Marriage Register, Christchurch Cathedral, Department of Archives, Nassau.

96. W. Johnson, *Race Relations,* 44.

97. *Bahama Gazette,* April 29, 1800.

98. *Bahama Gazette,* April 12, 1799.

99. W. Johnson, *Race Relations,* 43. Also *Bahama Gazette,* February 28, 1789.

100. *Bahama Gazette,* February 28, 1789.

101. *Bahama Gazette*, February 6, 1795.

102. *Bahama Gazette,* July 21, 1797.

103. Graham Russell Hodges notes that blacks in New York City lived in "Negro barracks" at 18 Broadway, 10 Church Street, 18 Great George Street, 8 Skinner Street, and 36 St. James Street, and in Brooklyn near the navy yard and the wagon yard. These dormitories were crowded: 64 laborers shared one set of five and a half rooms, 78 others had six and a half rooms, and 37 Black Pioneers shared three and a half rooms; *Roots and Branch*, 150.

104. White, "A Question of Style," 26.

105. See for example a runaway who apparently "plays well on the violin," *Royal Gazette*, September 26, 1778. Also *Royal Gazette*, December 18, 1779. Hodges notes that apart from "Ethiopian balls," Black Loyalists also mixed with whites at other secular public sites within the city, including taverns, gambling houses, and horse races; *Roots and Branches*, 151.

106. *Bahama Gazette,* October 4, 1799.

107. *Bahama Gazette,* October 4, 1799.

108. Studies of other Black Loyalist communities also indicate the presence of a cross-racial plebian culture. For New York see White, "A Question of Style," 23–44; Hodges, *Roots and Branches.* For Jamaica and the thirteen colonies in general see John Pulis, "Bridging Troubled Waters," 183–221.

109. *Bahama Gazette*, June 16, 1795.

110. *Bahama Gazette*, May 6, 1794.

111. *Bahama Gazette*, February 6, 1795.

112. Act printed in the *Bahama Gazette,* December 24, 1799.

113. Act printed in the *Bahama Gazette,* December 24, 1799.

114. Act printed in the *Bahama Gazette,* December 24, 1799.

Chapter 5. Codifying Power, Challenging the Law

1. See Peggs, *Dowson's Journal*, 102. See also Act of 57 Geo., III, c 9, cited in Craton and Saunders, *Islanders in the Stream,* I: 332.

2. Peggs, *Dowson's Journal*, 103.

3. Peggs, *Dowson's Journal,* 104

4. McWeeney, "Madding Crowd," 123, 133. McWeeney mentions a planter on Caicos Island who observed that it was but "6 hours sail from Cape Francois [*sic*]."

5. Childs, "Images," 142.

6. Drescher cites, for example, South Carolina, which reopened the slave trade in 1803 during the climax of the Haitian Revolution. This would also explain why two separate French regimes relaunched the slave trade within the French Caribbean before 1815. Drescher, "Limits of Example," 11. Roughly 40,000 slaves were imported into South Carolina between 1803 and 1807. See Davis, "Impact," 5.

7. The bond amounted to 400 pounds. Presumably a white sponsor would have advanced the bond payment. In such instances, this gesture would have undermined the autonomy that Black Loyalist preachers had envisioned for their congregations.

8. Peggs, *Dowson's Journal*, 104.

9. See notice of Prince Williams, posted in *Bahama Gazette,* October 4, 1799. Also notice of Judy Minors, cited in *Bahama Gazette*, March 22, 1799.

10. For Richard Allen and the founding of the AME, see Newman, "Richard Allen's Eulogy," 117. For black community development in Philadelphia, see also Nash, *Forging Freedom*; Julie Winch, *Philadelphia's Black Elite.*

11. Census data cited by W. Johnson, *Race Relations*, 39, 132.

12. W. Johnson, *Race Relations*, 11.

13. Whittington Johnson argues that with the collapse of the cotton kingdom, the mercantile elite became more concerned about the arrival of new groups of free blacks, most notably West Indian troops. Additionally, "whereas in the 1790s only Turks Island produced salt and many islands planted cotton, in 1831 the tables were turned with many islands producing salt while cotton was hardly mentioned," *Race Relations, 67.*

14. *Bahama Gazette*, May 9, 1795.

15. *Bahama Gazette*, January 1, 1796.

16. *Bahama Gazette*, January 1, 1796.

17. *Bahama Gazette*, January 22, 1796.

18. Craton and Saunders, *Islanders in the Stream*, I: 208–209.

19. Craton and Saunders, *Islanders in the Stream*, I: 211.

20. *Bahama Gazette*, December 13, 1800.

21. *Bahama Gazette,* December 13, 1800.

22. *Bahama Gazette,* December 13, 1800.

23. *Bahama Gazette,* December 13, 1800.

24. *Bahama Gazette,* December 13, 1800.

25. *Bahama Gazette,* December 13, 1800.

26. *Bahama Gazette,* December 13, 1800.

27. *Bahama Gazette,* December 20, 1800.

28. For vivid accounts of the destruction at Cap-Français, see Antoine Dalmas, "History of the Revolution," 92. While Dalmas' report can be corroborated with other accounts, some of his details differ. For example, C.L.R. James noted that two-thirds of the city was destroyed by fire, whereas Dalmas suggested a great deal more was burned to ashes. Coke suggests half the city was destroyed by fire. See James, *Black Jacobins,* 127. Coke, *History*, III: 459.

29. For estimates of refugees leaving La Cap see James, *Black Jacobins,* 127. For studies of the royalist refugees and their impact on various regions within the United States and Louisiana, then under French control, see Baur, "International Repercussions," 394–418.

30. Craton and Saunders, *Islanders in the Stream*, I: 228.

31. Craton and Saunders, *Islanders in the Stream*, I: 332.

32. See Nash, *Forging Freedom*, 2.

33. Douglas Egerton notes that in the United States even though no ballot was cast, former bond-people and even those still enslaved helped to shape the politics of the early Republic through their demands and actions; *Death or Liberty*, 14.

34. Brooks and Saillant, *Face Zion Forward*, 12.

35. Brooks and Saillant, *Face Zion Forward*, 12.

36. Brooks and Saillant, *Face Zion Forward*, 12.

37. Notice of Prince Williams, posted in *Bahama Gazette,* October 4, 1799.

38. Case of Samuel Lambert under death notices, cited in Johnston and Hallett, *Early Colonists,* 104.

39. Notice of Judy Minors, cited in *Bahama Gazette,* March 22, 1799.

40. Pybus, *Epic Journeys of Freedom,* 168.

41. In a letter written by James Jones and dated August 1, 1814, William Dowson described James Jones as "a leader and exhorter in our society in New Providence" who had arrived in the Bahamas from America with the Loyalist refugees. See Peggs, *Dowson's Journal,* 81–82; See also C. Williams, *Methodist Contribution,* 132.

42. Petition cited in C. Williams, "Methodist Contribution," 290–291.

43. Petition cited in C. Williams, "Methodist Contribution," 290–291.

44. Though not an exact replication of the experience of black and white women in the early republican period in the United States, there appear to be interesting parallels. According to Rosanne Zaggari, it was the contested battles between the Republican Party and the Democratic Federalist party that eventually paved the way for women being consigned to the domestic sphere; *Revolutionary Backlash,* 135.

45. Peggs, *Dowson's Journal,* 108.

46. Gilroy, *Black Atlantic,* 4, 17.

47. Morrison includes the covenant in her footnotes. "George Liele," 17. See also Holmes, "George Liele," 345–348. The practices embedded in the 1796 covenant were adopted by black evangelicals in Jamaica such as George Gibb, George Lewis, Thomas Swigle, and Moses Baker. It was also transmitted to congregations in the United States, where white and black evangelicals incorporated it in their efforts to appease planters. See Futrell, "Ethiopian Baptists," 82–83.

48. Liele and the other Black Loyalist evangelicals petitioned the government for the right to "worship Almighty God according to the tenets of the Bible." Although the Jamaican Legislature tacitly agreed to grant the license to black leaders Liele, Moses Baker, George Vinyard, and Thomas Swigle, it came at a price. In dispensing the authority to preach, the Jamaican legislation (later adopted by the Bahamian legislature) made it mandatory that a preaching license be required, to be renewed annually at considerable expense to the applicant. Liele, "Letters," 72; Liele, "Letter to John C. Rippon."

49. December 1, 1825, COP 23/81, folio 315.

50. The marriage of Prince Williams to Peggy Wilson is verified in the Christ Church Marriage Register. See Marriage Register, Christ Church Cathedral Marriage Register, 1791–1828, Department of Archives. 1807–1828.

51. Petition of Prince Williams, January 1826, COP 23/81.

52. Petition of Prince Williams, January 1826, COP 23/81.

53. Petition of Prince Williams, January 1826, COP 23/81.

54. Petition of Prince Williams, January 1826, COP 23/81.

55. Petition of Prince Williams, January 1826, COP 23/81.

56. Petition of Prince Williams, January 1826, COP 23/81.

57. Cassandra Pybus notes that Thomas Peters, a Black Loyalist with Yoruba origins, petitioned the British government to establish an alternative colony for blacks settled in Nova Scotia. In the petition, Peters argued that "blacks were refused the common rights

and privileges of other inhabitants, not being permitted to vote at any elections nor serve on juries." Thomas Peters' petition, FO 4/1/419, NA, cited by Pybus, *Epic Journeys of Freedom*, 23; Pybus, "Runaway Slaves," 124–125.

58. Petition of Prince Williams, January 1826, COP 23/81.

59. Petition of Prince Williams, January 1826, COP 23/81.

60. Petition of Prince Williams, January 1826, COP 23/81.

61. Petition of Prince Williams, January 1826, COP 23/81.

62. Petition of Prince Williams, January 1826, COP 23/81.

63. Petition of Prince Williams, January 1826, COP 23/81.

64. Canzoneri, "Early History," 10.

65. *Bahama Gazette,* March 29, 1792.

66. *Bahama Gazette*, March 29, 1792.

67. The petition is found among the collection of Brown family documents located at the New York Historical Society. Petition of Caesar Brown, addressed to Mrs. Sophia Brown, Amboy, near New York, Brown Family Correspondence.

68. Petition of Caesar Brown, addressed to Mrs. Sophia Brown, Perth Amboy, near New York, Brown Family Correspondence.

69. Will of Anthony Wallace, December 9, 1830, Supreme Court Wills, W, Department of Archives, Nassau.

70. For an extensive overview of the series of insurrections that occurred on Lord Rolle's plantations in Exuma, see Craton and Saunders. Of significance, the authors note that "the flogging of the Rolle women in April 1830 also created such a stir in antislavery circles that it accelerated protective legislation, if not the emancipation bill itself"; *Islanders in the Stream*, I: 383–386.

71. Craton and Saunders, *Islanders in the Stream,* I: 366.

72. Craton and Saunders, *Islanders in the Stream,* I: 367.

73. Craton and Saunders, *Islanders in the Stream,* I: 367.

74. Grant to Goderich, February 10, 1824, Duplicate correspondence, 5, 1834, Bahamas Archives, cited by Craton and Saunders, *Islanders in the Stream*, I: 332.

75. Craton and Saunders, *Islanders in the Stream*, I: 333.

76. Craton and Saunders, *Islanders in the Stream,* I: 334.

77. Adderley, *New Negroes from Africa,* 121.

78. Adderley, *New Negroes from Africa,* 162.

Conclusion

1. Symonette and Canzoneri, *Baptists in the Bahamas*, 13.

2. Craton and Saunders, *Islanders in the Stream*, I: 334.

3. Marrant was in fact ordained on May 15, 1785. See Brooks and Saillant, *Face Zion Forward*, 10–11. For work on John Marrant's radical theology, see Hinks, "John Marrant," 105–117. Marrant's republicanism was shared by other black evangelicals such as Lemuel Haynes. For work on Lemuel Haynes, see Saillant, *Black Puritan*; Saillant, "Revolutionary Origins," 79–102; Saillant, "Black Republicanism," 293–324; Roberts, "Patriotism," 569–588; R. Brown, "Extreme Poverty," 502–518.

4. Brooks and Saillant, *Face Zion Forward*, 17–20.

5. E. Wilson, *Loyal Blacks,* 228.

6. James Sidbury notes that black artisans and other working people living in American coastal cities founded a range of churches, schools, and fraternal organizations during the decades surrounding 1800, and many included the term "African" within their titles; *Becoming African in America,* 7.

7. Will of Frank Spence, Supreme Court Wills, Department of Archives, Nassau.

8. See Herman Bennett's work on colonial Mexico City, where descendants of Africans, though aware of Christian norms, exhibited alternative social practices with their Spanish lovers; *Colonial Blackness,* 37.

9. Bennett, *Colonial Blackness,* 76, 82–83; Gilroy, *The Black Atlantic,* 72–110.

10. Craton and Saunders, *Islanders in the Stream,* I: 185.

11. Craton, "Loyalists Mainly to Themselves," 63.

12. Governor's Dispatches. Vol. 2, May 8, 1838, no. 105, cited by Symonette and Canzoneri, *Baptists in the Bahamas,* 19.

13. Symonette and Canzoneri, *Baptists in the Bahamas,* 19.

14. Moving beyond oral history accounts that suggest a high concentration of Yorubas among Liberated Africans settling in the Bahamas, Adderley uses documents from Cuba's Anglo-Spanish Mixed Commission in order to determine the number of ethnic Yorubas processed in Cuba. Of the 10,391 Liberated Africans processed in Cuba, Yorubas were counted as the largest group, with 2,755 or 26.51%. As this cohort studied by Adderley only accounts for those tried in Cuba, the actual number of Yorubas entering the Bahamas is still difficult to determine. It is worth noting that many late-nineteenth-century travel writers in the Bahamas refer to distinct African ethnicities, including Nangoes [Yorubas], "Congoes," and "Egbas"; *New Negroes from Africa,* 101, 118.

15. Adderley notes that specific outcomes in Trinidad and the Bahamas were determined by environment and the degree of input by missionaries. She also notes that in the Bahamas, Wesleyan missionaries were relatively confined and more intensively focused on the missionary territory of New Providence, whereas in Trinidad there was a combination of autonomy and missionary neglect. Missing from her analysis is the role of Black Loyalists or other black missionaries—both Methodists and Baptists—who spearheaded work in New Providence and the Family Islands; *New Negroes from Africa,* 179–180.

16. Craton and Saunders, *Islanders in the Stream,* II: 457. Craton and Saunders have argued that in more recent years a shift from the employment of black Bahamians to Haitians has occurred. Hence, by the 1980s, each of the Abaco cays had its small resident group of Haitian migrants, informally assigned a location for their settlement in the remotest spot, at Man-O-War Cay, adjacent to the garbage dump.

17. Craton and Saunders, *Islanders in the Stream,* II: 188.

18. See for example Craton, "Bay Street," 71–94; Hughes, *Race and Politics*; Saunders, *Bahamian Society after Emancipation.*

19. LaFlamme, "Green Turtle Cay: A Bi-racial Community in the Out Island Bahamas," cited in Hughes, *Race and Politics,* 23.

20. Craton, "Bay Street," 84.

BIBLIOGRAPHY

Primary Sources

Bahama Gazette, 1784–1802

Book of Negroes, BHP Box 44, #10427. Rare Book and Manuscript Room, New York Public Library, Stephen A. Schwarzman Building, New York City.

[BHP] British Headquarters Papers, Boxes 31–43, Rare Book and Manuscript Room, New York Public Library, Stephen A. Schwarzman Building, New York City.

Brown Family Correspondence and Miscellaneous Items, 1 box, New York Historical Society.

Census Records, 1784–1814, East Florida papers, microfilm reel 148, list of Negroes with Certificates of Freedom, University of Florida Special Collections Library.

Charleston Royal Gazette 1782–1783, The South Carolina Historical Society, Charleston, South Carolina.

Christ Church Cathedral Marriage Register, 1791–1828.

Coke, Thomas. *A History of the West Indies: Containing the Natural, Civil and Ecclesiastical History of Each Island.* Vol. III. London: T. Blanshard, 1811.

[COP] Colonial Office Papers 23/25–30; 23/81, Special Collections, Department of Archives, Nassau, Bahamas.

[COP] Colonial Office Papers 5/557, Saint Augustine Historical Society, St. Augustine, FL.

Dowson, W. "Letter from Mr. Dowson to the Methodist Conference." *Methodist Magazine* 37 (Dec. 1814): 952. http://britishperiodicals.chadwyck.com.ezproxy.lib.uconn .ed u/journals/(accessed Nov. 5, 2009).

George, David. "An Account of the Life of Mr. David George, from Sierra Leone in Africa; Given by himself in a conversation with Brother Rippon of London, and Brother Pearce of Birmingham, 1793." Reprinted in *Face Zion Forward: First Writers of the*

Black Atlantic, 1785–1798, edited by Joanna Brooks and John Saillant. Boston: Northeastern University Press, 2002.

Graves, John. *A Memorial: or, a Short Account of the Bahama Islands . . .* London: 1707. Gale Eighteenth Century Collections Online. http://galenet.galegroup.com.ezproxy.lib.uconn.edu/servlet/ECCO (accessed January 12, 2010).

Liele, George. "Letters Showing the Rise and Progress of the Early Negro Churches of Georgia and the West Indies," *Journal of Negro History* 1:1 (1916): 69–92.

Liele, George. "Letter to John C. Rippon," December 19, 1791. *Baptist Annual Register* (1791): 1: 334.

Marrant, John. "A Narrative of the Lord's Wonderful Dealings with John Marrant, A Black." London: Gilbert and Plummer, 1785. Reprinted in *Face Zion Forward: First Writers of the Black Atlantic, 1785–1798,* edited by Joanna Brooks and John Saillant. Boston: Northeastern University Press, 2002.

Methodist District Meeting Minutes, Special Collections, Department of Archives, Nassau, Bahamas.

Miller, William Hubert, ed. *Peter Townsend's Journal: The Diary of a Physician from the United States Visiting the Island of New Providence, 1823–24.* Nassau: Bahamas Historical Society, 1968.

Oldmixon, John. *The History of the Isle of Providence.* Reprint of a chapter in the 1741 ed. Nassau: The Providence Press, 1966.

Pascoe, C. F. *Two Hundred Years of the SPG: An Historical Account of the Society for the Propagation of the Gospel in Foreign Parts, 1701–1900.* London: Society for the Propagation of the Gospel in Foreign Parts, 1901.

Peggs, Dean, ed. *A Mission to the West India Islands: Dowson's Journal for 1810–17.* Nassau: The Deans Peggs Research Fund, 1960.

Proceedings and other records of the Board of Police, 1780–1782, South Carolina State Archives, Columbia, South Carolina.

Report of John Wilson acting engineer, New York, July 14, 1783, Box 5, file 4, Saint Augustine Historical Society.

Royal Gazette (New York) 1777–1783

Royal Georgia Gazette 1776–1779

Schoepf, Johann David. *Travels in the Confederation, 1783–1784.* Vol. II. Philadelphia: William J. Campbell, 1911; originally published in 1788.

SPG Records, The West Indies/Bahamas 1710–1908, Special Collections, Department of Archives, Nassau, Bahamas.

Supreme Court Wills, P–Y, Special Collections, Department of Archives, Nassau, Bahamas.

Townsend, P., *The Diary of a Physician from the United States visiting the Island of New Providence, 1823–24.* Nassau: Bahamas Historical Society, 1968.

Turton, William. "New Providence" *Methodist Magazine* 27 (Aug 1804): 382. http://britishperiodicals.chadwyck.com.ezproxy.lib.uconn.ed u/journals/ (accessed Nov. 5, 2009).

Ward, Joseph. "Letter from Mr. Ward to Mr. Buckley." *Methodist Magazine,* 39 (Jan

1816): 71. http://britishperiodicals.chadwyck.com.ezproxy.lib.uconn.edu/journals / (accessed Nov. 5, 2009).

Williams, Prince. Claim in the Loyalist Claims Commission, Sept 1, 1783, Great Britain Public Records Office, Audit Office, Class 12, Volume 99, folios 353–354. Cited at On-line Institute for Advanced Loyalist Studies. "Claims and Memorials; Decision on the Claim of Prince William of Georgia." http://www.royalprovincial.com/military /mems/ga/clmwilliam.htm (accessed April 12, 2010).

Wills, Deeds and Records, Nassau, Bahamas, 1700–1845, Georgia Historical Society.

Wylly, William. *A short account of The Bahama Islands, their climate, productions, &c. To which are added, some strictures upon their relative and political situation, the defects of their present government, &c. &c. By a barrister at law, late His Majesty's Solicitor General of those islands.* London: 1789. Eighteenth Century Collections Online, Gale Group. http://galenet.galegroup.com/servlet/ECCO (accessed January 11, 2010).

Secondary Sources

Adderley, Rosanne M. *New Negroes from Africa: Slave Trade Abolition and Free African Settlement in the Nineteenth-Century Caribbean.* Bloomington: Indiana University Press, 2006.

Albury, Paul. *The Story of The Bahamas.* London: Macmillan, 1975.

Aptheker, Herbert. *American Negro Slave Revolt.* New York: Columbia University Press, 1943.

Baum, Rosalie Murphy. "Early American Literature: Reassessing the Black Contribution." *Eighteenth-Century Studies* 27:4 (1994): 533–549.

Baur, John E. "International Repercussions of the Haitian Revolution," *The Americas* 26:4 (1970): 394–418.

Beckles, Hilary. *Centering Woman: Gender discourses in Caribbean Slave Society.* Kingston, Jamaica: Ian Randle, 1999.

———. "An Economic Life of Their Own." In *The Slaves' Economy: Independent Production by Slaves in the Americas,* edited by Philip Morgan and Ira Berlin. London: Frank Cass, 1991.

———. "Freedom without Liberty: Free Blacks in the Barbados Slave System." In *Slavery without Sugar: Diversity in Caribbean Economy and Society since the 17th Century,* edited by Verene Shepherd. Gainesville: University Press of Florida, 2002.

———. "Caribbean Anti-slavery: The Self-Liberation Ethos of Enslaved Blacks." In *Caribbean Slavery in the Atlantic World: A Student Reader,* edited by Verene Shepherd and Hilary Beckles. Kingston, Jamaica: Ian Randle, 2000.

Beckles, Hilary, and Verene Shepard. *Liberties Lost: The Indigenous Caribbean and Slave Systems.* Cambridge: Cambridge University Press, 2004.

Bennett, Herman. *Africans in Colonial Mexico: Absolutism, Christianity, and Afro-Creole Consciousness, 1570–1640.* Bloomington: Indiana University Press, 2005.

———. *Colonial Blackness: A History of Afro-Mexico.* Bloomington: Indiana University Press, 2009.

Berlin, Ira. *Many Thousands Gone: The First Two Centuries of Slavery in North America.* Cambridge, MA: Harvard University Press, 2000.

Berlin, Ira, and Philip Morgan, eds. *The Slaves' Economy: Independent Production by Slaves in the Americas.* London: Frank Cass, 1991.

Besson, Jean. "Religion as Resistance in Jamaican Peasant Life: The Baptist Church, Revival Worldview and Rastafarian Movement." In *Rastafari and Other African-Caribbean Worldviews,* edited by Barry Chevannes. London: Macmillan, 1995.

Blackburn, Robin. *The Overthrow of Colonial Slavery: 1776–1848.* London: Verso, 2011.

Blanck, Emily. "The Legal Emancipations of Leander and Caesar: Manumission and the Law in Revolutionary South Carolina and Massachusetts." *Slavery and Abolition* 28:2 (2007): 235–254.

Brereton, Virginia. *From Sin to Salvation: Stories of Women's Conversions, 1800 to Present.* Bloomington: Indiana University Press, 1991.

Brooks, Joanna, and John Saillant, eds. *Face Zion Forward: First Writers of the Black Atlantic, 1785–1798.* Boston: Northeastern University Press, 2002.

Brooks, Walter. "The Priority of the Silver Bluff Church and Its Promoters." *Journal of Negro History* 7:2 (1922): 172–196.

Brown, Christopher Leslie. *Moral Capital: Foundations of British Abolitionism.* Chapel Hill: University of North Carolina Press, 2006.

Brown, Kathleen. *Good Wives, Nasty Wenches and Anxious Patriarchs: Gender, Race and Power in Colonial Virginia.* Chapel Hill: University of North Carolina Press, 1996.

Brown, Lois. "Memorial Narratives of African Women in Antebellum New England." *Legacy* 20: 1&2 (2003): 38–61.

Brown, Richard D. "'Not Only Extreme Poverty, but the Worst Kind of Orphanage': Lemuel Haynes and the Boundaries of Racial Tolerance on the Yankee Frontier, 1770–1820." *New England Quarterly* 61:4 (1998): 502–518.

Bundy, David. "The African and Caribbean Origins of Methodism in the Bahamas." *Methodist History* 53:3 (2015): 173–183.

Bush, Barbara. *Slave Women in Caribbean Society, 1650–1838.* Bloomington: Indiana University Press, 1990.

Buskirk, Judith Van. *Generous Enemies: Patriots and Loyalists in Revolutionary New York.* Philadelphia: University of Pennsylvania Press, 2002.

Cahill, Barry. "The Black Loyalist Myth in Atlantic Canada." *Acadiensis* 29:1 (1999): 76–87.

Canzoneri, Antonina. "Early History of the Baptists in the Bahamas." *Bahamas Historical Society Journal* 4:1 (1982): 9–16.

Cash, Philip, Shirley Gordon, and Gail Saunders, eds. *Sources of Bahamian History.* London: MacMillan, 1991.

Catron, John W. "Evangelical Networks in the Greater Caribbean and the Origins of the Black Church." *Church History* 79:1 (2010): 77–114.

Childs, Matt. "Images of the Haitian Revolution in Cuba's 1812 Aponte Rebellion." In *The Impact of the Haitian Revolution in the Atlantic World,* edited by David Patrick Geggus. Columbia: University of South Carolina Press, 2001.

Cleve, George Van. "Somerset's Case and its Antecedent in Imperial Perspective." *Law and History Review* 24:3 (2006): 601–646.

Craton, Michael. "Loyalists Mainly to Themselves: The 'Black Loyalist' Diaspora to the Bahamas, 1783–c.1820." In *Working Slavery, Pricing Freedom: Perspectives from the Caribbean, Africa and the African Diaspora,* edited by Verene A. Shepherd. New York: Palgrave, 2002.

———. *A History of the Bahamas.* London: Collins, 1968.

———. "Historiography of the Bahamas, Turks and Caicos, Cayman Islands and Belize." In *General History of the Caribbean: Methodology and Historiography of the Caribbean,* vol. 6, edited by B. W. Higman. London: UNESCO/Macmillan Caribbean, 1999.

———. "Bay Street, Black Power and the Conchy Joes: Race and Class in the Colony and Commonwealth of the Bahamas, 1850–2000." In *The White Minority in the Caribbean,* edited by Howard Johnson and Karl Watson. Kingston, Jamaica: Ian Randle, 1998.

———. "The Evolution of Bahamian Land Tenures." In *Land and Development in the Caribbean,* edited by Jean Besson and Janet Momsen. London: Macmillan Caribbean, 1987.

———. "Hobbesian or Panglossian? The Two Extremes of Slave Conditions in the British Caribbean, 1783 to 1834." *William and Mary Quarterly,* 3rd ser. 35:2 (1978): 324–356.

———. "We Shall Not Be Moved: Pompey's Slave Revolt in Exuma Island, Bahamas, 1830." *New West Indian Guide* 57:1/2 (1983): 19–35.

Craton, Michael, and Gail Saunders. *Islanders in the Stream: A History of the Bahamian People.* 2 vols. Athens: University of Georgia Press, 1992–1998.

Curry, Christopher. "A History of the Baptists' Contribution to Education in the Bahamas." *American Baptist Quarterly* 26: 4 (2007): 374–387.

———. "Christianity and Slavery in The Bahamas: A Catalyst for Revolutionary Change or a Quest for Respectability." M.A. thesis, University of Waterloo, 1996.

Dalmas, Antoine. "History of the Revolution of Saint Domingue," originally published in Paris in 1814. In *Slave Revolution in the Caribbean 1789–1804: A Brief History with Documents,* edited by Laurent Dubois and John D. Garrigus. Boston/New York: Bedford/St. Martin's, 2006.

Davis, David Brion. "Impact of the French and Haitian Revolutions." In *The Impact of the Haitian Revolution in the Atlantic World,* edited by David Patrick Geggus. Columbia: University of South Carolina Press, 2001.

Dayton, Cornelia Hughes. *Women Before the Bar: Gender, Law and Society in Connecticut, 1639–1789.* Chapel Hill: University of North Carolina Press, 1995.

Degler, Carl. *Neither White nor Black: Slavery and Race Relations in Brazil and the United States.* Madison: University of Wisconsin Press, 1971.

Dodd, Dorothy. "The Wrecking Business on the Florida Reef 1822–1860." *Florida Historical Quarterly* 22:4 (2008): 171–199.

Dodge, Steve. *Abaco: The History of an Out Island and its Cays.* Decatur, IL: White Sound Press, 1995.

———. *Carleton: Refugee Loyalist Settlement in Abaco, 1783–c.1790.* Abaco: Abaco Archaeological Survey–Carleton project, 1985.

Drescher, Seymour. "The Limits of Example." In *The Impact of the Haitian Revolution in the Atlantic World,* edited by David Patrick Geggus. Columbia: University of South Carolina Press, 2001.

Dyer, Justin Buckley. "After the Revolution: Somerset and the Antislavery Tradition in Anglo-American Constitutional Development." *Journal of Politics* 71:4 (2009): 1422–1434.

Egerton, Douglas. *Death or Liberty: African Americans and Revolutionary America*. New York: Oxford University Press, 2009.

Engerman, Stanley L., and B. W. Higman, "The Demographic Structure of the Caribbean Slave Societies in the Eighteenth and Nineteenth Centuries." In *General History of the Caribbean: The Slave Societies of the Caribbean*, vol. 3, edited by Franklin W. Knight. London: UNESCO/Macmillan, 1997.

Finkenbine, Roy E., and Richard S. Newman. "Black Founders in the New Republic: Introduction." *William and Mary Quarterly*, 3rd ser. 64:1 (2007): 83–94.

Frey, Sylvia. *Water from the Rock: Black Resistance in a Revolutionary Age*. Princeton, NJ: Princeton University Press, 1991.

Fuente, Alejandro de la. "Slave Law and Claims-Making in Cuba: The Tannenbaum Debate Revisited." *Law and History Review* 22:2 (2004): 339–369.

Futrell, Samantha. "They Came Up Out of the Water: Ethiopian Baptists in the Southern Low-country and Jamaica, 1737–1806." M.A. thesis, Liberty University, 2013.

Genovese, Eugene. *Roll Jordon Roll: The World the Slaves Made*. New York: Pantheon Books, 1974.

Gilroy, Paul. *The Black Atlantic: Modernity and Double Consciousness*. Cambridge, MA: Harvard University Press, 1993.

Gomez, Michael. *Reversing Sail: A History of the African Diaspora: New Approaches to African History*. New York: Cambridge University Press, 2005.

———. *Exchanging Our Country Marks: The Transformation of African Identities in the Colonial and Antebellum South*. Chapel Hill: University of North Carolina Press, 1998.

Harris, Leslie. *In the Shadow of Slavery: African-Americans in New York City, 1626–1863*. Chicago: University of Chicago Press, 2003.

Harris, Leslie, and Ira Berlin, eds. *Slavery in New York*. New York: New Press, 2005.

Harris, Marvin. *Patterns of Race in the Americas*. Westport, CT: Greenwood, 1980.

Hinks, Peter P. "John Marrant and the Meaning of Early Black Free Masonry." *William and Mary Quarterly*, 3rd ser. 64:1 (2007): 105–117.

Hodges, Graham Russell, ed. *The Black Loyalist Directory: African Americans in Exile after the American Revolution*. New York: Garland Publishing in association with New England Historic Genealogical Society, 1996.

———. *Roots and Branch: African Americans in New York and East Jersey: 1613–1863*. Chapel Hill: University of North Carolina Press, 1999.

———, ed. *Black Itinerants of the Gospel: The Narratives of John Jea and George White*. Madison, WI: Madison House, 1993.

———. "Liberty and Constraint: the Limits of Revolution." In *Slavery in New York*, edited by Leslie Harris and Ira Berlin. New York: New Press, 2005.

———. *Slavery, Freedom and Culture among Early American Workers*. Armonk, NY: M.E. Sharpe, 1998.

Holmes, E. A., "George Liele: Negro Slavery's Prophet of Deliverance, *Baptist Quarterly*. London: Baptist Historical Society, 1964.

Hughes, Colin. *Race and Politics in the Bahamas.* London: University of Queensland Press, 1981.

Hulsebosch, Daniel J. "Nothing but Liberty: 'Somerset's Case' and the British Empire." *Law and History Review* 24:3 (2006): 647–657.

Isaac, Rhys. *The Transformation of Virginia.* Chapel Hill: University of North Carolina Press, 1982.

James, C.L.R. *The Black Jacobins: Toussaint L'Ouverture and the San Domingo Revolution.* New York: Vintage, 1989.

Jasanoff, Maya. "The Other Side of Revolution: Loyalists in the British Empire." *William and Mary Quarterly,* 3rd ser. 65:2 (2008): 205–233.

Johnson, Howard. *The Bahamas in Slavery and Freedom.* Kingston, Jamaica: Ian Randle, 1991.

———. *The Bahamas from Slavery to Servitude, 1783–1933.* Gainesville: University Press of Florida, 1996.

Johnson, Whittington. *Race Relations in the Bahamas, 1784–1834.* Fayetteville: The University of Arkansas Press, 2000.

Johnston, Francis Claiborne, and C.F.E. Hollis Hallett. *Early Colonists of the Bahamas: A Selection of Records.* Bermuda: Juniper Hill Press, 1996.

Joyner, Charles. *Down by the Riverside: A South Carolina Slave Community.* Chicago: University of Illinois Press, 1984.

Kelley, Robin. *Race Rebels, Culture, Politics, and the Black Working Class.* New York: Free Press, 1996.

Kerber, Linda K. *No Constitutional Right to be Ladies: Women and the Obligations of Citizenship.* New York: Hill and Wang, 1998.

Knight, Franklin, ed. *General History of the Caribbean: The Slave Societies of the Caribbean.* Vol. 3. London: UNESCO/Macmillan, 1997.

Kramnick, Isaac. *Republicanism and Bourgeois Radicalism: Political Ideology in Late Eighteenth-Century England and America.* Ithaca, NY: Cornell University Press, 1990.

Landers, Jane. *Black Society in Spanish Florida.* Chicago: University of Illinois Press, 1999.

———. "Black Community and Culture in the Southeastern Borderlands." *Journal of the Early Republic* 18:1 (1998): 117–134.

MacIntosh, Roderick J. "Trades and Occupations of Runaway Slaves in the Bahamas." *Journal of the Bahamas Historical Society* 6:1 (1984): 7–14.

Mangan, Jane E. *Gender, Ethnicity, and the Urban Economy in Colonial Potosi.* Durham, NC: Duke University Press, 2005.

May, Cedric. "John Marrant and the Narrative Construction of an Early Black Methodist Evangelical." *African American Review* 38:4 (2004): 553–570.

McKinley, Michelle. "Fractional Freedoms: Slavery, Legal Activism and Ecclesiastical Courts in Colonial Lima, 1593–1689." *Law and History Review* 28:3 (2010): 749–790.

McWeeney, Sean. "Not Far from the Madding Crowd: Bahamian Reaction to the Revolutionary Upheaval in Haiti and the Intensification of Racial Control." *Journal of Haitian Studies,* 10 (2004): 122–145.

Mintz, Sidney W. *Caribbean Transformations*. New York: Columbia University Press, 1989.

Mintz, Sidney W., and Douglas Hall. *The Origins of the Jamaican Internal Marketing System*. New Haven, CT: Dept. of Anthropology, Yale University, 1960.

Mitchell, Michelle. *Righteous Propagation: African Americans and the Politics of Racial Destiny after Reconstruction*. Chapel Hill: University of North Carolina Press, 2004.

Morgan, Philip D., and Andrew Jackson O'Shaughnessy. "Arming Slaves in the American Revolution." In *Arming Slaves from Classical Times to the Modern Age,"* edited by Christopher Leslie Brown and Philip D. Morgan. New Haven, CT: Yale University Press, 2006.

Morrison, Doreen. "George Liele and the Ethiopian Baptist Church: The First Credible Baptist Missionary Witness to the World." Self-published, 2014.

Mullin, Michael. *Africa in America: Slave Acculturation and Resistance in the American South and the British Caribbean, 1736–1831*. Chicago: University of Illinois Press, 1992.

Nash, Gary B., *Forging Freedom: The Formation of Philadelphia's Black Community, 1720– 1840*. Cambridge, MA: Harvard University Press, 1988.

Newman, Richard. "'We Participate in Common': Richard Allen's Eulogy of Washington and the Challenge of Interracial Appeals." *William and Mary Quarterly,* 3rd ser., 64:1 (2007): 117–128.

Norton, Mary Beth. "The Fate of Some Black Loyalists of The American Revolution." *Journal of Negro History* 58:4 (1973): 402–426.

Olwell, Robert. "'Loose, Idel and Disorderly': Slave Women in Eighteenth Century Charleston Marketplace." In *More than Chattel: Black Women and Slavery in the Americas*, edited by David Barry Gaspar and Darlene Clark Hine. Bloomington: Indiana University Press, 1996.

Paley, Ruth. "After Somerset: Mansfield, Slavery and the Law in England, 1772–1830." In *Law, Crime and English Society, 1660–1830*, edited by Norma Landau. New York: Cambridge University Press, 2002.

Parish, Lydia Austin. "Records of Some Southern Loyalists . . . Being a Collection of Manuscripts about some eight families most of whom immigrated to the Bahamas during and after the American Revolution" [original 1953]. Department of Archives, Nassau, Bahamas.

Peters, Thelma. "The American Loyalists and the Plantation Period in the Bahama Islands." Ph.D. diss., University of Florida, 1960.

Piecuch, Jim. *Three Peoples, One King: Loyalists, Indians, and Slaves in the Revolutionary South, 1775–1782*. Columbia: The University of South Carolina Press, 2008.

Pulis, John W., ed. *Moving On: Black Loyalists in the Afro-Atlantic World*. New York: Garland, 1999.

———. "Bridging Troubled Waters: Moses Baker, George Liele, and the African American Diaspora to Jamaica." In *Moving On: Black Loyalists in The Afro-Atlantic World*, edited by John W. Pulis. New York: Garland, 1999.

Pugh, Alfred L. "The Great Awakening and Baptist Beginnings in Colonial Georgia, the Bahama Islands, and Jamaica (1739–1833)." *American Baptist Quarterly* 26:4 (2007): 374–387.

Pybus, Cassandra. *Epic Journeys of Freedom: Runaway Slaves of the American Revolution and their Global Quest for Liberty.* Boston: Beacon Press, 2005.

———. "From Epic Journeys of Freedom: Runaway Slaves of the American Revolution and their Global Quest for Liberty." *Callaloo* 29:1 (2006): 114–130.

Quarles, Benjamin. *The Negro in the American Revolution.* Chapel Hill: University of North Carolina Press, 1961.

Reily, D. A. "William Hammett: Missionary and Founder of the Primitive Methodist Connection," *Methodist History* 10 (1971): 30–44.

Riley, Sandra. *Homeward Bound: A History of the Bahama Islands to 1850.* Miami: Island Research, 1983.

Roberts, Rita. "Patriotism and Political Criticism: The Evolution of Political Consciousness in the Mind of a Black Revolutionary Soldier." *Eighteenth-Century Studies* 27:4 (1994): 569–588.

Rodriguez, Felix V. Matos. "Domestics, Urban Enslaved Workers, and the Abolition of Slavery in Puerto Rico." In *Slavery without Sugar: Diversity in Caribbean Economy and Society since the Seventeenth Century,* edited by Verene Shepherd. Gainesville: University Press of Florida, 2002.

———. *Women and Urban Change in San Juan Puerto Rico, 1820–1868.* Gainesville: University Press of Florida, 1999.

Rooke, Patricia T. "The Pedagogy of Conversion: Missionary Education to Slaves in the British West Indies, 1800–1833." *Paedagogica Historica* 18:1 (1978): 356–372.

Saillant, John. "Antiguan Methodism and Antislavery Activity: Anne and Elizabeth Hart in the Eighteenth-Century Black Atlantic." *Church History* 69:1 (2000): 86–115.

———. "Lemuel Haynes's Black Republicanism and the American Republican Tradition, 1775–1820." *Journal of the Early Republic* 14:3 (1994): 293–324.

———. "Lemuel Haynes and the Revolutionary Origins of Black Theology, 1776–1801." *Religion and American Culture* 2:1 (1992): 79–102

———. *Black Puritan, Black Republican: The Life and Thought of Lemuel Haynes, 1753–1833.* New York: Oxford University Press, 2003.

Saunders, Gail. *Bahamian Loyalists and their Slaves.* London: Macmillan Caribbean, 1983.

———. *Slavery in the Bahamas.* Nassau: Media Publishing, 1995.

———. *Bahamian Society After Emancipation.* Kingston, Jamaica: Ian Randle, 2000.

———. "Slavery and Cotton Culture in the Bahamas." In *Working Slavery, Pricing Freedom: Perspectives from the Caribbean, Africa and the African Diaspora,* edited by Verene A. Shepherd. New York: Palgrave, 2001.

Schmidt-Nowara, Christopher. "Still Continents (and an Island) with Two Histories?" *Law and History Review* 22:2 (2004): 377–382.

Scott, James C. *Domination and the Arts of Resistance: Hidden Transcripts.* New Haven, CT: Yale University Press, 1990.

Scott, Joan. *Gender and the Politics of History.* New York: Columbia University Press, 1988.

Scott, Rebecca. *Degrees of Freedom: Louisiana and Cuba after Slavery, 1862–1914.* Cambridge, MA: Harvard University Press, 2009.

———. *Slave Emancipation in Cuba: The Transition to Free Labor, 1860–1899.* Pittsburgh: University of Pittsburgh Press, 2000.

Shepherd, Verene, ed. *Slavery without Sugar: Diversity in Caribbean Economy and Society since the Seventeenth Century.* Gainesville: University Press of Florida, 2002.

Shirley, Paul. "Tek force wid force." *History Today* 54:4 (2004): 30–36.

———. "Migration, Freedom and Enslavement in the Revolutionary Atlantic." Ph.D diss., University College of London, 2011.

Sidbury, James. *Becoming African in America: Race and Nation in the Early Black Atlantic.* New York: Oxford University Press, 2007.

———. *Ploughshares into Swords: Race, Rebellion, and Identity in Gabriel's Virginia, 1730–1810.* New York: Cambridge University Press, 1997.

Siebert, Wilbur Henry. *The Legacy of the American Revolution to the British West Indies and Bahamas: A Chapter out of the History of the American Loyalists.* Boston: Gregg Press, 1972.

Sio, Arnold. "Marginality and Free Coloured Identity in Caribbean Society." *Slavery and Abolition* 8:2 (1987): 166–182.

Sobel, Mechal. *The World They Made Together: Black and White Values in Eighteenth-Century Virginia.* Princeton, NJ: Princeton University Press, 1989.

———. *Trabelin' On: The Slave Journey to an Afro-Baptist Faith.* Westport, CT: Greenwood Press, 1979.

Sparks, Randy. *The Two Princes of Calabar: An Eighteenth-Century Odyssey.* Cambridge, MA: Harvard University Press, 2004.

Stuckey, Sterling. *Slave Culture: Nationalist Theory and the Foundations of Black America.* New York: Oxford University Press, 1988.

Symonette, Michael C., and Antonina Canzoneri. *Baptists in the Bahamas.* El Paso, TX: Baptist Spanish Publishing House, 1977.

Tannenbaum, Frank. *Slave and Citizen: The Negro in the Americas.* New York: Alfred A Knopf, 1947.

Troxler, Carole. "Refuge, Resistance, and Reward: The Southern Loyalists' Claim on East Florida." *Journal of Southern History* 55:4 (1989): 563–596.

———. "Hidden From History: Black Loyalists at Country Harbour, Nova Scotia." In *Moving On: Black Loyalists in The Afro-Atlantic World,* edited by John W. Pulis. New York: Garland, 1999.

———. "Re-enslavement of Black Loyalists: Mary Postell in South Carolina, East Florida, and Nova Scotia." *Acadiensis* 37:2 (2008): 70–85.

Truett, Samuel, and Elliot Young, eds. *Continental Crossroads: Remapping U.S.-Mexico Borderlands History.* Durham, NC: Duke University Press, 2004.

Underhill, Edward Bean. *The West Indies: Their Social and Religious Condition.* Westport, CT: Negro Universities Press, 1970.

Vianna, Fernando, ed. *The American Heritage Desk Dictionary.* Boston: Houghton Mifflin, 1981.

Walker, James W. St. G. *The Black Loyalists: Search for a Promised Land in Nova Scotia and Sierra Leone 1783–1870.* New York: Africana Publishing, 1976.

———. "Myth, History and Revisionism: The Black Loyalists Revisited." *Acadiensis,* 29:1 (1999): 88–105.

Welch, Pedro L. V. "The Urban Context of the Life of the Enslaved: Views from Bridgetown Barbados in the Eighteenth and Nineteenth Centuries." In *Slavery without Sugar: Diversity in Caribbean Economy and Society since the 17th Century,* edited by Verene Shepherd. Gainesville: University Press of Florida, 2002.

White, Shane. "A Question of Style: Blacks in and around New York City in the Late 18th Century." *Journal of American Folklore* 102:403 (1989): 23–44.

Wigger, John. "Taking Heaven by Storm: Enthusiasm and Early American Methodism, 1770–1820." *Journal of the Early Republic* 14:2 (1994): 167–194.

Wilkinson, Henry C. *The Adventurers of Bermuda: A History of the Island from Its Discovery until the Dissolution of the Somers Island Company in 1684.* 2nd ed. Oxford: Oxford University Press, 1958.

Williams, Colbert. *The Methodist Contribution to Education in the Bahamas.* Gloucester, UK: Alan Sutton, 1982.

———. "The Methodist Contribution to Education in the Bahamas." Ph.D. diss., St. David's University College, Lampeter, Wales, 1977.

Williams, Eric. *Capitalism and Slavery.* Chapel Hill: The University of North Carolina Press, 1994.

Wilson, Ellen. *The Loyal Blacks.* New York: G.P. Putnam and Sons, 1976.

Wilson, Marcelle. "Loyalists: Economic, Gendered and Racial Minorities Acting Politically for King and Country." Ph.D. diss., West Virginia University, 2003.

Winch, Julie. *Philadelphia's Black Elite: Activism, Accommodation, and the Struggle for Autonomy, 1787–1848.* Philadelphia: Temple University Press, 1993.

Zaggari, Rosemarie. *Revolutionary Backlash: Women and Politics in the Early American Republic.* Philadelphia: University of Pennsylvania Press, 2007.

INDEX

Born in the Bahamas, Christopher Curry serves as associate professor of history and chair of the School of Social Sciences at the University of The Bahamas. Curry has published a number of significant books and articles. In 2006 he coauthored a three-volume series titled *Social Studies for Bahamian Secondary Schools.* In 2004, he researched and coproduced a thirteen-week television series on Bahamian history titled "Time Longer Than Rope: The History of the Bahamian People."

CONTESTED BOUNDARIES

Edited by Gene Allen Smith, Texas Christian University

The Maroons of Prospect Bluff and Their Quest for Freedom in the Atlantic World, by Nathaniel Millett (2013; first paperback printing, 2014)

Creole City: A Chronicle of Early American New Orleans, by Nathalie Dessens (2015; first paperback printing, 2016)

Entangling Migration History: Borderlands and Transnationalism in the United States and Canada, edited by Benjamin Bryce and Alexander Freund (2015)

Endgame for Empire in the Southeast: British-Creek Relations in Georgia and Vicinity, 1763-1776, by John T. Juricek (2015)

Freedom and Resistance: A Social History of Black Loyalists in the Bahamas, by Christopher Curry (2017; first paperback printing, 2018)

Borderland Narratives: Negotiation and Accommodation in North America's Contested Spaces, 1500–1850, edited by Andrew K. Frank and A. Glenn Crothers (2017)

James Monroe: A Republican Champion, by Brook Poston (2018)

www.ingramcontent.com/pod-product-compliance
Lightning Source LLC
LaVergne TN
LVHW091608270225
804733LV00004B/129